The Road to Down Street

The Story of North Bath

by Nancy Dearborn Lovetere

Other books from Islandport Press

Old Maine Woman: Stories from The Coast to The County
by Glenna Johnson Smith

Where Cool Waters Flow
by Randy Spencer

Shoutin' into the Fog
by Thomas Hanna

down the road a piece: A Storyteller's Guide to Maine,
and *A Moose and a Lobster Walk into a Bar*
by John McDonald

Windswept, Mary Peters, and *Silas Crockett*
by Mary Ellen Chase

Nine Mile Bridge
by Helen Hamlin

The Story of Mount Desert Island
by Samuel Eliot Morison

The Cows Are Out! Two Decades on a Maine Dairy Farm
by Trudy Chambers Price

Hauling by Hand: The Life and Times of a Maine Island
by Dean Lawrence Lunt

These and other Maine books are available at:
www.islandportpress.com.

The Road to Down Street

by Nancy Dearborn Lovetere

ISLANDPORT PRESS

YARMOUTH • MAINE

ISLANDPORT PRESS
P.O. Box 10
Yarmouth, Maine 04096
www.islandportpress.com
books@islandportpress.com

ISBN: 978-1-934031-407
Library of Congress Card Number: 2011922197

Book jacket design by Karen F. Hoots / Hoots Design
Book designed by Michelle A. Lunt / Islandport Press
Publisher Dean L. Lunt
Cover image courtesy of Marilyn Wright

To John, of course.

Table of Contents

" . . . a history of a place is no different from the toughness and brightness of its people. These men and women have always been many-sided creatures. They farmed while they fished, hunted while they hayed, lumbered while they manufactured, kept cows and chickens and horses while they built ships and went around the world. And they were filled with sharp wisdom and tart proverbs, full of lustiness and unpuritanic liveliness. They were cranky and independent and witty all at once . . . these people of the Kennebec are people of the heart of Maine . . . "

—Robert P. Tristram Coffin,
Kennebec, Cradle of Americans

From the Author

I grew up in Bath with a keen sense of its historical importance. My fifth-grade teacher, Laleah Snyder, and my uncle, George Barker, were very influential in my mission. Several years ago, research work with two friends made me aware that several small settlements surrounding Bath proper had fascinating histories about which little or nothing had been written. Interviews with a number of people reinforced this fact. I became greatly encouraged to compile my research into a collection that could be enjoyed by everyone.

Nancy Dearborn Lovetere
Bath, Maine
June 2008

Nancy Dearborn Lovetere Collection

Florence and George Barker

A Special Note

Our mother, Nancy Dearborn Lovetere, was raised in the 1940s and '50s on a beautiful peninsula surrounded by the Androscoggin and Kennebec rivers. This paradise, with Merrymeeting Bay at the headland, is known as North Bath, Maine.

With a great love and respect for the people and places that made her childhood so special, she researched and wrote this book about the settlement and history of rural Bath. She was patiently awaiting its release when her life suddenly ended in the summer of 2009.

There are so many people we know she would want us to thank for helping to make this book possible—too many for us to list here. Personally we can thank our dad, John, her ever supportive and loving husband; and her best friend and research assistant, Anne Vadakin, who was an immense help to editors after our mother's death.

Our mother was as passionate about this project as she was about her family and her running. Her spirit will forever be a source of strength and inspiration to us as we travel down life's new paths.

Duke and Lissa

Prologue

Bath, Maine, had set the stage for greatness long before it became a city. In 1607, Captain John Popham and Sir Raleigh Gilbert sailed up the Kennebec and praised its length and depth. The first English ship built in North America, the *Virginia*, was launched on this river in 1607. Many acts followed, but between December 7, 1941, and August 15, 1945, Bath Iron Works, for a curtain call, spit out a destroyer every twenty days, for a total of sixty-eight, more than any other American shipyard. It is no wonder that Bath's progress was contagious, spreading the buzz of shipyards and mills to surrounding communities. Farms were needed, too, and the north of Bath, unlike its sister, West Bath, which left home over a sidewalk dispute and independently incorporated, stayed on and didn't cause a family squabble. This area owes its scenarios to Bath, although no one has really noticed its performance.

Bordered by the Kennebec and Androscoggin rivers, a rural community known as North Bath thrived for many years alongside its maternal city, Long Reach, or Bath, with its own farms, shipyards, mills, tanneries, blacksmith shops, tub factory, school, chapel, and post office. Homesteads were noted here as early as 1650. Maps in 1718 indicate ownership of hundreds of acres of land by colonial entrepreneurs. Riding the court circuit on horseback in 1765, John Adams, lawyer, farmer, and soon-to-be second president of the United States, passed through the woods of northwest Bath to a ferry crossing near the Chops on his way to the Pownalborough Courthouse in Dresden. The first governor of Maine, William King, owned much of this property, including Lines Island. A long-forgotten bridge spanned Topsham and East Brunswick; only a few pieces of granite remain.

Little Whiskeag Creek ran through the heart of East Brunswick and Bath and sent ripples beyond—to the north, Swan Island and Bowdoinham; to the east, Woolwich and Dresden; and to the west, New Meadows, West Bath, Brunswick, and Topsham. The cast of significant characters in the making of this grand finale included Native Americans, African-Americans, Franco-Americans, English, and Scot-Irish.

In the seventeenth century, the Kennebec and Androscoggin rivers supported agricultural-based communities, but the Indian Wars curtailed expansion and decades passed before sounds of progress were heard again. Then, urban development caused the rivers to lose their importance; ice and fish were no longer in great demand, and shipbuilding shifted to larger cities. These tiny neighborhoods were left with just a few dog-eared photographs and blurry memories to share.

On the back of an old black-and-white photograph of a view looking down from Varney Mill Road, Dorris Wing had written "the road to down street." A phrase still used here in New England, "going down street" meant you were going into town. The North Bath Road was that road you took to downtown Bath, and it is still the road to down street. As the book title, *The Road to Down Street* is a metaphor for all the communities up and down the Kennebec and Androscoggin rivers; once unremarkable, often unnoticed and, until recently, undocumented.

The Road to Down Street has an extensive reference list, bibliography, and previously unpublished maps. Family genealogies, diaries, journals, detailed census data, rare vintage photographs, and cemetery records round out the program.

Courtesy of Calvin Wing

Dorris Wing wrote "The road to down street" on the back of this photograph, which shows the south end of what is now Varney Mill Road, with the old schoolhouse in the background to the right.

Introduction

A great deal of history is verbally passed down through generations, and, if the information is skewed in any way, it often becomes fact. Many New England historians of the eighteenth century were ministers and, with no disrespect to men of the cloth, their historical writings became gospel. Some of their accounts were not from primary sources, which become more and more difficult to find. If this information continues to be repeated and rewritten, the truth is lost. Ministers were, for the most part, well-educated, itinerant men who became disciple-like in spreading their historical knowledge.

The reverends Henry Thayer, William Hubbard, and Edward Ballard, and attorney Levi Lemont are four such historians. It is not that their ambitious works are completely incorrect; rather, it is that errors do exist and sometimes statements are created to suit the writer and the audience. Maps cannot be accepted at face value, either, for most contain a mistake or two. The *United States Department of the Interior Geological Survey of 1941* shows Thorne Head at the Chops location on the Bath side of the Kennebec River. Another current map shows Lovers Retreat Road (Ridge Road) as Lower Retreat Road. Personal names as well as place names have often been copied incorrectly. On the *1858 Chace Map*, Wittum and Whittum are spelled two ways; they refer to the same family, which also spelled its name Whittam. Because the Butler family had property in two spots at different times, Butler Cove is legitimately depicted in two locations. In Arrowsic, Dublin Point became Doubling Point.[1] It is the reader's responsibility to question the authenticity of what he reads and to allow for human error. There have been countless incidents in history where erroneous information is cited in order to conceal certain facts or locations. For many years there have been several theories as to the final destination of George Waymouth's visit in 1605. Was it to the Kennebec River, the Penobscot River, or the St. George Islands in the Muscongus? The few supporters of the Kennebec hypothesis feel the location was disguised purposely with several oversights, including unmentioned latitude and longitude. This may have been to limit rival trading. I absolve myself early in this work for any errors, omissions, or inaccuracies.

On some twentieth-century maps, North Bath is shown as the upper Washington Street area. Now it is commonly known as the area northwest of the city from Whiskeag Creek extending to Merrymeeting Bay. It is impossible to present a complete historic picture of this area without spilling over to Woolwich, Richmond, Bowdoinham, Brunswick, Topsham, West Bath, and New Meadows, as history has no boundaries. The immigrants who came here settled regionally, like the Scot-Irish who, with British Army officer Robert Temple as proprietor, settled North Bath, Topsham, and Dresden. The early communities were connected by necessity and industry. This book has been organized into five geographical sections so that the reader can envision where the photographs, maps, and text are leading: After an overview of the entire area of North Bath, Part One begins with Big Whiskeag Creek and Thorne Head, also known as Telegraph Point; Part Two follows the North Bath Road to the Ireland district; Part Three, the Ireland district along Varney Mill Road; Part Four, the Butler Head tip of North Bath at Merrymeeting Bay; and Part Five, Bayshore Road to New Meadows.

The Road to Down Street is a reflection of the individuals and institutions that endured here after the initial settlements. It tells of want, prosperity, and family connections. These areas were often overlooked as Bath has always been one of the brightest stars of towns and cities in Maine. The settlements north and west of Bath had more than farmers over a 400-year period. And yes, ships were built there, too.

To research each cited home's deeds would be, although very interesting, an exhaustive job. Some past and present owners have been listed to give some bearing to the reader. Most homes have changed hands many times; a few have had only several families inhabiting them since the 1800s.

The Many Names of Whiskeag

Where is Whiskeag Creek? If you ask one hundred people in Bath, ninety-five of them will say that it is near town, not far from Oak Grove Cemetery. Perhaps a few would know that there are two Whiskeag Creeks. Early eighteenth-century maps depict "Whigby," one of the many spelling variations of this interesting area, as the whole peninsula of northern Bath from the familiar area of Big Whiskeag Creek to Butler Cove in the Merrymeeting Bay area and over to the New Meadows River.

Listed below are thirty-three varieties of the ancient word, mostly of Native American origin. The earliest, Wisqueg, dates back to 1677. It has several different interpretations, many of which are incorrect, from "rapidly running water" to "Smoking Fish Point." Fannie Eckstorm,[2] who remains the leading authority on Indian place names in the area, says that the same title can apply to several locations. The name of a place is a description, not a location. Therefore, more than one Whiskeag exists.

Eckstorm agrees with her contemporaries that part of the root word of Whiskeag applies to the Abenaki word meaning "tide running out." Other parts refer to grass or hay, which would account for the low tide and salt marsh. These separate roots, used in other locations in Maine, all have a commonality. Since Little and Big Whiskeag share a similar topography, it is easy to understand why they have the same title with various spellings. The Weskeag River in South Thomaston is another good example of a tidal river or salt creek.

(The word Kebec[3] also has an interesting word origin. A common belief is that the name of the Chops at Merrymeeting Bay signifies choppy water; most likely it is derived from the old English word "chops," which means "jaws." The word Quebec comes from the Indian word Kebec, with the root "keb" or "kep," which looks like jaws, something that is closed in. *The United States Geodetic Survey Map of 1862* shows the title of Kebec at the Chops.)

Some of the names for Whiskeag became anglicized, such as Whisby, Whidby, Weswick, Wisbee, Whisgig, and Whigby. Fish Gig is the most unusual and descriptive. Often times these names appear on maps at both

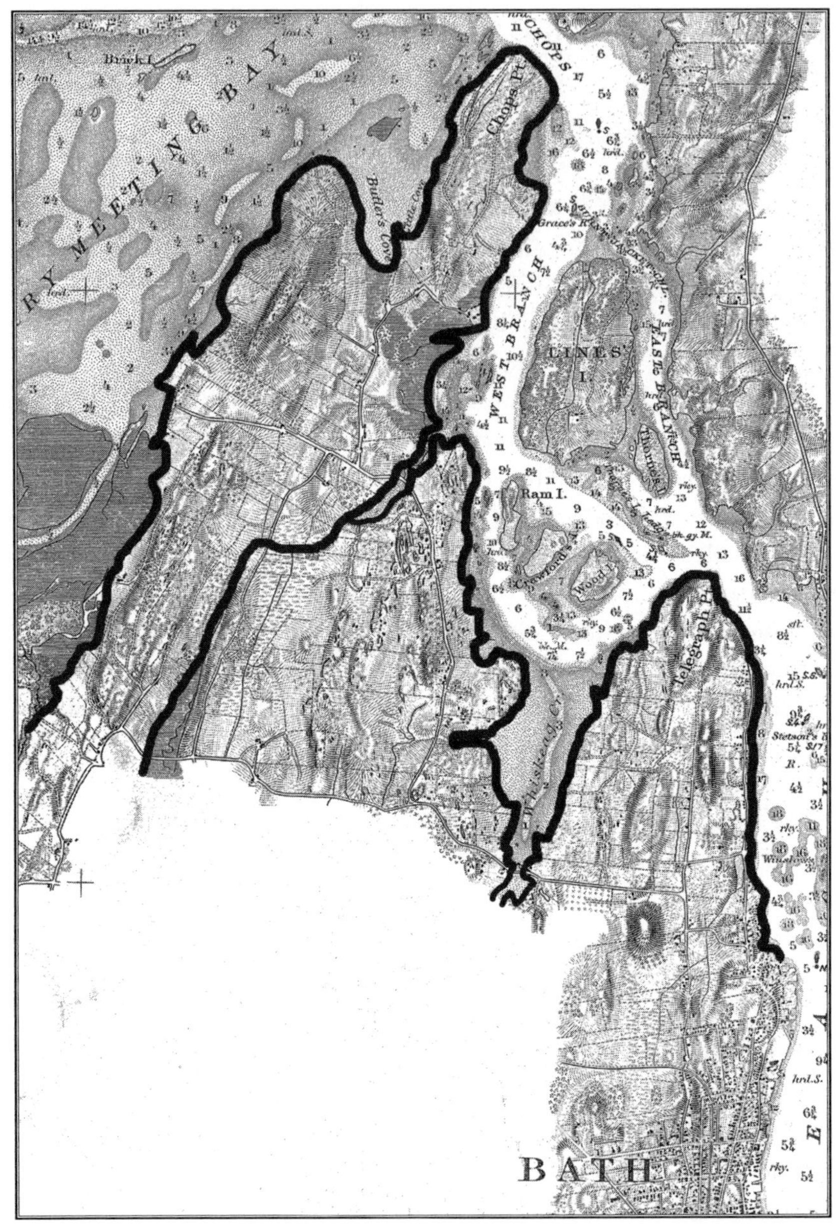

National Oceanic and Atmospheric Administration

North Bath. 1878 U.S. Coast and Geodetic Survey

the upper and lower locations. Deeds to property as recent as 1960 mention Wisbee Creek, leaving no doubt by its description that it is the smaller stream a bit below the Varney Mill Road, a little less than three miles northwest of Oak Grove Cemetery. Earl E. Wing had a farm there in the 1940s and '50s, the first house on the left on Varney Mill Road, with two barns on the opposite side. The name of his dairy was Wisbee Farm. Over time this creek was given the names of a succession of property owners, including Welch's Creek and Crawford's Creek. The name Whiskeag was nearly forgotten, and the larger Whiskeag Creek near the Oak Grove Cemetery and the Stone House became dominant.

An article in the August 14, 1922, edition of the *Bath Daily Times* featured "Emery's Mountain and Land Bordering." "The mountain lies west of Centennial Avenue, just before reaching North Bath Road and is the highest land in that locality; from its top one gets a view of sweeping valleys and wooded land, while beyond, to the west, lies Whiskeag Creek, that pretty winding stream known to so many generations of Bath boys who have loved to dip in its waters on hot summer days.

"Circling the mountain or driving up the North Bath Road and then turning and driving along its east bank, through the east side of Oak Grove, across the more recent Sewall extension, to the state highway connecting Bath and Brunswick will someday become one of the most beautiful drives which will be shown summer guests when they visit this city."

Little Whiskeag appears on maps and deeds as early as 1677, where more ancient activity took place. Indian occupation was very apparent at the more northwest site, whereas colonial mills were the more dominant interest near Big Whiskeag in the seventeenth century. Confusion over the location of the Peterson Canal lay with the fact that it was at the smaller Whiskeag Creek in North Bath.

Some of the titles below apply to Big Whiskeag; others apply to Little Whiskeag, while some belong to both. More information on the sources cited can be found throughout this book and in the bibliography.

1. Cape Lewis—Henry O. Thayer's *Sagadahoc and Kennebec Collected Papers, Notes, Abstracts, Copies*, p. 167.
2. Fish Gig—*1750 Kennebec Proprietors Map.*

3. Fisgigg—Thayer, p. 169.

4. Fishgege—*History of Dresden, Maine*, p. 69.

5. Little Whisbee—*History of Bath, Maine*, p. 366.

6. Waskeag—*Memorial Volume of the Popham Celebration*, pp. 310–311. Refers to Big Whiskeag with this spelling.

7. Wesquag—*Indian Place Names of the Penobscot Valley and the Maine Coast*, p. 134.

8. Weswick—*Pejepscot Papers* 8:54.

9. Whesgig—*Plan of the Town of Bath by Dummer Sewall, Surveyor*, 1795.

10. Whidby—*Wheeler's History of Brunswick, Topsham and Harpswell*, p. 747.

11. Whigby and Upper Whigby—*History of Dresden, Maine, History of Bath, Maine*, and York Deed 8:122.

12. Whisbee—(See Little Whisby)

13. Whisby and Little Whisby—*Memorial Volume of the Popham Celebration*, pp. 310–311 refers to upper Little Whiskeag with this spelling; also Whisby Creek Bridge.

14. Whisgeag—*Indian Place Names of the Penobscot Valley and the Maine Coast*, p. 134.

15. Whisgig—*Ancient Dominions of Maine*, p. 136.

16. Whiskeag—*Memorial Volume of the Popham Celebration*, p. 308.

17. Whiskege—*Owen's History of Bath*, p.44.

18. Whisky Creek—*Sagadahoc and Kennebec Collected Papers, Notes, Abstracts, Copies*, p. 169.

19. Whisqueag—Ibid.

20. Whizby—_________________

21. Whizgeag—*History of Bath & Environs*, p. 19.

22. Whizgig—*History of Bath & Environs*, p. 19.

23. Wigby—*Genealogical Dictionary of Maine and New Hampshire*, page 420.

24. Wisbeck—An 1891 letter to the editor of a Bath newspaper; filed at Sagadahoc. History & Genealogy Room, Patten Free Library, Bath.

25. Wisbee—Sagadahoc Deeds. 1:61 and 378:840.

26. Wisby and Wisbee Creek Bridge—Sagadahoc Deed 48:289.

27. Wisgig—*The History of the State of Maine*, Vol.1, p. 47.

28. Wiskeag—Ibid.

29. Wiskege—*History of Brunswick, Harpswell and Topsham*, p. 19;

Genealogical Dictionary of Maine and New Hampshire, p. 20.
30. Wiskig—*Length and Breadth of Maine*, p. 267; *History of the State of Maine*, Vol. 1, p. 47.
31. Wisqueg (earliest form)—York Deed 3:80. 1677.
32. Worsequeage—York Deed 8:123. 1892.
33. Worsqueage—*Pejepscot Proprietors Map*, 1718; *Pejepscot Papers* 8:63.

Notable People and Deeds

"A general land tangle and grab and controversy and a harvest for lawyers."
—Rev. Henry O. Thayer[4]

Many of the deeds to land in Wisqueg, the whole peninisula of North Bath, were inaccurate, overlapping, and sold more than once to various people. The Indians, having no concept of land ownership or boundaries, deeded the same land to different people for different "rights of the land," such as fishing, farming, hunting, timber trading, and trapping. One person would receive the deed for fishing rights, for example, while another would hold a deed for hunting rights on the same plot of land. The kings of England granted tracts of the same land to individuals for colonizing. Early developers, groups of men called "the proprietors," came with the responsibility to sell lots, develop communities, and make money. This confusion of ownership and unspecific boundaries created several chains of title and many lawsuits. The individuals or groups noted below had some part in the dissemination of Wisqueg's 1,000 acres. Whether through a royal grant, Indian deed, or proprietor's claim, the people named below became entangled in legalities that tied up the court system for many years.

Sir Ferdinando Gorges, born in 1566 in Somersetshire, England, became military governor of Plymouth, England. As a colonizer, he and his partner, John Popham of the Plymouth Council of New England, were given the territory of Maine in 1620 from King James I of England. Both backed the Sagadahoc Colony in 1607. A lack of funds prevented Gorges from colonizing his domain. His grant was passed on to his heirs, who sold all rights for Maine to Massachusetts in 1677. Maine may have been named by Gorges for an ancestral estate known as Shipton Gorges in Dorset, England, where there is a small village called Broadmayne, southeast of Dorchester, and once known as Maine. This is a logical consideration, as Gorges named a smaller patent Lygonia, for his mother, Cecily Lygon Gorges.[5] Although he never saw New England, he is often called "the Father of Maine." Gorges granted the Plymouth Council 1,000 acres with the king's approval; for this he was given a monopoly on fishing rights.

Christopher Lawson was born in 1616 and lived in Exeter, New Hampshire, with his wife, Elizabeth James. The first settler of North Bath, Lawson was a barrel maker who bought 1,000[6] acres from the Indians in 1640, as well as land on Swan Island and all of Lines Island. He owned land adjacent to Thomas Purchase and reportedly lived above what became the old Peterson Canal. In 1665, he was listed as a constable's deputy.[7]

Major Thomas Clarke and **Captain Thomas Lake**, Massachusetts Bay merchants, purchased timberland (which had been patented to the Pilgrims for trade) on both sides of the Kennebec and Androscoggin rivers from Indians in the mid-1600s. They sued the Kennebec and Pejepscot Proprietors over jurisdictional conflicts. The pair's trading post and fort was on the eastern shore of Arrowsic on the Sasanoa River.

Thomas Purchase, originally from Dorchester, England, was engaged in fishing at New Meadows and the Androscoggin along with Lawson, about 1628. He may have owned Lines Island at one time. Merrymeeting Bay was called Purchase's Bay.

Robert Gutch, from Wincanton, England, settled in Bath about 1665[8] and was Sagadahoc's first minister (Presbyterian). His meetinghouse was somewhere on Long Reach. A hand-drawn map[9] in the Sagadahoc History and Genealogy Room in Bath shows that Gutch "occasionally preached at this Place" on the Sasanoa River (Preble Point). His house was on the Bath side as well. Gutch was related to Dr. S. F. Dike, who became a clergyman in Bath in the early 1800s.[10] Gutch bought from the sachem Robin Hood the territory of what is now Bath. Gutch had one son and six daughters.

The Plymouth Company or **Kennebec Company** was originally a royal patent for trade granted in 1629 to William Bradford and the

Pilgrims of the Colony of New Plymouth. In 1661, the Plymouth patent was sold to a group of proprietors: John Winslow, Antipas Boies (Boyce), Edward Tyng, and Thomas Brattle. It later was reorganized as the Kennebec Company, with a tract of land called the Kennebec Purchase. The owners of this land were called the Kennebec Proprietors. Its primary investors were half-brothers James and William Bowdoin, Samuel Goodwin, and Silvester Gardiner. They were the driving force behind the successful development of Maine.

Thomas Stevens moved from North Yarmouth to become the first settler of Brunswick, where he acquired two square miles of property from New Meadows to Merrymeeting Bay to the Atlantic Ocean. In 1675 he lived on the north side of the New Meadows River in the area that became known as Stephen's Carrying Place and the Peterson Canal. He was listed in 1665 as "a grayn [sic] jury man."[11]

Pejepscot Proprietors was a group of eight merchants with the responsibility to develop communities and support industry. They encouraged immigrants to settle land in 1714, laying out four towns or plats: Topsham, Brunswick, Harpswell, and Lewiston. As with the Kennebec Proprietors, they were in charge of the sale of home and farm lots. The eight original proprietors, who were the founding fathers of Brunswick, were: John Rusk (Ruck), John Watts, David Jeffries, Oliver Noyes, Adam Winthrop, Stephen Minot, Thomas Hutchinson, and John Wentworth. All were from Boston with the exception of Wentworth, who was from Portsmouth, New Hampshire. The Pejepscot Proprietors sold the land in North Bath to British Army officer Robert Temple, who, as proprietor, settled many Scot-Irish families there from 1714–20.

Joseph Heath was a surveyor from Roxbury, Massachusetts, whose title to 400 acres came to him from the Pejepscot Proprietors in 1718. His land between the Kennebec and New Meadows rivers was then owned in part by Captain Simeon Turner, and later by John Tarp in 1731. The property where William King resided at his Stone House near Whiskeag Creek was previously part of this parcel.

Job Lewis, Esquire, from Boston, owned land on both sides of the Kennebec. He lived in Boston most of his life, where he was a constable and town auditor.[12] The Whiskeag area in his time was known as Cape

Lewis.[13] He first appears on the Woolwich side of the Kennebec in 1724–26. Not an original Pejepscot Proprietor, he acquired his land from the Clarke and Lake heirs. Lewiston, Maine, may have been named for him. Married to Sarah Palmer, their children were Hannah (Waterhouse) and Abigail (Bethune).[14]

John Tarp was a farmer who resided in Bath c. 1731 and lived at the foot of Harward Street at what became the old Peterson home. This is the location of Kings Dock and Mast Landing. He later owned the land occupied by the Stone House.

Silvester Gardiner, born in South Kingston, Rhode Island, was a Boston physician. In 1761 he invested with the Kennebec Proprietors in a million and a half acres in Maine. In 1761 he was granted almost all of the Second Parish of Georgetown. Gardiner, Maine, is named for him.

Deed Succession

A property on the Varney Mill Road loosely follows this chain of title, below, with approximate dates. LW indicates Lincoln (County) West. YD indicates York (County); all others are filed in Sagadahoc County. The volume or book is listed first, with the page or folio listed second.

1. King George I of England.
2. The Council for New England, Sir John Popham, and Sir Ferndinando Gorges, 1620.
3. Christopher Lawson (1,000 acres), 1640.
4. Edward Camer [Keemer] (Listed as an owner of Lines Island, then called Purchase's Island) about 1660.
5. Thomas Purchase, 1628.
6. Obadiah Walker and Edward Nailor [Naylor], partners, 1679.
7. Sarah Walker (widow of Obadiah) married Ephraim Savage.
8. Ephraim and Elizabeth Savage: attorney and shopkeeper from Boston, 1714–15. [YD 8:122]
9. John and Hannah Butler (Savage's daughter), 1718–19 and in 1723, (admeasurement discovered at this point). They convey "the farm." [YD 11:136].
10. Thomas and Jane Selby, 366 acres, 1723. Thomas dies intestate. [Y.D.

15:2]. Selby son sells to Job Lewis.

11. Job Lewis conveys "farm," 1731, from Selby heirs.

12. Kennebec Proprietors to Silvester Gardiner, 1762, [LW 1:287].

13. Silvester Gardiner, 1763.

14. Abigail Whipple (Gardiner's daughter), 1797.

15. Oliver Whipple and Abigail Whipple to John Crawford, 1797 (*being one-half of what was set off to us as our share of what is called the Chops Farm*) [43:63].

16. William (who became Maine's first governor) and Ann King, 1828 (*being the farm which I purchased of John Crawford with the buildings & improvements*) [LW 2:252] He may have obtained this property by fore-closure.

17. Anna Kelley (daughter of Joseph Edgecomb and granddaughter of Pendleton Edgecomb) to Elizabeth Edgecomb, 1858 [12:459] (*home-stead farm*).

18. Samuel Edgecomb (widower), administrator of the estate of Elizabeth Edgecomb, to John G. Rogers, 1874 [41:99].

19. James R. Wright and Albert Ward to Hiram Cornish, 1879 [52:259].

20. Hiram Cornish to Ellen A. Cornish, 1894 [85:237].

21. Cornish to Ralph E. Wright, 1921 [147:138].

22. Ralph E. Wright—Federal Land Bank of Springfield, 1930 [169:443].

23. Federal Land Bank of Springfield to Joseph Robinson, 1938 [210:120].

Maine Indians on the Lower Kennebec and Androscoggin Rivers

The term *Wabanaki* refers to all natives of the Maritime Peninsula (Maine, New Brunswick, and Quebec south of the St. Lawrence River), according to the Abbe Museum, a Native American heritage museum in Bar Harbor, Maine. *Wabanaki* means "People of the Dawn," or "Dawnlanders." This term was coined during the 1700s to describe the Wabanaki Confederacy, disbanded in the nineteenth century. It included the four exist-ing Maine groups: Micmacs, Maliseets, Penobscots, and Passamaquoddies.

Seventeenth-century English colonists oversimplified Indian names by identifying them with the rivers on which they lived. They called the Indians who lived along the Kennebec the Kennebecs, for example. Seventeenth-century French sources are more reliable, according to Bruce Bourque, chief archaeologist at the Maine State Museum, because they "continued to apply ethnic names current among their native associates."

Inland tribes traveled to the shore in summer months. Merrymeeting Bay was a great mixing ground. Bath was the western limit of the Etchemins, or Maliseets. Near the Androscoggin and perhaps farther west were the Arasuntacooks or Almouchiquois, which meant "dog people." Micmac (known by the English as Tarrentines) territory ran from Nova Scotia west to the St. John River. In addition to guiding the French expeditions of Pierre de Monts and Samuel D. Champlain, the Micmacs provided information to Jesuit Pierre Biard around 1610–11. The Almouchiquois may have died from the plague in 1617–18, or retreated south.

Christopher Lawson bought Purchase's Island (also known as Camer Island and Lines Island) from the Indian Sagamore Derumkin. Lawson claimed that the deed to the island was lost during the Indian Wars, which began in 1675. It is not stated whether the deed was physically lost or if Lawson meant the Indians had reclaimed the island. Derumkin, chief sachem of the Androscoggins, and his son Cateramogus (also listed as Agamogus), were well known. Terramugus Cove, between Ferry Point and Granny-Hole Mill on the Topsham side of the Androscoggin, was named in Cateramogus's honor. Derumkin and Abonhammon, a lesser chief also known as Absalom, deeded to Thomas Stephens land nearby called Aguahadongoneek from Grape Island to Wigwam Bay, which included the whole neck to Merrymeeting Bay in December 1654.[15]

Derumkin and Abonhammon conveyed to Lawrence Dennis in 1685 what later became known as Thorne Head at the most northern tip of Bath. Other land transactions involved Swan Island and Winslow's Rocks, just off the city of Bath proper.

Mohotoworomet, a Sagamore from the Nequasset Falls area in Woolwich, was called Robin Hood by the English and was a friend of the colonists for many years. It is unknown if he belonged to the Etchemin-Maliseet tribe that lived nearby. Robin Hood was involved with many land transactions; his name appears on more than twenty-five deeds, and he was witness to more. He may have been a shaman, or spiritual leader. It is possible that the name of Merrymeeting Bay was attributed to his witchcraft and roles as a medicine man and sorcerer, of which the colonists neither understood nor approved.

Robin Hood sold the island of Georgetown to John Parker in 1648. Other land transactions involved John Richards, Edward Tyng, William Dyre, Thomas Stephens, John Parker, Henry Curtis Land, Nicholas Cole, and John Purrington,[16] and, in 1660, the reverends Robert Gutch and Alexander Twaite. Several dealings involved both Robin Hood and Derumkin. The last conveyance they made was for land near the Merrymeeting Carrying Place, on July 2, 1675. One week later, King Philip's War began, the first of the five Indian Wars that would last until 1763.[17]

Robin Hood's circle of travel was not limited to Maine, according to Harald Prins, a noted anthropologist and Indian rights activist. Robin Hood and his tribe stole pigs while raiding a colonists' settlement in the Connecticut River Valley. The pigs and other livestock had been previously "earmarked" by their owners for identification, and when the stolen pigs' pursuers tracked down Robin Hood's campsite, all of the pigs in his possession were found with their ears cut off. The Indians said this was their method of marking "their" pigs. Who could argue with that?

Robin Hood died about 1675. He allegedly is buried on Gunner's Nose on the Barley Neck Road on the Sasanoa River in Woolwich. Robinhood Bay and Robinhood Village in Georgetown, the area of his summer home, are named for him.

Private Burial Grounds

In Maine, an ancient burying ground is defined as a private cemetery established before 1880.[18]

Seven cemeteries with headstones are visible today in the North Bath area, all on private property. They are located along the North Bath Road from the corner of Whiskeag Road going north, west on Bayshore Road, and southwest of the intersection of Ridge and Whiskeag roads. In the last forty years, two cemeteries have become difficult to find. One is the Welch-Wise burial ground, on North Bath Road in a pasture on the west side. It holds the oldest headstone in the area. Elizabeth Wise died in 1749 at age thirty-four. Two other headstones are those of Captain William Welch and his wife Molly Smith; they, no doubt, gave the creek one of its many names, Welch's Creek.

The other burial ground is opposite the Hawkes Farm and Greenhouse; it had several headstones, which apparently have become part of the earth. Albert Whittam, age two years, six months, son of Charles and Jane, was buried there. Charles owned land in that area.

Harold Brown, a Morse High School teacher for thirty-four years and first curator of the Maine Maritime Museum in Bath, gave the burial grounds their location descriptions. Brown, along with his sister, Helen McPhee, and friend, Doris Rowland, spent many years documenting old cemeteries. This trio's work, enhanced by the earlier records of Mary Pelham Hill, are combined herein as the USGenWeb Project, with Lorelei Gustafson, compiler. Brunswick cemetery records are maintained by webmaster Barbara Desmarais. The information on gravestones sometimes contain errors in date, ages, and spelling of names, and there may be discrepancies between compilations, but these are the complete records of burials in this area.

(Anyone interested in visiting a private family burying ground should ask permission from the landowner. The owner may provide an easement for a direct route from the public way nearest to the burying ground site.)

As North Bath Road was once known as Ireland Road, it is likely that the land would hold several Irish burial grounds. On the east side of Varney Mill Road near the Kennebec River, a small island of earth rises up, encircled with mayflowers. In this little cemetery, nameless fieldstones are configured as head- and foot-markers. Brown theorized that these were Irish graves. It seems that most old burial grounds were high and dry with a good view, revealing lives lost from hard work, disease, and disasters at sea.

Maps and Their Makers

The following original maps, as a record of a place and a time, are priceless resources that show the area's development and changes in names and spellings over the years. The maps are too large to reproduce here with clear detail, but a written description of their highlights is included below.

1718 Pejepscot Proprietors Map

Joseph Heath, Surveyor, Brunswick 1718–19

"This Plott of land Called in Indian Aquehadongonock and Described by ye yellow & black lines is bounded by a Line running South 30 Degrees East from a Small Ashe Tree landing on ye Middle of Grape Island in Merrimeeting Bay one mile and ___ chain unto a white oake tree landing on wigwam point on ye westerly side of a Creek Coming out of Casco Bay; From ye Said White oak North 40 degrees East 148 Chain To the Head of Weswick Creek and from said Creek Sagadahock River and Merrimeeting Bay is ye bound unto forementioned Grape Island. The Contents of this plott is Eight Hundred & Twenty Acres and was Plotted by the Scale of 40 perch in an Inch. Brunswick in the Late Province of Mayne In New England Jan 28 1718."

Joseph Heath was the surveyor for the Christopher Lawson title, established by the Pejepscot Proprietors. Heath lived on a 200-acre farm at the Harward Street location in Bath proper in 1759.[19] This property stretched between the Kennebec and New Meadows rivers and sections of it belonged at various times to Captain Simeon Turner, John Tarp, and William King.

This map encompasses part of the Pejepscot Proprietors' land. Actually, it is most of North Bath today, excluding Thorne Head. It encroaches a bit on the New Meadows side. This area was called "Aquehadongonock, alias Whigby," in Indian. According to Fannie Eckstorm, the first part of the title means "drag my canoe out of the

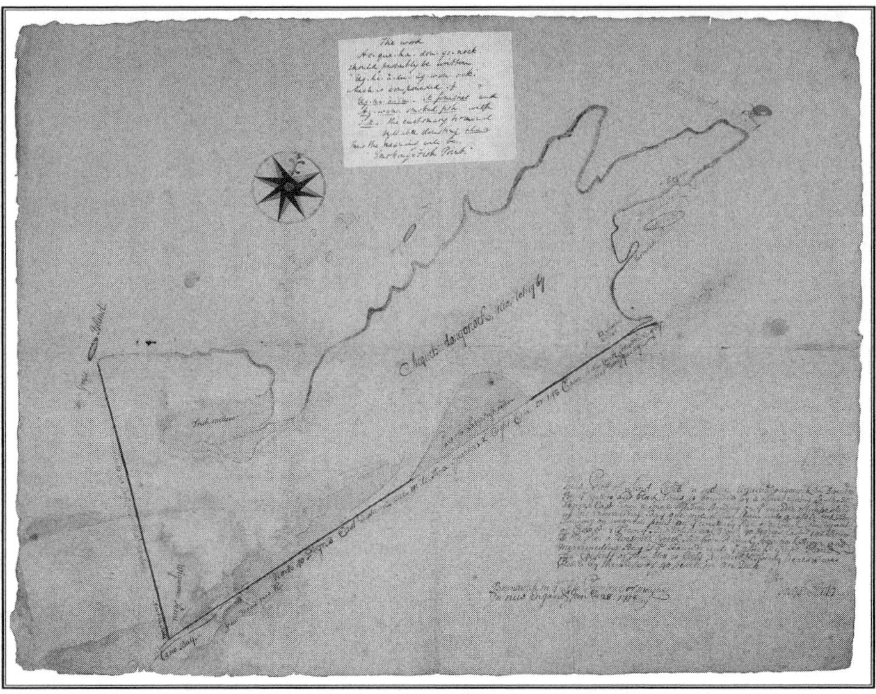

Collection 61, Map 53, Maine Historical Society

Pejepscot Proprietors Map

water and make a landing." The last part is a root word meaning a landing
for portage or the end of a carry.[20] Conor McDonough Quinn, a postdoc-
toral researcher at the Massachusetts Institute of Technology, gives a contemporary translation similar to Eckstorm's.

The survey includes land from the center of Grape Island[21] on
Merrymeeting Bay; part of the Androscoggin River to Wigwam Point at
the head of the New Meadows River, just north of the present-day Old
Bath-Brunswick Road bridge to the head of Weswick Creek (Whiskeag);
and to the Sagadahoc River (or Kennebec). *Pejepscot Papers, VIII*: 53 state
that the location of Aquehadongonock is " . . . a point on the west side of
the Chops, Kebec, where the Kennebec leaves Merrymeeting Bay."[22]

The names Lemont and Rogers, the notation of New Meadows River,
and the large note at the top of the map are nineteenth-century additions,

possibly made by John McKeen (1789–1861), a Brunswick town clerk who organized documents and other material in order to give them to the Maine Historical Society. The designation "Fresh Meadow" is assigned to two places, at the open fields where the buffalo graze today, including parts of the fairways of the Bath Country Club, and on the Brunswick side, near Bonney Brook. Also noted is House Island, known today as Stony or Stoney Island.

Mr. Lawson's Cellar is the only mark on the map suggesting a home. There are several symbols that may represent Indian encampments. Christopher Lawson owned all of this land, surveyed at 820 acres.

1750/1 Kennebec Proprietors Map

John North, Surveyor, copied by William Alline, 1785

"This is a Plan of a Tract of Land lying fifteen English miles on each side of Kennebeck River, purchased from the late Colony of New Plymouth by Antipas Boies, Edward Tyng, Thomas Brattle and John Winslow in the year 1660, and now owned by their Heirs and Survivors, who are distinguished by the names of The Proprietors of the Kennebeck Purchase from the late Colony of New Plymouth measured and laid down by a scale of 640 poles or two miles to an inch the 3rd Feb 1750/1.[23]

"By John North Surveyor Copied Nov. 1785 by William Alline."

John North prepared this map on February 3, 1750/1. The section shown here was later copied from the original, which measures 366 centimeters by 274 centimeters, or 12 by 9 feet, done in nine sections.[24] John North's daughter, Mary, was married to John McKechnie, also a surveyor for the Kennebec Proprietors (see following map), but obviously North was not fond of her choice in husbands. Lincoln County Probate Records, July 6, 1763, state North's last will and testament to say . . . "and I give my Daughter no More of my Estate by reason of her undutifullness in contracting marriage with a Man who is Not to my good liking."

Shown on this map are the boundaries and grants of the Kennebec Proprietors or the Kennebec Purchase Company, which owned fifteen English miles on both sides of the Kennebec River. The land originally was

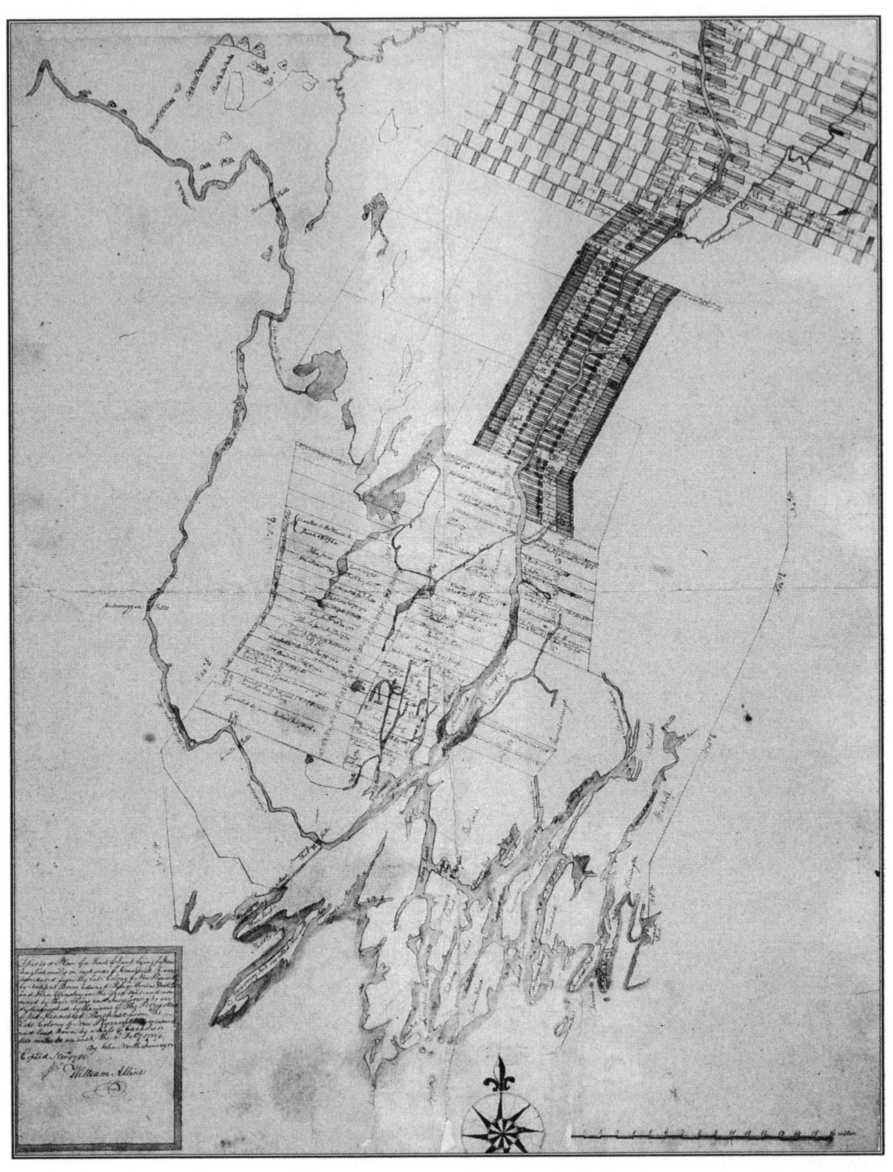

Copied by William Alline, 1785, Bowdoin College Collection

1750/1 Kennebec Proprietors Map

Copied by William Alline, 1785,
Bowdoin College Collection

Seal of the Kennebec
Proprietors

bought for the late colony of New Plymouth (Plymouth Company), the Pilgrims, who received the deed from King George I of England. A great deal of acreage was deeded to James Bowdoin, whose widow became the third wife of General Henry Dearborn. Dearborn accompanied Aaron Burr and Benedict Arnold on their trek to Quebec. Also shown here is land deeded to William Bowdoin, half-brother of James, for whom Bowdoin, Bowdoinham, and Bowdoin College are named.

The road from Mequoit and Mair Point (or Maquoit and Mare Point) in Brunswick was originally a carrying place between that area of Casco Bay and Fort St. George, built in 1715; it is depicted at the end of the carry by the falls. This route, also known as Twelve Rod Road, was built for the Pejepscot Proprietors to be 200 feet wide (twelve rods). The fort is noted at the Upper Carrying Place. The upper Androscoggin is curiously depicted as the Kennebeck River.

The Whiskeag area is noted as Fish Gig. Frankfort Fort is located near the Eastern River in Pownalborough. The Chops are marked as well.

The Kennebec Proprietors Seal displays an anchor and a codfish. The crown represents the King with the motto, *Nec frustra dedit rex,* or "The King has never given in vain." It is a wonderful composite of the Proprietors' accomplishments.

1764 Plymouth Company Plan of Georgetown

John McKechnie, Surveyor for Silvester Gardiner

"The annexed Plan represents an Actual Survey of a Tract of land to Doct. Silvester Gardiner of Boston lying in GeorgeTown, bounded as follows: Viz, beginning on Whisgig bay opposite to the Middle Island there,

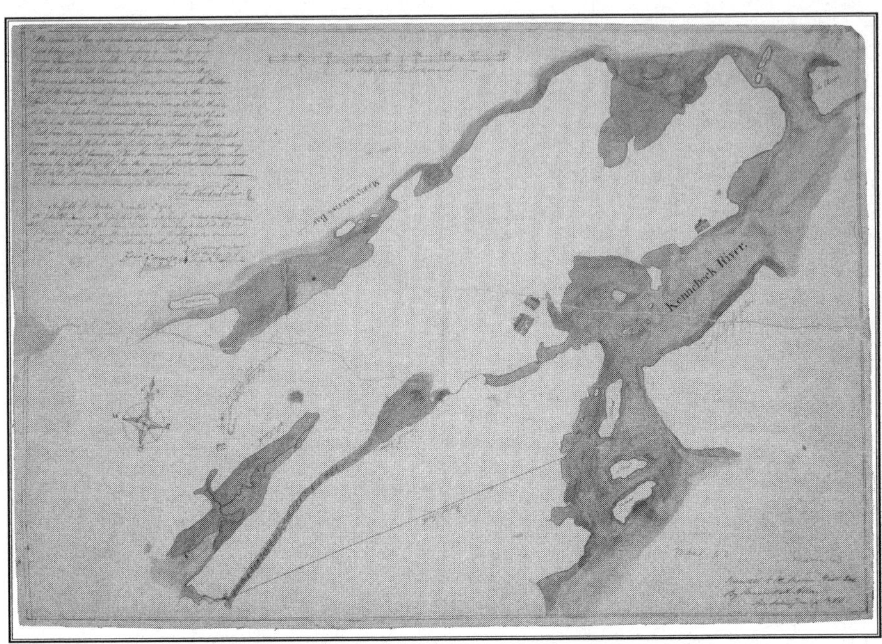

Plymouth Company Papers, Collection 60, Map 81, Maine Historical Society

1764 Plymouth Company Plan of Georgetown

from thence running West, 37 Degrees South to a White Oak Stump &
heap of Stones on the Northern Side of the Falls at Smelt Brook near to a
large rock, then down to Smelt Brook as the Brook runs to Stephen's
River, so Called, then up to Said River to a brook that runs round
Wigwam Point & up said Creek to the Head thereof which leads into
Stephen's Carrying Place or Path from thence running along the Carrying
Path or place as the Path goes on the South Westerly Side of a large ledge
of rock running to merrymeeting bay at the end of the Carrying Place,
then running northeasterly on merrymeeting bay to the Chop of said Bay
then running Southerly down Kennebeck River to the first mentioned
bounds in Whisgig bay. This plan is laid down by a scale of 40 Poles to one
Inch. John McKechnie surveyor. John Hill Justice of the Peace for the
County of Suffolk."

This survey was prepared for Dr. Silvester Gardiner, a Kennebec Proprietor. Surveyor John McKechnie, born in Scotland in 1703, married Mary North, daughter of surveyor John North, and had thirteen children.

The Plymouth Company Plan of Georgetown shows Bath before it became a separate parish; this area is almost exclusive to North Bath. It begins on Whisgig Bay (Big Whiskeag, which holds Crawford, Woods, and Ram Islands)[25] opposite Middle Island (Crawford), then runs to the north side of Smelt Brook (a resident recalls smelts there in the 1960s). Shown also are the small falls and large rock formation in back of the former Dunton's Store, near the intersection of Ridge Road and the Old Brunswick Road. The brook runs to Wigwam Point, up the small creek to the end of the New Meadows River, just north of the bridge, to the head of Stephen's Carrying Place or Path, which goes along the southwest side of the large ledge running to the bay to the end of the Carry, then northeast to Merrymeeting Bay to the Chops and then back to Whisgig Bay.

This tract of land was under dispute by several men in 1763. Boston attorney Job Lewis had homes on the Woolwich and Bath banks of the Kennebec River. Although none of the four homes depicted on this map is designated to a certain person, Lewis, Christopher Lawson, Thomas Stevens, Thomas Purchase, Ephraim Savage, and Gardiner have been noted as living in this vicinity at one time or another. The smallest house on this map may have been the home of Thomas Stephens, spelled Stevens on the map. Gardiner also had homes on both sides of the river and allegedly another on Line's Island. Varney's Island, a twentieth-century title, is shown with a connecting neck to the mainland.

1774 Sproule Chart

"A Plan of the Coast From Kennebeck River to Round Pond, on the West Side of Muscongus Bay including the Islands, Rivers, etc. Within that Extent. Surveyed Agreeably to the Orders and Instructions of the Right Honorable the Lords Commissioners for Trade and Plantations to Samuel Holland, Esq., Surveyor General of the Lands for the Northern District of North America, by his Deputy Ensign George Sproule of His Majesty's 59th Regiment."

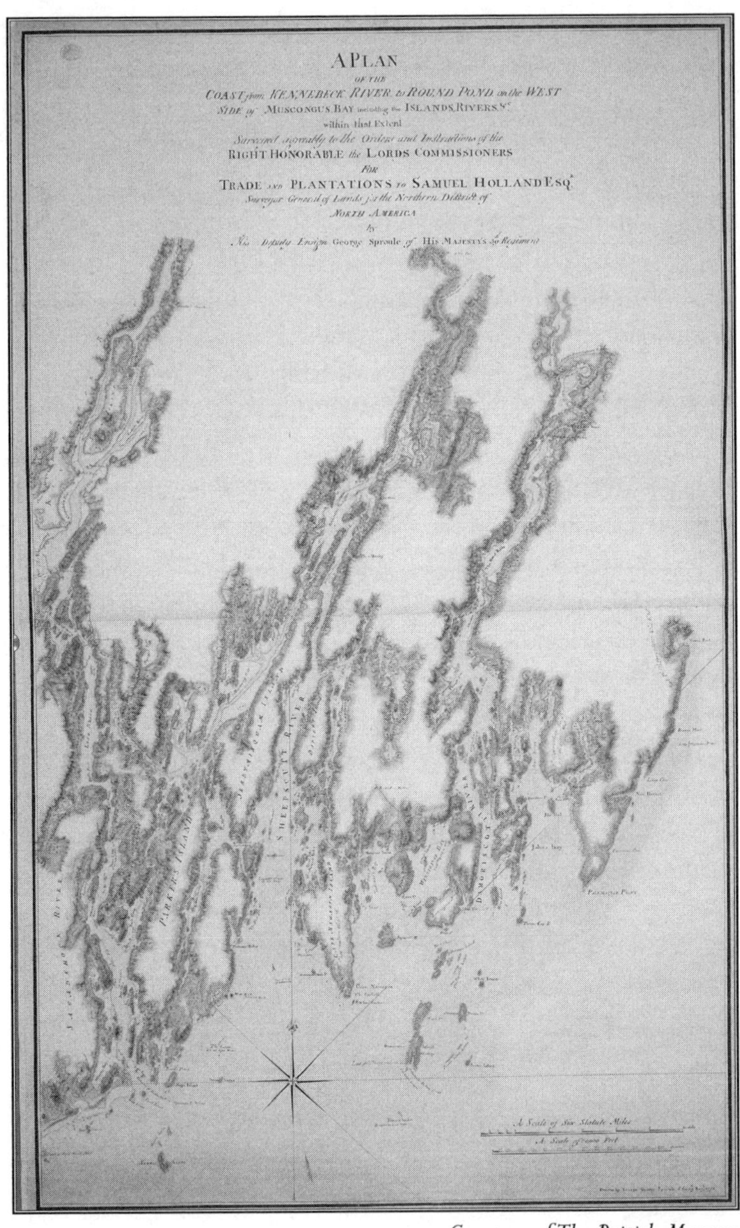

Courtesy of The British Museum

1774 Sproule Chart

The *Sproule Chart* is considered pre-Neptune in that it preceded the *Atlantic Neptune Atlas*, charts drawn from surveys for the British admiralty. This pre–Revolutionary War era chart illustrated land and water details and was similar in style and accuracy to the *1776 Des Barres Chart*. The *Sproule Chart* depicts Sturgeon Island just above Butlers Cove. On the Bath shore, Mast Dock is shown. Whisgig Creek is plotted along with a mill. Farther south on the left fork of the Whisgig is another mill. Little Whisgig is noted, as well as two separate buildings at the beginning of the Varney Mill Road and two more at the end.

The Chops, Chops Point, and Chops Creek are all on the Woolwich shore. Lyne's Island is slightly north of Middle Ground, home of Whisgig Islands. A ferry is shown here near Arnodl's [sic] Narrows. Across from the ferry landing in Woolwich is the Road to Pownalborough, now Dresden. At least eleven houses are shown on Swan Island. Cork Cove is depicted in Dresden. A Garrison House is noted to the east on the Woolwich shore, as well as Pownalborough, the Pownalborough Church, and Frankfort.

1776 Des Barres Chart

"Charts of the Coast and Harbours of New England, composed and engraved by Joseph Frederick Wallet Des Barres, Esq., in Consequence of an Application of the Right Lord Viscount Howe, Commander in Chief of His Majesty's Ships in North America—from the Surveys taken by Samuel Holland, Esq." London, 1776, first publication.

This chart of Casco Bay was one of many nautical surveys that comprised the five volumes of the *Atlantic Neptune Atlas*. Joseph Frederick Wallet Des Barres, a Swiss, was born in 1721/2. He and fellow surveyors compiled the works for the British Admiralty. Des Barres became a British subject and, in 1756, came to America as an engineer and surveyor. After fighting in the French and Indian Wars, he began surveying parts of New England, Nova Scotia, the Gulf of St. Lawrence, and Cape Breton. After nine years of charting, he returned to England in 1774 to begin production of his marine atlas, which showed great water and land detail. These navigational charts were completed by 1776, and later revised. Reproductions of many of his maps were printed from more than 250 copper plates, then

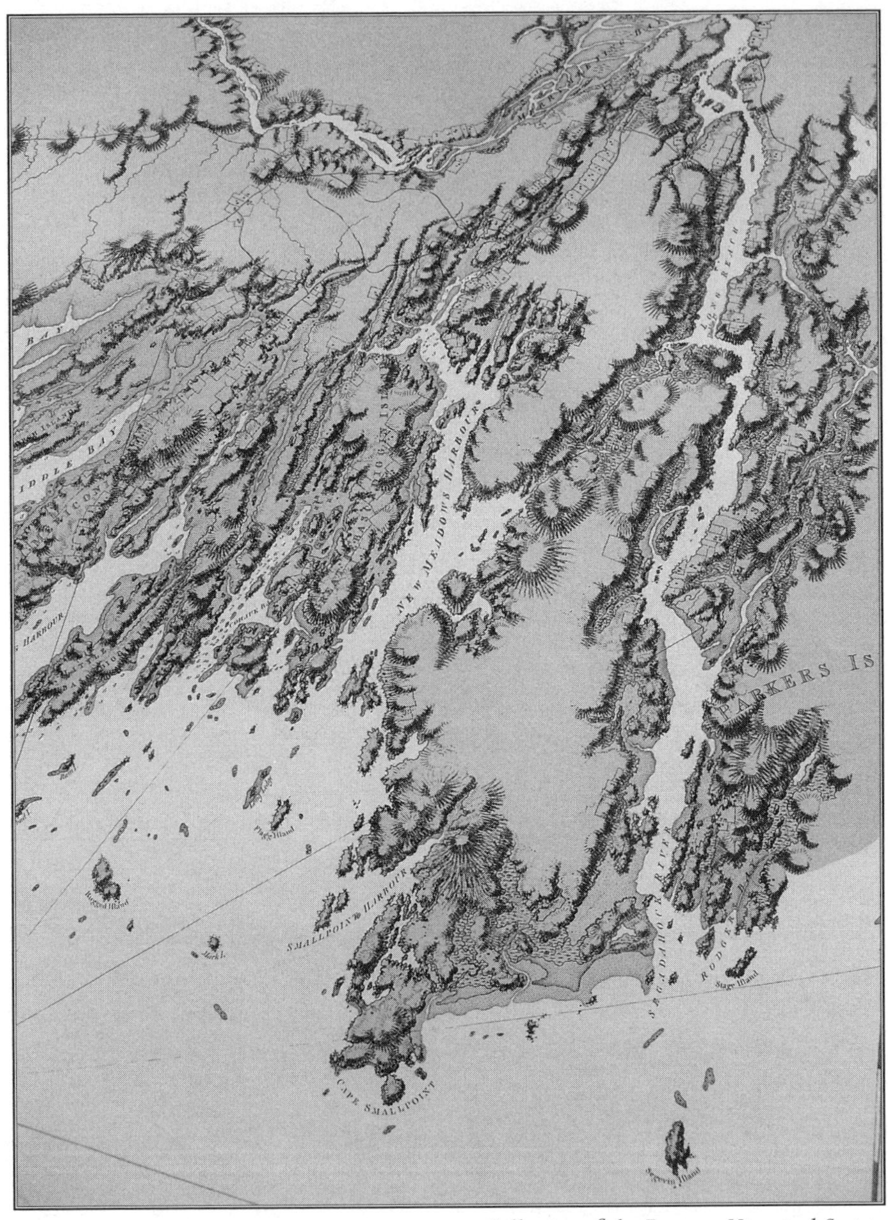

Collection of the Freeport Historical Society

1776 Des Barres Chart

hand-colored in watercolors, as were the originals. Des Barres died in Halifax in 1824 at age 102 after serving as lieutenant governor of Cape Breton Island and lieutenant governor of Prince Edward Island.

The Whiskeag Road was known as East Brunswick Road. It goes past the Bath Country Club to the intersection of the eighteenth tee. This second-oldest crossing to Brunswick followed the course of this road straight across the intersection, down the hill, with the Ham Cemetery on the right. Passage then went up and to the East Brunswick side, thus establishing its name, coming out on Bridge Road.

The *Des Barres Chart* shows that the original crossing followed a course of a right turn at this intersection, headed north on the Lover's Retreat or Ridge Road, then made a sharp turn partway through the wooded ridge to cross the Peterson Canal. (Remains of a stone bridge represent what may have been an unresolved corporate boundary dispute between Bath and Brunswick). The course this road takes is apparent on the chart by the "swirl," which diverges to the meadow, leading to the North Bath Road and Rocky Reach area we know today. At this point there are several squares depicting homes. There also are many homes noted along Ridge Road and on Bridge Road on the East Brunswick side, all favoring water frontage. The high water table on the New Meadows River in 1776 shows the convenience of an Indian carry at this point.

An interesting square on the map representing a home is shown near the banks of the Androscoggin River, near Bayshore Road, and there are several others on the shoreline in East Brunswick. Also, at the beginning of Varney Mill Road, a complex of four buildings is depicted. There are several other properties at Big Whiskeag Creek, Thorne Head, and the Woolwich and Topsham shores.

1858 Chace Map

This section of the *Chace Map of 1858*, a plan prepared from surveys that show property ownership, was published by J. Chace Jr. of Portland and Philadelphia. It can be viewed at the Sagadahoc County Registry of Deeds, the Sagadahoc History and Genealogy Room at the Patten Free

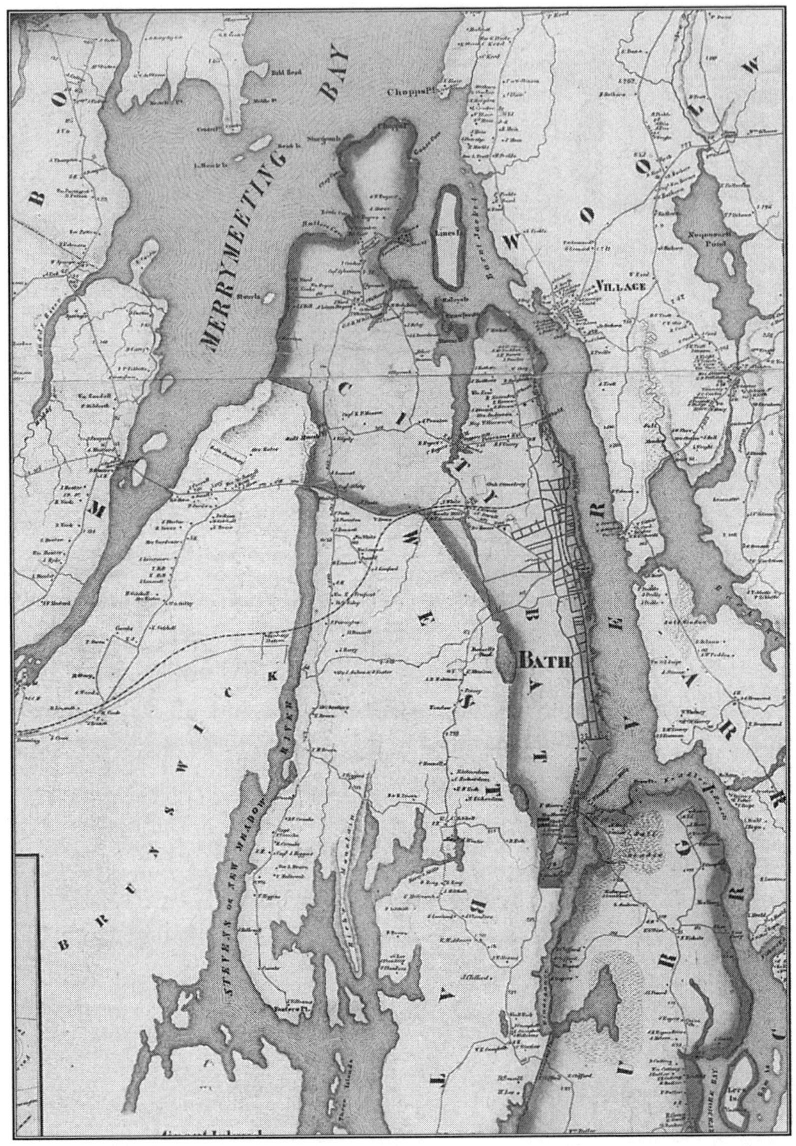

Courtesy of the Sagadahoc Genealogy and History Room, Patten Free Library

1858 Chace Map

Library in Bath, the Maine Maritime Museum in Bath, and at the Georgetown Historical Society.

1878 The United States Coast and Geodetic Survey

The *U.S. Coast and Geodetic Survey* has been the nation's official chart since 1807, initiated during President Thomas Jefferson's administration, when it was known as the *Survey of the Coast*. In 1871 a geodetic connection was made between the Atlantic and Pacific coasts (geodetic, meaning the ability to measure the curvature of the surface of the Earth). In 1878 it became the *Coast and Geodetic Survey*. Today it is known as the *National Geodetic Survey*, which is part of the National Oceanic and Atmospheric Administration within the United States Department of Commerce.

It is this 1878 survey that is used at the beginning of each section of this book.

Robert M. Thorson, in his book entitled *Stone By Stone*, says "Locating the exact boundaries of a tract, even for surveyors, was difficult because the straight-edged polygonal land divisions of British law (squares, rectangles, parallelograms, triangles) bore little, if any, relationship to the irregular and gradational shapes of nature." A good example of this is seen on the Rocky Reach portion of this map, which shows several different geometric shapes.

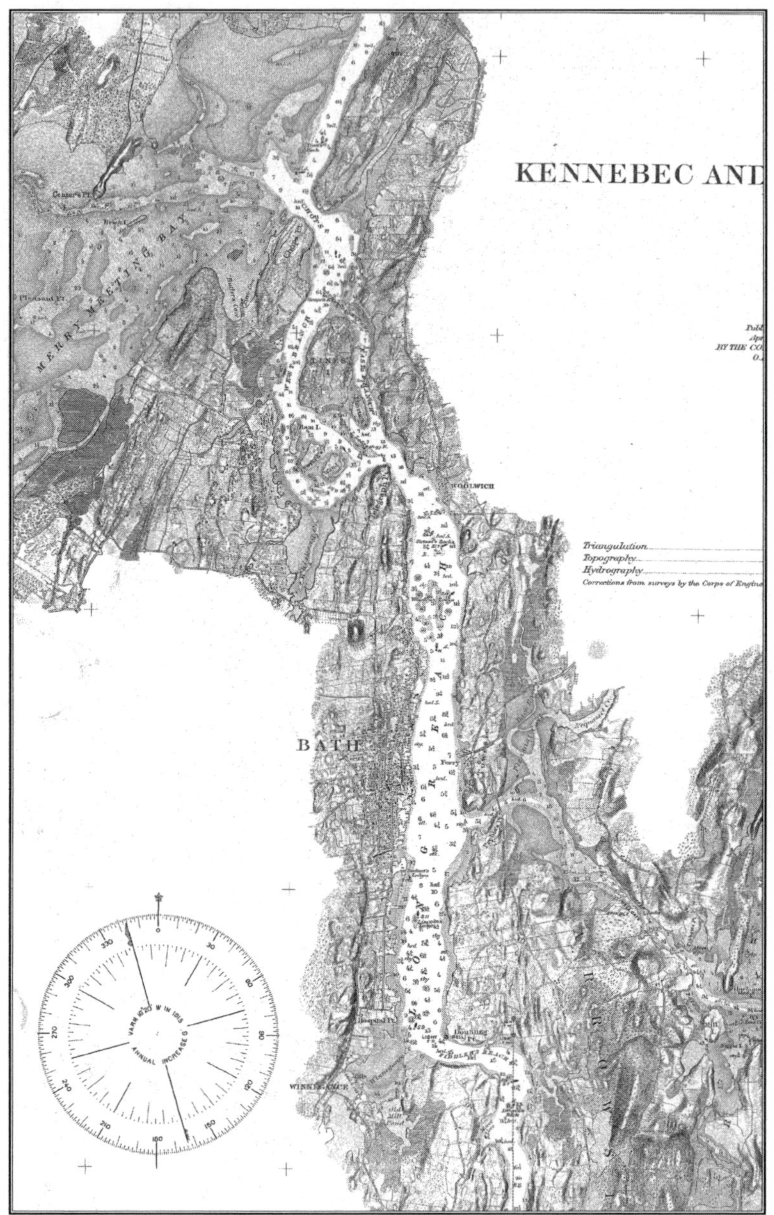

National Oceanic and Atmospheric Administration

1878 U.S. Coast and Geodetic Survey

Part One

Big Whiskeag Creek & Thorne Head

Big Whiskeag Creek became an early site of industrial development with several mills and ice harvesting.

Today, Thorne Head has a 96-acre preserve of walking trails, but its history is particularly interesting. It was here that a man hid out in a cave after murdering a Bath police officer, and where William King, the first governor of Maine, lived for a number of years and was active in the development of the area.

Big Whiskeag Creek

The original route between Bath and Brunswick was a course of stepping-stones across Whiskeag Creek. In 1790 a petition was presented to the town of Bath to build a bridge, at the cost of one hundred pounds, over the Whisgig River.[26] Below is a summary of the activity that took place at both ends of Whiskeag Creek, at the causeway and at the lower end near today's Bath Middle School.

Whiskeag Creek Mill Location

1732:   Wiscasset deed shows that Joseph Heath leased land to John Tarp and Robert Hayford; mentions possibility of building a "mill upon a creek called Weswick."

1774:   *Sproule Chart* shows a mill at this site and also below, which became Sewall's.

1797:   John Peterson moved from New Meadows to this location where he and his son, Levi, had a sawmill and gristmill.

1818:   Adam Lemont built a "fulling" and carding mill (fabric).[27]

1821:   Samuel Rogers rebuilt a mill here.

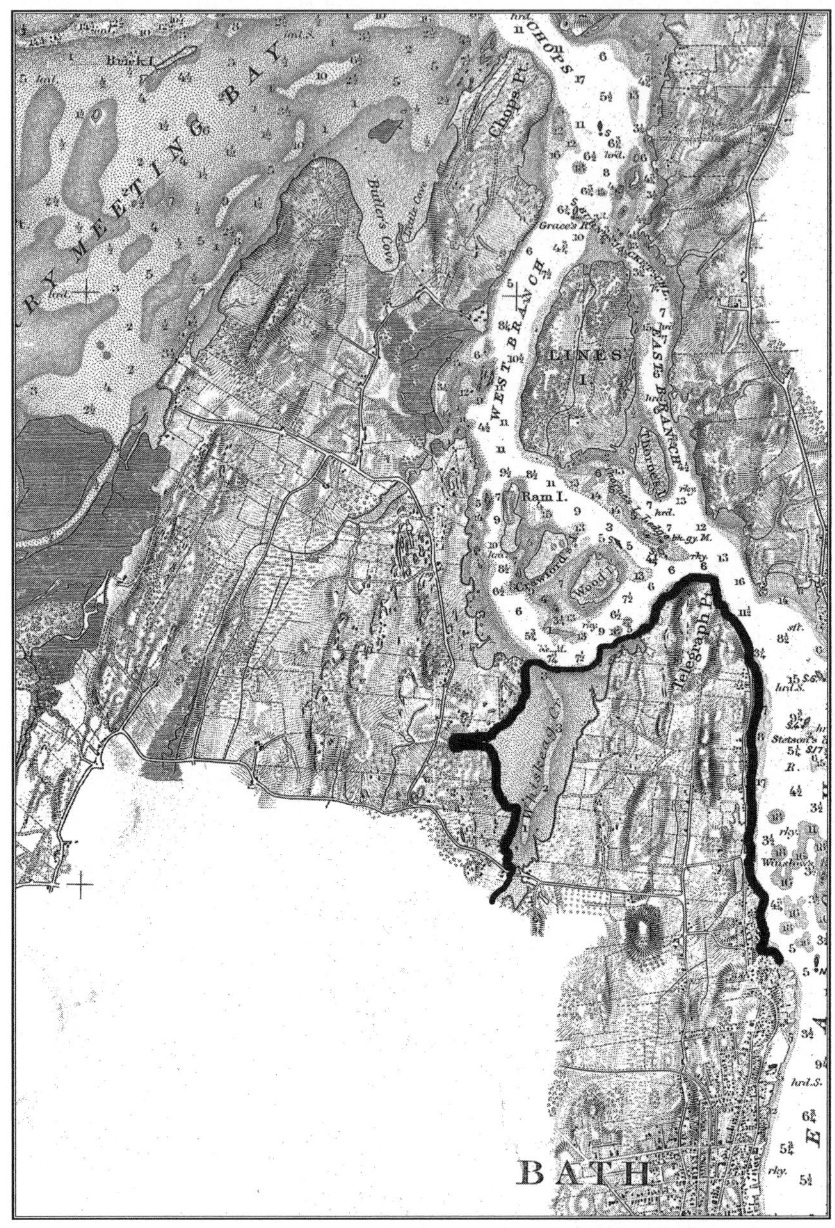

National Oceanic and Atmospheric Administration

North Bath's Whiskeag Creek and Thorne Head area

1858:   *Chace Map* shows Rogger's [sic] sawmill and gristmill here; also Peterson mill, canal, home nearby.

Sewall's Creek Mills Locations

1665:   Robert Gutch owned this tract and possibly had a mill here at an earlier date.

1763:   Henry Sewall of York, a house carpenter, and Dummer Sewall, of York, gentleman, acquired this tract. They rebuilt a mill that may have existed there one hundred years before.

1774:   *Sproule Chart* shows a mill here as well as the above Whiskeag Creek location.

1829:   Charles and Joshua Sewall enlarged the mill.

1849:   A railroad bridge was built across Sewall's Creek.

1858:   *Chace Map* shows Sewall as having a gristmill, sawmill, and icehouses.

1914:   Five thousand tons of ice was harvested here.[28]

Thorne Head

Thorne Head is a 96-acre preserve of public walking trails created by the Kennebec Estuary Land Trust with help from a land acquisition grant from the Maine Outdoor Heritage Fund in 2006. It is located at the north end of High Street in Bath.

The *1751 Kennebec Proprietors Map* shows Michael (Mickel) Thornton as dwelling at Thorne Head. James Grace acquired the Thorne Head property from the Kennebec Proprietors in 1759 and sold it in 1762 to James Thornton, for whom this region was named. In 1805, John Peterson was deeded property there belonging to James Thornton, north of Noah Innes's property. A James Thornton is listed as a "Scotch-Irish Pioneer" on Merrymeeting Bay between 1718 and 1722.[29] The land was logged into the 1900s, and old farmland is evident from extensive stone walls. Historian Henry O. Thayer also refers to this area as Thornton's Head at Narrows.

In 1761 James and Ann Thornton conveyed to James Michaels (Mitchell) 100 acres east of Whiskeag, called "lot #2"; this was in conveyance by the Kennebec Proprietors to Thornton, April 8, 1760. The 1803 Lincoln County Probate records refer to Michaels's property as bounded east by the heirs of James Thornton. Presumably, the James Michaels property stayed in the family because later records show Dot Michaels's home and cove at this location. Dot was a local hermit whose house stood on the cove, home to the Upper Ferry and Narrows. The Michaels's site, at the end of Upper Washington Street, was reached by following the original road, shown on various maps as both the Old Country Road and the County Road, until 1880.

Wilkinson's Cave, Smuggler's Cave, or Murderer's Cave

This 15-foot-deep cave is tucked on a steep hillside on the left of the trail leading to the "Scenic Overlook." It was discovered in 1853 by workmen setting telegraph poles, who also noticed that the cave was naturally ventilating smoke. (This type of rock formation is called a geothermal or hydrothermal vent, similar to a hot spring.) It is just to the west of what the *C&G S Map of 1878* and the *United States Department of the Interior Geological Survey of 1941* show as Telegraph Point. The cave was reportedly occupied at the time of its finding by a "hard character named Soule." It had, however, an even more intriguing history.

In 1883, Daniel Wilkinson, thirty-nine, a British "bearded merchant seaman," met Thomas Elliot at a "low" Irish boardinghouse in Philadelphia. They traveled to Maine by rail and boat, and arrived in Bath. While trying to rob Gould's grocery store, Wilkinson shot and killed a police officer, William L. Lawrence, sixty-three. Police spent several days trying to find Wilkinson and Elliot as they hid in the cave at Thorne Head that would soon bear the former's name. Dot Michaels, the hermit previously mentioned, supplied food for them at the cave.

The city of Bath hired Boston detective James R. Wood to solve the crime. The detective concluded that Wilkinson had stolen a boat from local resident John F. Dowe and taken it to Woolwich. There, he jumped on a Knox & Lincoln train to Rockland, then made his way to Bangor. Two weeks

Nancy Dearborn Lovetere Collection

The cave where convicted murderer Daniel Wilkinson hid

after the murder, policeman Dennis D. Tracey arrested Wilkinson in Bangor while he was loading lumber on a schooner at the Maine Central Wharf.

Wilkinson told the arresting officer that in 1880 he had been sentenced to serve three years for a burglary at Thwing's Point, Woolwich, but that he had escaped from the Sagadahoc County Court House shortly thereafter. (Three years later, while awaiting action of a grand jury on the murder charge, Wilkinson unsuccessfully tried to escape his Augusta jail cell using two razors and several small saws.) He said he had also done time in Massachusetts. Wilkinson said he was born in London, had four brothers, and went to sea when he was thirteen. He never revealed his parents' names.[30]

For the murder of William Lawrence, Wilkinson, wearing a suit of black alpaca, was found guilty and hanged at the Maine State Prison in Thomaston in 1885. The gruesome details of his demise caused the abolishment of capital punishment in Maine. Despite the reports of an unbroken neck being the reason for his slow seventeen-minute death, rumors circulated for many years that Wilkinson, with the aide of influential friends, had been replaced by a "dummy" at his hanging, and that he had escaped to northwest Canada where he was occasionally seen by "Maine men."

Wilkinson has the distinction of being the only person to receive the death sentence in Sagadahoc County.

Wilkinson denied knowledge of his accomplice's whereabouts and Elliot was never captured.

Details of this report came from *The American Sentinel*, 1883, and the *Bath Daily Times*, 1883, 1885, 1926, and 1961. Those microfilms can be found at the Sagadahoc Genealogy and History Room, Bath.

William King

Maine's first governor, William King, was born in Scarborough in 1768. His father died at an early age, and because of that, William did not have the opportunities of his half-brother, Rufus, the famed statesman. Nonetheless, he worked his way to Topsham with an inheritance of two oxen and eventually bought a sawmill.

He moved to Bath in 1800, and in 1808 purchased the property known as the Stone House on Whiskeag Hill.[31] No records indicate that King actually built this Gothic structure; it may have been constructed by English sportsmen for a hunting lodge.[32] Marion Jaques Smith, who wrote a King biography, thoroughly searched deeds but found no actual proof of its original owner. John Tarp was known to have lived on the property, which was part of the Heath tract, before King.

King was instrumental in the incorporation of the (Merrymeeting) Bay Bridge. He built ships and introduced the cotton trade between Maine and the South. At the Stone House he set out 500 fruit trees (as depicted by the small squares on the *Coast and Geodetic Survey of 1878*) and raised potatoes for export. He also owned many acres in North Bath, including Lines Island. which he purchased in 1808 from Robert Hallowell Gardiner.

King had an active role in Maine's separation from Massachusetts. He is buried at Maple Grove Cemetery in Bath.

From a tile by Ruth McKenn Jacob. Courtesy of Abbie Sewall.

The Stone House on Whiskeag Hill was home to Maine's first governor, William King.

Ferries on Thorne Head

Most ferry operators were farmers owning land on one side of the river, making just enough money to supplement their primary occupation. Less than a total of six months was optimal for ferrying due to floods, log drives (June, July, and August), and mechanical downtime. Although rope

ferries were common, water between the two landings had to be free of
current. This was not the case on the lower Kennebec.

The ferry known as the Upper Ferry, or the Upper Ferry and
Narrows,[33] had two locations, about a quarter of a mile apart. The ferry
farthest north, at the extreme end of Washington Street, was located at
Dot Michaels's Cove. Of the two landings on Thorne Head that served the
Woolwich side of Day's Ferry, the most northern location, with its deep,
swift water, was usually free of ice; that condition as well as tides dictated
which landing should be used. The south landing, more directly opposite
Day's Ferry, often froze. There are two houses there, originally identical,
which were built to accommodate ferry operators who worked in twelve-
hour shifts. One was called Ledge-O-Rocks Camp in 1924.[34]

Varney's Gazetteer of Maine (1881) mentions an upper and lower ferry
on the Woolwich side: "Woolwich has four small villages . . . Woolwich at
the Lower Ferry, post office and railroad station, and Woolwich Village at
the Upper Ferry, opposite the upper end of the city proper of Bath."

Captain Samuel Harnden operated the ferry between 1760 and 1769.
His son Samuel Jr. carried on the duties of ferryman until 1830, providing
transportation for travelers going to Pownalborough and Wiscasset. This
Upper Ferry Landing was also known as Arnold's Ferry and Arnold's
Ledge. Arnold's Narrows is depicted on the *1764 Sproule Chart*. Too early
to be named after Benedict Arnold, it is possible it was named for an early
Bath settler in the Second Parish of Georgetown in 1756, Samuel Arnold.
There is an Arnold mentioned in a deposition regarding Lines Island, and
Samuel is listed along with James Thornton of Thorne Head.

In 1778 this ferry location was purchased by Nathaniel Day and
Zebulon Smith, later operated by Nathaniel's sons, Joseph and Nathaniel
Day.[35] In 1795 Susanna Thorn (Thornton) was licensed to keep a ferry at
the landing near her house.[36] Lincoln County probate records show that
the "inventory of Daniel Peterson, Joseph Day and Peleg Delano, as
appraisers of the estate of William Thornton of Bath, deceased, presented
31 May 1822 by Jane Thornton, administrator. The estate included 7 acres
of land, $105; a dwelling, $250, and one-half a ferry boat, $20." *The 1794
Plan of the Town of Woolwich*, by surveyor David Gilmore, shows the
Kennebec Ferry, just below the Narrows, to be forty-four rods wide.

Courtesy of the Sagadahoc Genealogy and History Room, Patten Free Library

The Upper Ferry and Narrows had two locations.

In 1830 Thomas P. Stetson acquired the ferry and land on both sides of the river. Stetson's Rocks are shown on the *1858 Chace Map*. The Maine Legislature granted him a permit to operate a horse ferry in 1831. The horse-propelled ferry, using a great deal of deck space, was the forerunner to a steam-driven ferry. Through a tread wheel, then to a portable tread-mill, the horse walked on the deck of the ferry to generate power. There is no proof that Stetson actually implemented this method. Several seasoned Woolwich ferrymen, including Day, opposed Stetson's charter, perhaps for financial reasons, or the fact that they preferred the "gundalo" or gondola-style ferry.[37] Perhaps Stetson could not compete with a rival "downtown" ferry, which was soon abolished.

According to the *Seaside Oracle*, Wiscasset, Maine, February 26, 1876, "It is a beautiful walk or ride up Washington Street to [Day's Ferry], and after a walk or ride of eight miles, you may find yourself in Wiscasset. A good ferryboat has been built by Goss & Sawyer, and two small boats are kept, one on each side of the river, for the convenience of travelers, and the expense is moderate. Fare for a boat passenger, 10 cents, and for a single team and 2 persons, 25 cents. Teams loaded with wood or hay can pass directly over, the ferryboat being amply to accommodate them. Mr. Crooker, through whose influence this ferry had been re-established, is in attendance from 'sun to sun' on the eastern side and a man on the western side of the river stands ready the same length of time to convey passengers across."

Part Two

The Road to Ireland—North Bath Road

This area is home to four important ancient burial grounds memorializing some of the area's most important families, the Edgecombes, Robertses, Crawfords, Welches, and Wises. The Sagadahoc Rod, Gun & Skeet Club was incorporated here in 1934. Lines Island has changed hands many times over the years and has been the subject of property disputes. And, the land of Rocky Reach holds early homesteads along the Kennebec River north to Little Whiskeag Creek.

Purington Burial Ground

This burial ground is located at the top of the hill at the corner of Whiskeag and North Bath roads.

1. Joshua Purington, d. Oct. 29, 1842, age 74.
2. Sophia [Bryant], wife of Joshua Purington, d. Jan. 1, 1848, age 75.[38]

Nancy Dearborn Lovetere Collection

The Purington burial ground

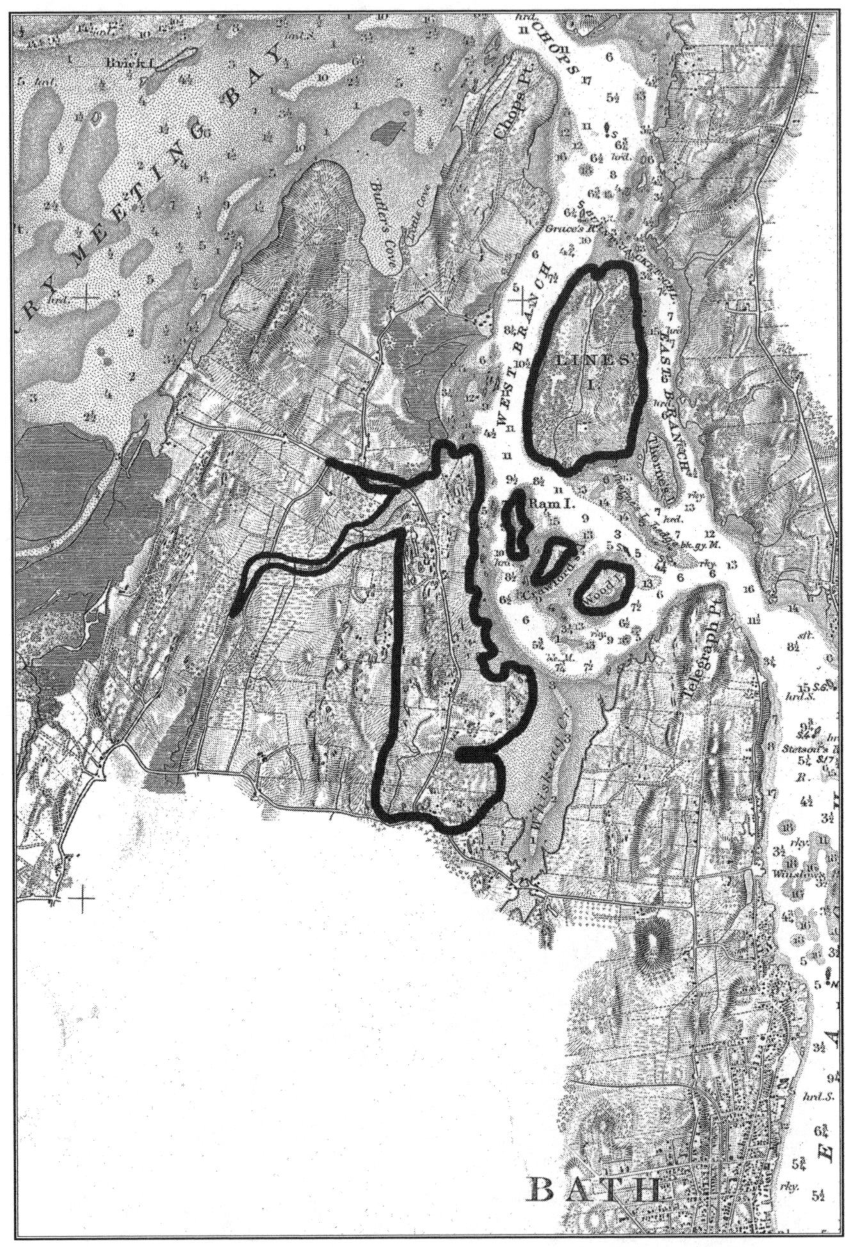

National Oceanic and Atmospheric Administration

Shown here are Lines Island and the North Bath Road area

Their children were: Martha, Huldah G., Nathaniel, Sophia, Hezekiah B., John H., Hezekiah (number two), Joshua, Lydia Clapp (married Hugh Rogers), Rebecca B., and Samuel F.

Compiled by Lorelei Gustafson for The USGenWeb Project.

Mount Edgecombe

Pendleton (Pembleton) Edgecombe,[39] with visions of the "Edgecumbe" lords in Cornwall, England, built a lovely Federal colonial farmhouse high above the Kennebec River in 1790 on the North Bath Road. The banks of the Kennebec were not the White Cliffs of Dover, but in those early days Mount Edgecombe must have been a stately, magnificent place. Edgecombe was deeded the land by his uncle, General Samuel Thompson,[40] a controversial figure who owned a great deal of land in the New Meadows–Bath area. Edgecombe was a farmer and lumberman; his religion was Congregationalist. He married Margaret Mains of Woolwich

Courtesy of Lorelei Gustafson

Mount Edgecombe was built on the North Bath Road in 1790. This photograph is from about 1925.

in December 1783. According to Edgecombe family genealogists, Pendleton was a descendant of the immigrant Nicholas, not Sir Richard Edgecombe of the celebrated British family that played major roles in Henry VII's reign.

Other Edgecombe relatives lived nearby, just up the road, on the Varney Mill Road, and other areas of North Bath and Bath proper. The James Grace Descendancy File includes many Edgecombe family members.

When Pendleton died, his brother Samuel inherited the home and property. Silas, Samuel's son, inherited the same property, which was subsequently deeded to his two sisters, Lydia Edgecombe and Mary Elizabeth Sylvester Edgecombe (Paine). Mary Paine's daughter, Ella, married William Kendall and bore the last child at Mount Edgecombe: "Theodore Paine Kendall was born at Mt. Edgecombe at 8 o'clock in the morning July 1, 1892. July 12 he was carried to the attic before being down stairs in order that he may rise in the world. This was nurse's suggestion."[41]

After Ella inherited the home, she sold it in 1926 to the Gillies family, which was also in the lumber business; they added gables and ells and named their home Fairfields. The homestead has since become the Fairhaven Inn.

Edgecombe Burial Ground

This burial ground and tomb is located on the west side of the North Bath Road on the grounds of the Fairhaven Inn, formerly Mount Edgecombe. A massive stone-dressed tomb holds two family members and commemorates a third.

Some family members have been moved to Oak Grove Cemetery in Bath.

Edgecombe
1. Pendleton Edgecombe, d. Mar. 5, 1839, age 69.
2. Margaret (Mains) Edgecombe, wife of Pendleton Edgecombe, d. Jan 4, 1849, age 80.
3. Anna Edgecombe, daughter of Pendleton and Margaret Edgecombe, d. Oct. 30, 1821, age 20.

4. William Edgecombe, son of Pendleton and Margaret Edgecombe, lost at sea, Oct. 5, 1856, age 52.
5. Abigail Edgecombe, daughter of Pendleton and Margaret Edgecombe, d. Nov. 9, 1811, age 1 yr., 3 mos.
6. Charles Edgecombe, son of Pendleton and Margaret Edgecombe, lost at sea, d. Nov 17, 1842, age 35.
7. Elizabeth Smith Edgecombe, daughter of Joseph Edgecombe and Abigail Smith, d. Nov. 13, 1873, age 53 yrs., 8 mos.
8. Joseph Edgecombe, son of Pendleton and Margaret, d. Oct. 25, 1856, age 62.
9. Abigail (Smith) Edgecombe, wife of Joseph Edgecombe, d. Mar 26, 1854, age 62.
10. James Edgecombe, son of Pendleton and Margaret Edgecombe, lost at sea, May 8, 1827, commemorated on tomb door.
11. Nancy (Chase) Edgecombe, buried in tomb, wife of James, d. Jan. 15, 1887.
12. Sarah Ann Edgecombe, buried in tomb, daughter of James and Nancy C. Edgecombe, d. Feb. 13, 1902.

Nancy Dearborn Lovetere Collection

The tomb, shown here in 2003, holds only two of the Edgecombe family members.

Kelley
13. Anna Kelley, daughter of Joseph and Abigail Edgecombe, wife of Robert R. Kelley, d. May 8, 1858, age 36.
14. Robert R. Kelley, husband to Anna, d. May. 23, 1897, age 80.

Sylvester

15. Elizabeth (Smith) Sylvester, wife of Marlborough Sylvester, Esq.;
    mother of Abigail Smith, wife of Joseph Edgecombe; and Elizabeth
    Smith, wife of Samuel Edgecombe; d. Feb 13, 1862, age 90 yrs., 5 mos.
16. Charles Sylvester, son of Elizabeth and Marlborough Sylvester, d. at
    sea, Nov. 29, 1813, age 36 yrs., 6 mos.

Compiled by Lorelei Gustafson for The USGenweb Project. Contributors to this and other cemetery records used various abbreviations. For the most part, parenthetical comments and bracketed comments are those of various compilers. Information was sometimes recorded on the stone itself.

Roberts-Edgecomb Burial Ground

This burial ground, also known as the Roberts Burial Ground, is located on the east side of North Bath Road, heading north, overlooking the Kennebec on the former Galen Ward property, just past Fairhaven Inn. Many headstones are now gone.

Peters

1. Lydia E. Peters, daughter of John and Reliance (Edgecombe) Peters
   (Reliance, daughter of John and Sarah Ham Edgecombe), d. Mar. 1,
   1848, age 17.

Roberts

2. Lydia Roberts, daughter of John and Sarah (Ham) Edgecomb, wife of
   John F. Roberts, d. Dec. 31, 1868, age 62 yrs., 2 mos., 16 days.
3. Abbie Edgecomb Roberts, daughter of John F. and Lydia (Edgecomb)
   Roberts, d. Sept. 20, 1918, age 79 yrs., 4 mos., 29 days.

Brimijin

4. Sarah R. Brimijin, child of Jesse I. and Sarah E. Brimijin, daughter of
   John & Sarah (Ham) Edgecomb, d. Sept 24, 1849, age 3 yrs., 4 mos.
5. Charles H. Brimijin, son of Jesse I. & Sarah E. Brimijin, d. Oct. 1,
   1849.

Edgecomb

6. Joel Edgecomb, son of Joel Sr. (son of John and Sarah Ham Edgecomb) and Charity (McKenney) Edgecomb; d. May 2, 1900, age 70 yrs., 3 mos.

Timmins

7. Martha Timmins, daughter of John and Sarah (Ham) Edgecomb, widow of Capt. Thomas Timmins, d. Aug. 12, 1863, age 65 yrs., 1 mo., 13 days.

Compiled by Lorelei Gustafson for the USGenWeb Project.

The Sagadahoc Rod, Gun & Skeet Club

The Bath City Directory of 1888 mentions two sporting clubs, the Sagadahock Gun Club and The Sagadahock Association for the Protection of Game and Fish. *Owen's History of Bath* shows the Bath Rod and Gun Club, incorporated in 1897, as having a range in Woolwich.

Courtesy of Barbara Marriner

Members practice their shots at the SRG&S Club.

The Sagadahoc Rod, Gun & Skeet Club was incorporated in Bath in 1934.[42] Before land was purchased on the North Bath Road in 1942, members shot at the location of the present-day Public Works Department on Oak Grove Avenue, near Whiskeag Creek. The land was bordered by property owned by George F. Wright, the Kennebec River, property owned by Albert Ward, and Whiskeag Road. Some names in the deed conveyance were Frank Ward, Eugene and Jesse Aderton, Lorin Eggleston, and Daniel Gleason. The *1858 Chace Map* shows several buildings on this spot.

The small blue building high on the hill overlooking the river was a canteen, or lunchroom, moved there after World War II from Bath Iron Works. It served as a clubhouse for many years. The small houses below on the range, also from Bath Iron Works, may once have been guardhouses or rigger shacks used beneath the cranes.

Before the North Bath Road land was acquired, the SRG&S Club met at various places in Bath, such as the YMCA Club Room, Winnegance Community Club, Central Church Parish House, State Armory, North End Community Club, and South End PTA Hall. Club minutes as far back as 1934 list clambakes; coon, bird-dog, and hound trials; pheasant and rabbit hunting; and fishing. Suppers featuring steaks, chicken pies, baked beans, and turkey generated funds for the club.

Nancy Dearborn Lovetere Collection

The old clubhouse at the Sagadahoc Rod, Gun & Skeet Club, acquired after World War II from Bath Iron Works.

Nancy Dearborn Lovetere Collection

From the Sagadahoc Rod, Gun & Skeet Club, one can see Crawford and Wood islands and Thorne Head.

The club was involved in state conservation measures pertaining to Merrymeeting Bay, Winnegance Creek, and Back Cove in Portland. Members participated in field trials at Merrymeeting Park, which was across from the Brunswick Naval Air Station. Still active today, the club meets on Sundays; familiar shots ring out once church bells stop pealing.

Lines and the Whiskeag Islands

Over the years the islands of the east and west branch of the Kennebec have changed names, usually because of new ownership. Lines Island, which divides the east and west branches, boasts at least eleven different titles. Folklore makes for an interesting interpretation of Lines: "The islands in that part of the Kennebec are all lined up!" Most historians would agree, however, that Lines is a corruption of Lynde's Island, later becoming Lyne's, as well as Lane's and Lyn's. There was a Lynde house, circa 1600s, in Melrose, Massachusetts, whose owner's name was pronounced as "lined."

The island is approximately eight-tenths of a mile long by three-tenths of a mile wide, encompassing about 138 acres.

Christopher Lawson bought Lines from Derumkin, an Androscoggin Indian, probably about 1649. It was then called Purchas' Island (perhaps after Thomas Purchase). Lawson later sold it to Edward Camer (Keemer). Camer's Island in turn was sold to Samuel Lyne (or Lynde) of Boston in 1677. Forty years later he gave the island to his granddaughter, Mary Ballantine. The island, which sat dormant for many years during the Indian Wars, was later claimed by the Plymouth Company, who referred to it as Linesses. That is the last we hear of the Ballantines, as Silvester Gardiner, a Kennebec Proprietor who seemingly got all the choice pieces of land, made it his island, Gardiner's Island. He had homes on both sides of the Kennebec with the island in the middle.

According to Henry Thayer,[43] in 1754 James Grace sued Samuel Harnden for trespass on Lynde's or Little Lynde's Island. James Blen testified that Harnden "sent sloop loads of cord wood from the island. Blen worked for him 6 years ago and Harden [sic] said he owned the island." Thomas Joy testified that he worked for Harnden and cut wood there. Samuel Harden's son, Samuel Jr., helped his father build a house on the island. Samuel Jr. also sold an "island near Harnden's narrows in the mouth of Whisgeg Creek" to Samuel Thompson of Topsham. In 1754 John Sullivan made staves for Harnden; Ebenezer Preble in the same year saw Harnden load a sloop there, and he himself fenced and cleared land and built a house on the island. The last sentence in the record says, "In suit Harnden got case 5 s[hillings] and costs."

William King purchased Lines in 1808 and crowned it King's Island, according to Lincoln County deeds. The deed then went to Ebenezer Arnold to Jacob C. Goss and to the Ledyard family, who owned the island for more than a century. Cellar holes, farm roads, and fences are shown on various maps of the island in the mid-1800s. There also is evidence of a brickyard in the southern part of the island. Woolwich farmers pastured sheep on Lines; grazing cows were sent from the North Bath side. The Ledyard family sold Lines Island in 1952.

In 1960, real estate entrepreneurs proposed a development for the island that never came to fruition. The "Kennebec Island Colony" was similar to a plan for an elaborate Florida community today. It featured almost enough lots for every day of the year, minus twenty. Eleven roads bisected the island, with a perimeter road just at the edge of the premier riverfront lots. A swimming pool with a water-controlled dike was planned for the north end of the island, while the south end was to feature a restaurant and marina. The blueprint reads: "The municipal offices of the City of Bath, Maine, unanimously approve this official map of the Kennebec Island Colony, on Wednesday, June 1, 1960, in accordance with section 14-5, Chapter 11, of the Statues of Maine 1954 revised. Attest: Harry E. Ring, Jr., City Clerk."[44]

For many years, Bath and Woolwich argued about who owned the island, but the river channel, which should have been the defining marker, ran around both sides. In 1966–67, the state legislature declared that the boundary should go through the center of the channel, bisecting the island, with Thorne Island included on the Woolwich side. In 2006, the Maine Department of Inland Fisheries and Wildlife purchased the island, making it state-owned.

The other islands, occasionally referred to as the Whiskeag Islands, Whigby Islands, and Middle Ground, have changed names less frequently than Lines. Thorne's (also Thorne) is the second largest, with seven and a half acres. It was sometimes called Little Lines, but today that title is reserved for the small island that is an appendage of Lines. On the *1858 Chace Map*, Thorne's is placed where we see Wood Island (spelled Woods today). Crawford Island, just off land owned by the Crawford family, was also shown as Sheep Island in the nineteenth century. Sheep is a sister island to Ram, shown as Haley's.

Rocky Reach

Two driveways several hundred feet apart divert off the North Bath Road near a little garage and eventually connect. Overlooking the Kennebec River, Rocky Reach, named in 1967, hides several homes. An old road left the shore of Little Whiskeag Creek and came up the hill, crossing the North Bath Road in the direction of Fresh Meadow. The Patridge home at the Rocky Reach promontory and the Woolwich shore is shown on the *1858 Chace Map*. The Patridge cellar hole is still visible.

The first home visible today from North Bath Road was previously the Oscar Wright farm, shown as that of O. A. Timmins on the *Chace Map*. Next in line is the "Crawford cape," originally a Federal-style house circa 1820, which has been disassembled and stored; the Edward Page home, built in Bath between 1790 and 1805, was moved to the foundation of the cape. At the end of the driveway is an old Federal-style farmhouse, shown as W. Hodgkins's. In 1907 all these homes, including the C. C. E. Whitham farm, could be seen on the hillside from the vantage point of the old schoolhouse on the corner of Varney Mill Road.

Nancy Dearborn Lovetere Collection

This garage on the North Bath Road sits between two roads that lead to Rocky Reach.

Courtesty of Judy Barrington

This home at the end of the driveway to the Crawford Cape belonged to W. Hodgkins, according to the Chace *Map of 1858. It is shown here in 1967.*

A letter from Captain John Crawford[45] was found in the attic beside a chimney in the old Hodgkins farmhouse, written on the fifth of April, the year unclear. A sheet of paper, folded in half to form two pages, was folded again to shape an envelope. It was sent from Charlestown to Thomas Crawford, Bath, Massachusetts, K.B. After leaving Kennebec, John mentions sailing on a ship, the *Florida*, and the severe gale that forced the crew to Trinidad to discharge their deck load. After returning to Charlestown, he left on the brig *Hiram*.[46] Other places noted were Mont Bourne and Collenberg, England. He closes his letter with: "Mr. Thomas Timmins[47] and Joseph send their love to you all. William Crawford was well the last time . . . I have not seen him this fair day for we dropped down to the roads a week ago. I sent twenty dollars home to William. I expect we shall get home in eight months. I hope this finds you all in good health. I expect we shall sail tomorrow if the wind is fair. Remember me to all inquiring friends, Yours, John Crawford."

Captain John Crawford, having no fair winds, died at sea from yellow fever on April 22, 1819, at age thirty-two; he was on passage from the West Indies to Bath.

Crawford Burial Ground

The Crawford Burial Ground is off the North Bath Road in a back pasture on the bank of the Peterson Canal at the location of the old Oscar Wright Farm, now the Taggert property.

Crawford

1. Capt. James G. Crawford, d. Apr. 1, 1867, age 72.
2. Margaret M. Rogers, wife of Capt. James G. Crawford, d. Aug. 12, 1830, age 34.
3. Rebecca (Chandler) Mereen, second wife of Capt. James G. Crawford, d. Mar. 26, 1876, age 68.
4. Thomas O. Crawford, killed in battle of Antietam, Sept. 17, 1862, age 20.
5. Capt. Thomas Crawford, d. Apr. 12, 1837, age 81, DAR marker.
6. Frances (Grace) Crawford, wife of Thomas Crawford, d. Oct 25, 1826, age 71.
7. Capt. Thomas Crawford, son of Frances, lost at sea, Sept. 1811, age 31.
8. John G. Crawford, son of Frances, d. Apr. 22, 1819, age 32.
9. Frances Crawford, d. Aug. 26, 1876, age 86 yrs., 6 mos.
10. Capt. William Crawford, d. Sept 2, 1851, age 69.
11. Mary L. (Pease) Crawford, wife of Wm. Crawford, d. Oct 20, 1859, age 66 yrs., 5 mos., 8 days.
12. Thomas Crawford (in memory of), son of Capt. Wm. and Mary L. Crawford, d. at sea, July 30, 1835, age 19.
13. John G. Crawford, son of Capt. Wm. and Mary L. Crawford, d. May 20, 1836, age 7 yrs., 8 mos.

Timmins

14. James C. Timmins, son of Thomas and Sukey (Susannah) Timmins, d. Feb. 14, 1816, age 11 mos.
15. Mrs. Sukey Crawford, wife of Capt. Thomas Timmins, d. Mar. 22, 1826, age 42.
16. Catherine F. (Fox) Timmins, daughter of Thomas and Sukey Timmins, d. Mar. 6, 1829, age 21.
17. Franklin W. Timmins, son of O. A. (Owen Augustus) and Lucy Timmins, d. Sept. 18, 1849, age 15 mos.
18. Frank A. Timmins, son of O. A. and Lucy Timmins, d. Aug 5, 1868, age 14.

Haley

19. Mary F. Haley, daughter of Josiah D. and Mary S. Haley, d. Aug. 24, 1863, age 15.
20. Mary S. Haley, wife of Josiah D. Haley, d. May 23, 1875, age 83 yrs., 9 mos.
21. Catherine F. T. Haley, daughter of Josiah D. and Mary S. Haley, d. May 24, 1832, age 18 mos.

Mereen

22. Rebecca (Chandler) Mereen, widow of Capt. Samuel Mereen, d. Sept. 26, 1849, age 72.
23. John Orin Mereen, son of John and Lucia Mereen, d. Aug. 25, 1844, age 2 mos.

Arnold

24. Mrs. Margaret, wife of Nathanial Arnold, d. _________.

Foster

25. Winfield S. Foster, son of George and Susan Foster, d. May 30, 1853, age 2 yrs., 4 mos.

Varney

26. Lunette, daughter of William W. and Rebecca C. Varney, d. July 1, 1861, age 3 yrs., 4 mos.

Compiled by Lolelei Gustafson for The USGenweb Project.

Welch-Wise Burial Ground

As noted previously, the Welch-Wise burial ground has the oldest headstone in the area, that of Elizabeth Wise, who died in 1749 at age thirty-four. Two other headstones are those of Captain William Welch and his wife Molly Smith.

Wise

Elizabeth, wife of John, d. Oct. 24, 1749, age 34.

Welch

Capt. William, d. 1844, age 93 (removed to Richmond, Maine).

Smith

Molly, wife of Capt. William Welch, d. about 1844, age 86.

Compiled by Harold Brown, Doris Rowland, and Helen McPhee.

Little Whiskeag Creek

Because there is little written history of this area, one must look at deeds and maps to chronicle the events of the past four hundred years. The names on these documents mark the location of proprietors, farmers, and immigrants. From Casco Bay to the New Meadows River,[48] also known as Stephen's (Steven's) River and Purchase's (Purchas') River, came water which flowed into Little Whiskeag Creek by way of the Peterson Canal, a man-made waterway partially visible today. Depending upon the period of history in which its waters flowed and who lived on its banks, Little Whiskeag was called Welch's Creek, Wittum's (Whittam's) Creek, and Crawford's Creek. A cemetery or two along the way memorialize its people.

On the geodetic map, a very distinct road or way across the inlet at Little Whiskeag Creek is shown, a bit to the north of the causeway used today. At low tide it is apparent that many large stones still loosely bridge the two shores. Perhaps this was the original crossing; another theory is that the rocks were placed there to prevent the fields from flooding. Or perhaps a stone fish weir? Deeds and books mention that various people lived "above the old dike," both at this location and New Meadows. Modern navigational maps show a "dike" at this spot. The flow of water here possibly powered a tidewater mill, as millstones have been found less than a quarter-mile away.

Little Whiskeag is the end of the Peterson Canal where it spills into the Kennebec. It may have been an important Indian carry, or portage, as it presents a perfect location to launch a canoe carried from Merrymeeting Bay at the Androscoggin River, westerly. This would quickly place Native Americans on the Kennebec River, thus eliminating passage around the northern tip of Butler Head.

The Crawford family, whose name is on many documents, owned a great deal of property from the Kennebec River to Merrymeeting Bay. Ancestors of Grace and Crawford still have homes in this location. The *Survey Map of the Crawford Farm of 1837*[49] shows The Ireland Road. Thomas Crawford is listed in the *Wigwam Point Deposition* as a weaver. Perhaps Little Whiskeag provided the source of power for his occupation? The *1718 Pejepscot Proprietors Map* shows "Mr. Lawson's Cellar." Christopher Lawson owned all of this North Bath property, which is shown on the *Map of Ancient Sagadahock*, from the Chops to Little Whigby. A cooper by trade, Lawson was considered an Antinomian, a "Christian by faith not law." One of the former Grace-Edgecomb homes on the Varney Mill Road was part of a large farm that had a cooper's building. The Crooker family, living near the end of Varney Mill Road, was also engaged in barrel making.

The *1764 Plymouth Company Plan* shows just four buildings; two are located very close to the shores of Little Whiskeag Creek.

Part Three

Ireland—North of Bath

North Bath drew numerous immigrants from Ireland. The descendancy file of one such immigrant couple, the Graces, shows they were the progenitors of more than fifteen other family names in the area. Meanwhile, the Irish built their own church, school, and post office. Dairy farming, barrel making, and mills were early industries in this part of North Bath.

The Irish and the Ulster-Scots

Beckoned by better agricultural land and religious freedom, hundreds of Protestant Presbyterians left their homes in Scotland to settle in the north of Ireland, known as the Ulster Plantation, between 1605 and 1697. By 1718, however, increased rents, religious persecution, drought, and poor crops—the very reasons they had abandoned their homeland— necessitated another move. Encouraged by influential religious leader Cotton Mather to create "good Scotch Colonies," they set off for New England in what is known as the Great Migration of 1718. By 1720, more than five hundred of them had made the trip.

Colonists already in the new world, overwhelmed by the influx of these immigrants and hoping to buffer their own settlements from the French and Indians, sent them on to the frontier lands of Maine, New Hampshire, and western Massachusetts. These settlers have collectively been called Scot-Irish, although John Mann, in his book *Ulster-Scots on the Coast of Maine*, explains that the Ulster-Scots were commonly referred to as Scotch Irish or simply Irish. As a result, there was confusion as to the identity of the origins of many in Maine who had migrated primarily from Scotland through the Ulster Plantation and then on to the American colonies.

A portion of the first group of Ulster-Scots who arrived spent their first winter in Falmouth (now Portland), Maine. Others soon followed

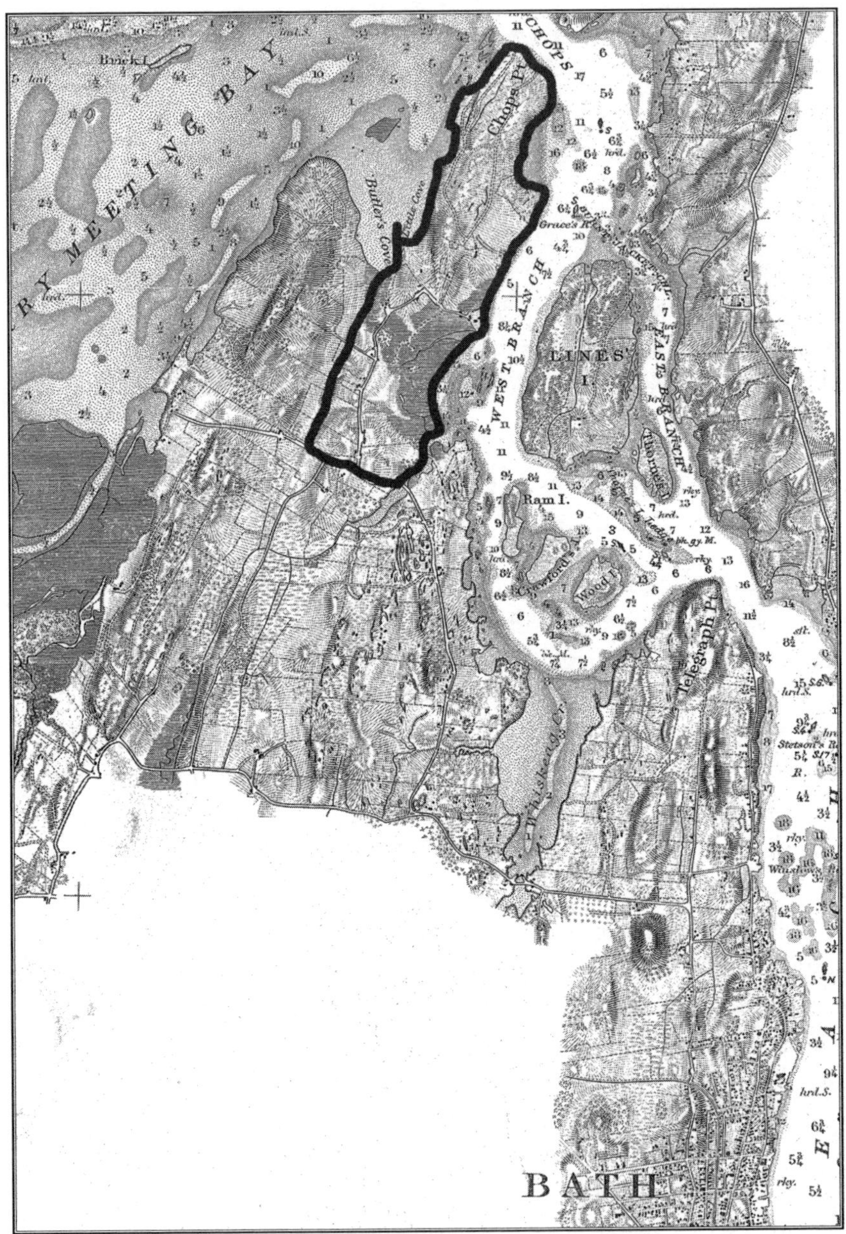

National Oceanic and Atmospheric Administration

The Ireland area of North Bath

and eventually settled throughout the Casco Bay area and the lower Kennebec River valley, including Brunswick, Woolwich, and Bowdoinham. This group was known as the Kennebec Settlement and the Merrymeeting Bay Settlement.[50]

In describing a new meeting house in Pleasant Cove in Phippsburg in 1736, proponents of the church wrote: "the house for none other use but for public Worship of God according to form of discipline used in the church of Scotland." Today the only written remnants of the Scot-Irish in North Bath are the Crawford Farm maps layout names—Ireland Road or the Ireland District—and old journals and diaries that mention the Ireland District.

The Grace Family

James Grace, a Scotch-Presbyterian, emigrated from Cappa, County Clare, Ireland, to Woolwich, and married Jane Kneely, granddaughter of Alexander Drummond.[51] In 1759 Grace bought from the Kennebec Proprietors many acres of land known as the Chops Farm, the upper property purchased by Christopher Lawson from the Indians in 1640. Grace drowned in the Kennebec River, opposite his property, at the location of Grace Rock, just a little north of Lines Island. This is marked on most navigational maps and noted in Drummond family history.

The James Grace Descendancy File[52] is included here to show several of the Bath and North Bath families that have evolved from this one couple: Main, Crawford, Ward, Whittam, Witham, Rogers, Rook, Kelley, Batchelder, Mereen, Edgecomb, Timmons, Haley, Thornton, Perry, Percy, and Purington.

John Grace, James's son, married Hannah Hallowell Rogers in 1799. John and Hannah adopted their nephew, Samuel Wiley (Wylie) Rogers, whose parents were Martha Wiley and Samuel Hallowell Rogers. Samuel inherited the property from his adoptive father and married Lucinda Owen[53], with whom he had three sons. Samuel and Lucinda Rogers's first son, John Grace Rogers, married Catherine Smith Edgecombe and was a farmer and postmaster. That couple's son, Owen Rogers, inherited the family farm and home shown below. Owen married Lillian Sarah Mallett of Topsham on June 25, 1895. He was a Bath city councilman and a member of the West Bath Grange and the Winter Street Congregational Church. Owen was the first person in North Bath with a Delco generator that provided electricity to his barn. His water supply was gravity fed from a tower behind the house. Owen and Lillian took in boarders, serving them generous meals, which probably lessened their profits. Owen was known to serve his guests "Thanksgiving-style" from the head of the table at every meal.[54]

Nancy Dearborn Lovetere Collection

The Grace home

The James Grace Descendancy File

1 James Grace b: ABT 1725
  + Jane Kneely
    2 Mary Grace b: ABT 1748
    2 Margaret Grace b: ABT 1750 d: 14 Mar 1831
      + Samuel Main b: ABT 1750 d: 9 Jun 1810
        3 Samuel Main b: 20 Jan 1774 d: 24 Jan 1851
          + Abigail Moulton b: ABT 1774 d: 11 Aug 1870
            4 Dorothy Main b: 3 Feb 1799

4 Catherine Moulton Main b: 3 May 1801
4 Wealtha Moody Main b: 15 Oct 1804
4 Samuel Augustus Main b: 10 Jul 1806 d: 26 Sep 1806
4 Emeline Margaret Main b: 30 Aug 1808
4 Loyalist Brown Main b: 10 May 1810
  + Charlotte
    5 Loyalist Brown Main b: 1850
4 Abigail Ann Main b: 17 Jun 1812 d: 1 Sep 1812
4 Thomas Crawford Main b: 3 May 1814
4 Miranda Main b: 2 Jun 1817
4 Abigail Francis Main b: 2 May 1820
3 Amos Main b: ABT 1776
3 Joseph Main b: ABT 1779
  + Margaret McKay b: ABT 1780
4 Warren Main b: 11 Jul 1813
4 Franklin Main b: 9 Feb 1815
4 Lucinda Main b: 5 Nov 1816
4 Susan Main b: 9 Jan 1819
4 Margaret Main b: 9 Apr 1821
4 Lewis Main b: ABT 1823
4 Otis Main b: ABT 1825
4 Ann Main b: ABT 1827
4 Lydia Main b: ABT 1829
3 Dorothy Main b: 5 Jun 1783 d: 1889
3 Susan Main b: 5 Aug 1784 d: 10 Sep 1857
  + John Marble b: 27 Jul 1784
4 Amos Marble b: 23 Jan 1806
4 John Marble b: 23 May 1807
4 Mary Ann Marble b: 10 Jan 1810 d: BEF 1821
4 Charles Winslow Marble b: 30 Apr 1812
4 Lucinda Marble b: 30 Apr 1812
  + Stillman Linsdey b: ABT 1810
4 William Harrison Marble b: 15 Apr 1814
4 Benjamin Flagg Marble b: 28 Nov 1818
4 Mary Ann Marble b: 12 Feb 1821

4 Levi Emery Marble b: 5 Aug 1823
3 James Main b: 8 Mar 1787 d: 2 Jul 1863
  + Martha Blair b: ABT 1788
    4 James Main b: 21 Jan 1808
    4 Caroline Main b: 23 Oct 1809
    4 Amos Main b: 12 Apr 1812
    4 Robert Blair Main b: 13 Dec 1813
      + Louisa Dorcus Buswell b: 6 Oct 1827
    4 Andrew Jackson Main b: 8 May 1817
    4 Iram Main b: 13 Jan 1820
    4 Harrison Main b: 9 Jun 1822
    4 Martha Ella Main b: 17 Oct 1824
    4 Mary Main b: 31 Mar 1826
    4 Elinor Main b: ABT 1828
2 Elsie Grace b: ABT 1751 d: 12 May 1825
 + Eban Ward b: ABT 1750 d: 25 Dec 1774
  3 James Ward b: 8 Jan 1774 d: 29 May 1862
   + Ruth Brown b: 6 Jul 1783 d: 11 Dec 1863
    4 Fanny Grace Ward b: 1 Apr 1802
    4 Ebenezer Ward b: 1 Feb 1804 d: Jan 1831
    4 Daniel Brown Ward b: 27 Feb 1806 d: 1836
      + Margaret Elliott b: ABT 1810
    4 Thirza Maria Ward b: 7 Mar 1808
    4 Robert Ward b: 22 May 1810
    4 Asa Ward b: 23 Jul 1812 d: 3 Sep 1812
    4 Candace Ward b: 16 Sep 1813
    4 Narcissa Stone Ward b: 12 Feb 1817
    4 Hannah Parker Ward b: 12 Oct 1819
    4 James Brown Ward b: 17 Jul 1825
  3 Jane Grace Ward b: 19 May 1775 d: 2 Feb 1848
   + Mathew Whittam b: ABT 1775 d: 24 Apr 1817
    4 Jesse Grace Whittam b: ABT 1803
    4 Charles Whittam b: 17 Apr 1805
    4 Matthew Whittam b: 13 Jul 1807
    4 Margaret Jane Whittam b: 27 May 1812

    4 Thomas Timmins[55] Whittam b: 2 Mar 1816 d: 14 Jun 1898
2 Thomas Grace b: ABT 1752 d: ABT 1776
2 Jane Grace b: 1753 d: 2 Sep 1825
  + Robert Rogers b: 10 Apr 1752 d: 9 Jan 1815
   3 Thomas Grace Rogers b: 12 Jul 1775 d: 18 Aug 1840
    + Martha Hunter b: 20 Nov 1778 d: 21 Oct 1865
     4 Robert Rogers b: 11 Feb 1799
     4 Martha Rogers b: 11 Mar 1801
     4 Lydia Rogers b: 2 Feb 1803
     4 Jane Rogers b: 22 Feb 1805
     4 Frances Ann Rogers b: 13 Sep 1807
     4 Rebecca Rogers b: 2 Mar 1810 d: 18 Jul 1839
     4 William Rogers b: 16 Mar 1813
     4 Ephraim Rogers b: 26 Apr 1815
     4 Agnes Campbell Rogers b: 14 Apr 1817
     4 John Jeremiah Rogers b: 22 Aug 1819
   3 George Rogers b: 23 Feb 1777 d: 24 Dec 1799
   3 William Rogers b: 1 Mar 1779
   3 Frances Rogers b: 17 Feb 1781 d: 23 Jul 1862
    + John Rook b: ABT 1780 d: Aug 1806
     4 George Rogers Rook b: 6 May 1802
     4 Mary Rook b: 4 Apr 1804
      + Francis Kelley b: ABT 1800
     4 John Rook b: Nov 1806
      + Thomas Kelley b: ABT 1780 d: 1 May 1815
   3 James Grace Rogers b: 12 Jun 1783 d: 9 Oct 1855
    + Ann Rogers b: ABT 1785
     4 Jane Rogers b: 20 Nov 1808
     4 George Alexander Rogers b: 17 Apr 1814
     4 Robert Rogers b: 12 Feb 1819
      + Elizabeth Mary Batchelder b: ABT 1820
   3 Ruth Rogers b: 26 Oct 1785 d: 23 Nov 1870
    + John Kelley b: 17 Oct 1786 d: 29 Jul 1867
     4 John Kelley b: 13 Nov 1813
      + Maria Mereen b: 13 May 1814 d: 8 Oct 1836

4 Robert Rutherford Kelley b: 25 Mar 1816 d: 23 May 1897
  + Anna Edgecomb b: 5 Jul 1824 d: 8 May 1858
    5 Charles S. Kelley b: ABT 1852
      + Cora E. Hutchins
    5 Rogers P. N. Kelley b: ABT 1858
4 Thomas Kelley b: 7 Jun 1818
4 William Kelley b: 6 Apr 1821 d: 7 Aug 1849
4 Jane Grace Kelley b: 25 Sep 1823 d: 30 Apr 1908
  + Waldron Cushing b: ABT 1823
4 Edward Allen Kelley b: 7 Apr 1828 d: 19 Mar 1872
3 Ann Allen Rogers b: 23 Mar 1787 d: 3 May 1871
  + Ballard Bartlett b: 10 May 1779 d: 9 May 1854
  4 William Rogers Bartlett b: 31 May 1810
  4 Lydia Bartlett b: 3 Jul 1812
  4 Ballard Bartlett b: 15 Dec 1814
  4 Drusilla Bartlett b: 31 Dec 1816
  4 Jeremiah Bartlett b: 20 Sep 1819 d: 24 Apr 1888
    + Almira Pinkham b: ABT 1820
  4 Henry Bartlett b: 15 Mar 1822 d: 14 Jun 1889
  4 Frances Mary Bartlett b: 15 Apr 1824
  4 Rufus King Bartlett b: 15 Apr 1826
  4 Hannah Ann Bartlett b: 14 Nov 1828
3 Jane Grace Rogers b: 18 Jul 1790 d: Nov 1868
  + Spencer Dingley b: ABT 1790 d: 23 Apr 1845
3 Mercy Rogers b: 9 Jan 1794
  + Benjamin Foster b: ABT 1794
3 Margaret Miller Rogers b: 16 May 1796 d: 12 Aug 1830
  + James Grace Crawford b: 21 Mar 1795 d: 1 Apr 1867
  4 Susan Timmons Crawford b: 30 Mar 1819
2 James Grace b: ABT 1755 d: ABT 1776
2 Frances Grace b: 10 Jun 1755 d: 25 Oct 1826
  + Thomas Crawford b: 23 Aug 1756 d: 12 Apr 1837
  3 Thomas Crawford b: 12 Sep 1780 d: Sep 1811
  3 William Crawford b: 12 Jul 1782 d: 2 Sep 1851
    + Mary T. Pease b: 12 Jul 1793 d: 20 Oct 1859

4 Mary Jane Crawford b: 3 May 1814

4 Thomas Crawford b: 28 Sep 1816 d: 30 Jul 1835

4 Lois P. Crawford b: 19 May 1819

4 William Henry Crawford b: 19 Mar 1824

4 John Grace Crawford b: 10 Sep 1828 d: 20 May 1836

3 Susannah Crawford b: 8 Jul 1785 d: 22 Mar 1826

+ Thomas Timmons b: ABT 1785 d: 25 Dec 1832

4 Catherine Fox Timmons b: 30 Sep 1807 d: 6 Mar 1829

4 Thomas Crawford Timmons b: 13 Jun 1812 d: 13 Dec 1812

4 James Grace Timmons b: 15 Dec 1814 d: 15 Feb 1816

4 Owen Augustus Timmons b: 7 Jan 1817

+ Lucy

5 Franklin W. Timmons b: ABT 18 Jun 1848 d: 18 Sep 1849

5 Frank A. Timmons b: ABT Aug 1854 d: 5 Aug 1868

4 Frances Mary Timmons b: 11 Mar 1819

4 Huldah Grace Timmons b: 11 Apr 1821

+ Samuel Wylie Grace Rogers b: Aug 1820

3 John Grace Crawford b: 17 Mar 1787 d: 22 Apr 1819

3 Frances Crawford b: 27 Feb 1790 d: 26 Aug 1876

3 Mary Smith Crawford b: 17 Aug 1793 d: 25 May 1875

+ Josiah Dill Haley b: ABT 1793

4 Mary Frances Haley b: 6 May 1828 d: 24 Aug 1863

4 Catherine Fox T. Haley b: 8 Nov 1830 d: 24 May 1832

4 Catherine J. Augusta Haley b: 9 Feb 1833

4 John Thomas Haley b: 9 Feb 1835

3 James Grace Crawford b: 21 Mar 1795 d: 1 Apr 1867

+ Margaret Miller Rogers b: 16 May 1796 d: 12 Aug 1830

4 Susan Timmons Crawford b: 30 Mar 1819

+ Rebecca Chandler Mereen b: 3 Feb 1808 d: 28 Mar 1876

4 James Wylie Crawford b: 21 Oct 1832

4 Rebecca Chandler Crawford b: 30 Jul 1834

4 Margaret Ann Crawford b: 3 May 1836

4 Hannah Melissa Crawford b: 21 Jun 1838

4 Lorenzo Mereen Crawford b: 11 Aug 1840

4 Thomas Orin Crawford b: 5 Sep 1842 d: 17 Sep 1862

4 Ellen Adelia Crawford b: 5 Apr 1845

2 Patrick Grace b: 1758 d: 21 Sep 1829

+Huldah Purington [possibly sister of Joshua Purinton]

2 John Grace b: 1761 d: 19 Jan 1831

+ Hannah Hallowell Rogers b: 23 Dec 1773

  3 Samuel Wylie Grace Rogers b: Aug 1820

  + Huldah Grace Timmons b: 11 Apr 1821

2 William Grace b: 13 Apr 1764

+ Sarah Andrews b: 30 May 1757 d: 23 Feb 1837

  3 Thomas Grace b: 1785

  3 William Grace b: ABT 1787

  3 Jane Grace b: ABT 1789

    + William Thornton b: ABT 1790

  3 Hannah Grace b: 1791

    + Samuel Witham b: ABT 1790

  3 Elsie Grace b: 21 Feb 1796 d: 3 Jan 1866

    + David Percy b: 29 Nov 1791 d: 9 Feb 1867

      4 Rachel G. Percy b: 8 Apr 1817 d: 25 Sep 1818

      4 Rachel Jane Percy b: 12 May 1819

      4 Mary Elizabeth Percy b: 22 Feb 1822

      4 John Grace Percy b: 14 Jun 1824

      4 Marcus D. Percy b: 22 Sep 1826 d: 4 Jul 1828

      4 Andrew Jackson Percy b: 14 Mar 1829

      4 David Thomas Percy b: 15 Aug 1831

      4 Alice Joanna Percy b: 22 Apr 1834 d: 1 May 1836

      4 William Percy b: 14 Aug 1836 d: 4 Sep 1836

  3 Rachel Grace b: ABT 1798

    + Amasa Smith b: ABT 1795

  3 John Grace b: ABT 1800

    + Percy

The Union Chapel

The Union Chapel, between the two intersections of Varney Mill–North Bath roads and Bayshore–Ridge roads, was set back from the road alongside a private driveway. Built in the 1880s, it likely was developed so that the Irish residents of North Bath, most of them Scotch-Presbyterian, didn't have to travel to Bath to worship. It was demolished in the 1960s. According to records at Bath's Patten Free Library, several community chapels, such as the one at Parker Head and Dromore, were organized as "Free Union" with denominations of Baptist and Methodist. A Bath City Directory of 1927 lists a Union Church in Popham.

Annie E. Wylie of Sanford Road in West Bath, in a diary[56] entry dated March 14, 1886, mentions that she "Heard an awful thing. A big boat exploded and two of Warren Crooker's sons were killed."[57] She writes that their funeral was "at the chapel in Ireland." In 1892 records show Frederick E. Wright, clerk; George F. Wright, treasurer; John G. Wright, superintendent of Sunday school; John H. Morse, assistant Sunday school teacher; and George T. Ward, librarian.

The North Bath School

Diagonally across the road from the Union Chapel, on the site of the log cabin home that sits today at the corner of Varney Mill and North Bath roads, was the original North Bath schoolhouse, built in 1808. It was later demolished, and rebuilt in 1858. In 1862 it was called the Ireland School. *The City of Bath Almanac and Directory of 1902* lists it

Courtesy of Calvin Wing

The North Bath School

Courtesy of Martha Rea and Millie Simpson Stewart

A North Bath School class, c. 1905. Those identified are Lester and Carl Crooker, in the front row wearing the boutonnieres; Lucy Ward Simpson, in the second row wearing a plaid dress; Thomasine (Thoma) Crooker, in the back row, far right.

as the North Bath Mixed School. It was demolished in 1935. In the 1940s a horse-drawn school wagon was discovered at the top of the pasture lane dividing the former Peters-Rogers property, just around the corner from the schoolhouse site.

Fourteen boys and twenty-one girls attended the school in 1891. The reading curriculum for the sixth grade in 1904 was *The Story of the Thirteen Colonies*, *Evangeline*, and *Hiawatha*, "with selections memorized."

Some of the grade-school teachers and principals were:

1851–66   Lydia Curtis, principal (with a salary of $214 and a fuel bill of $27.77 in 1862)

1864–68	Miss S. M. Springer
1866	E. Rich (the Rich family lived in the present-day Hawkes house)
1871	Miss Jennie R. Rich
1872	Josephine A. Haley
1876, 1877	Fred. E. C. Robbins; Miss J. A. Haley
1879–83	Miss Sophia M. Rich
1881–84	Miss M. Tabor, principal; A. W. Rogers, assistant; James W. Kelley, instructor of penmanship
1887	Miss Sarah Purington
1888	Miss J. Dunton, principal
1891–1903	Miss L. E. LaRock, principal
1906	Ella C. Whitney[58]

Nancy Dearborn Lovetere Collection

The old post office, as seen in 2003

The North Bath Post Office

The first official post office was established in America in 1639. In 1775, initial post offices in Maine were located in Kennebunk, Falmouth, and Bath. Richard Kimball delivered the mail to Bath from the Falmouth (Portland) office every two weeks. Prior to the Revolution and then until 1780, Luke Lombard carried mail on horseback to Boston twice a month. Dummer Sewall was the first postmaster in Bath, serving from 1791 until 1806; for a time he kept an office at his house just north of the railroad bridge at 1110 High Street, which remains a Sewall homestead. Later the postal facility was moved to Front and Summer streets in downtown Bath.

Little is known about early postal service in North Bath. The post office for the area, finally razed in 2007, was on the Grace-Rogers/Dearborn/Sutherland property. At that time the homestead was a dairy farm adjacent to the pasture lane shared with the Wisbee Dairy Farm. Letter slots were found in the building in 1940. *Maine Postal History and Postmarks* lists a post office in North Bath from 1890 to 1898. Records from Washington, D.C., show the request form for the proposed post office and subsequent documentation of its establishment. Sagadahoc County post offices and masters also are listed on the same page.[59] A Bath directory of 1892–97 shows John Grace Rogers, farmer and postmaster, living in North Bath.

Many early post offices were private, making their own connections with the major Post Road post offices until they became profitable or important. The North Bath Post Office was private and not profitable, closing after eight years of operation.

Nancy Dearborn Lovetere Collection

The Wing milk label

Nancy Dearborn Lovetere Collection

The old Wisbee dairy farm

Nancy Dearborn Lovetere Collection

The Wing family cemetery

Courtesy of Marilyn Wright

Pat Wing and Richard LeBlanc play on a hay wagon at the Wisbee Farm.

Courtesy of Marilyn Wright

Adeline Wing feeds chickens at the Wisbee Farm, started by her husband, Earl.

The Wing Family

Deborah (Bachiler)[60] Wing, widow of the Reverend John Wing,[61] left England in March of 1632[62] with her father, the Reverend Stephen Bachiler, and her four sons, settling in Saugus (now Lynn), Massachusetts. In 1637 they moved to a new settlement in Sandwich, Massachusetts.

Simeon, Deborah's great-great-grandson, had a daughter, Elizabeth, who married a fellow from Wayne, Maine. Her seven brothers followed her to Wayne and settled around Wing's Pond.[63] High above the pond, they built a cemetery, locally known as the Wing Ring. A tall monument stands in the center of concentric circles with the names of Simeon's sons: Simeon, Ebenezer, Aaron, Allen, Moses, William, and Thomas. In the past, Wing family members gathered here each spring. Today the family has its annual reunion in Sandwich, called the *Wing Ding*; their publication is *The Owl*.

Earl Edward Wing left Wayne to settle in the Bath area around 1900. That year's census places him at the home of a relative, Emery Wing, working as a farmhand. Earl was a resident farmer for the Stone House near Whiskeag Creek; he and his bride, Adeline B. (Blair), honeymooned in the white caretaker's cottage there. Adeline was one of the first students graduating from the Bath City Hospital Training School for Nurses. Earl later started his own dairy operation, the Wisbee Farm, at the start of Varney Mill Road. In 1937 his brother, (James) Carroll Wing, moved to North Bath from Farmington. Several close family members still live on Varney Mill Road; others are nearby in West Bath and Bath. Earl, who was known as "Wingy" to neighborhood children, is buried at the cemetery in Wayne, as are his wife and parents.

The Crooker Family

Francis Crooker was born in England in 1622, and settled in Marshfield, Massachusetts, where he married Mary Gaunt. One of their three children, Jonathan, was born in 1654. He lived in Marshfield with his wife, Mary Burroughs, with whom he had ten children.

Crooker Mill advertisement

Courtesy of Hazel Tardiff

The Crooker mill, circa 1897–1916

Courtesy of Hazel Tardiff

The former home of Zacheus Crooker

Courtesy of Martha Rea

Lumber stacks at the Crooker mill, taken over by Zacheus's son, Charles William

Courtesy of Martha Rea

In back of the Crooker home, Lester Crooker sits on a barrel made by his family.

Jonathan and Mary's son, Francis, was born in 1687. He married twice, his second wife being Patience Childs. Their fourth child, Isaiah, was born in 1729/30, also in Marshfield; Isaiah came to Bath about 1750. He was first married to Elizabeth (Betsey) Philbrook, daughter of Jonathan Philbrook. Isaiah's second wife was Hannah Harding McKenney, a widow from Truro, Massachusetts. With his two wives, Isaiah fathered eleven children.

Zacheus,[64] one of the eleven, married Polly Merritt, who was related to the Stockbridge family from Scituate, Massachusetts. They were the first Crookers to live in North Bath. They had twelve children, including Isaiah, named after his grandfather, born in 1807. The Crookers' neat brick home, tucked into the hillside facing east, saw early-morning sea smoke on the Kennebec, followed by the sun's glow as it rose above Lines Island.

Known as an expert joiner who made wooden tanks for Bath-built ships, Isaiah also operated a sleigh factory and a steam sawmill right across the road from his home. His obituary mentions "a sunshiny, happy Christian gentleman . . . almost his last words were to his wife about attending to some little church duty that had been his custom." The district school and Joseph Varney's mill were closed during his funeral service. Isaiah and his wife, Mary Benner, were predeceased by six children, whose names were not included in his obituary. Isaiah was survived by a daughter, Ellen Crooker Cornish, and a son, Charles William Crooker, who carried on his trades.

Charles married Adrianna Abigail Cornish. They had three children. The *1858 Chace Map* shows several buildings at the very end of Varney Mill Road with the name Crooker, as well as a tub factory in the same location of the Crooker lots in North Bath. Isaiah was listed as a cooper in the 1860 census. Included in Charles's lumber business was the manufacture of shingles and clapboards. It was dismantled in 1916.

Ellen A. Crooker Cornish was born in the brick home; her passing occurred on the second anniversary of the death of her brother, Charles. She and her husband, Hiram Cornish, lived a few houses south from where she grew up on the Varney Mill Road. Her obituary said she "had been an invalid for the past two years and was uncomplaining to the end."

Varney's Island

Three-and-a-half-acre Varney's Island is east of Varney Mill Road and northwest of Line's Island on the West Branch of the Kennebec River. It is privately owned and accessible at low tide by walking about fifty yards through shallow water. The *1764 Plymouth Company Plan of Georgetown* shows the island connected to the mainland. On the map at the chapter head, structures on the island are depicted as small black shapes, and eight buildings are indicated there on the *1858 Chace Map*.

One of the original deeds to Varney's Island dates back to Kennebec Proprietor Silvester Gardiner. Various deeds mention Robert Hallowell Gardiner, Zacheus Crooker, Hugh and Samuel Wiley Rogers, Adam Lemont, and Joseph Varney. It was also known as Black Island and Lemont's Island.

Alfred Lemont established the Lemont Shipyard for wood transportation as well as a large steam lumbermill at Lemont's Island from 1851 until 1865. Alfred was the great-grandson of John[65] and Elizabeth (McLanathan) Lemont of Londonderry, Ireland. Samuel Morse was Lemont's master ship-builder. Alfred, brother of Levi P. Lemont, was married to Malinda

Hodgdon. Alfred retired to West Bath to his farm overlooking Campbell's Pond. He died in 1896.

In 1650, the progenitors of most of the Varneys in New England were William and Brigit, who came from England to Ipswich, Massachusetts. Their children were Rachel, Humphrey, Thomas, and Sarah. Eight generations later, in 1824, Joseph Varney, a progeny of Humphrey, was born in Topsham, Maine. As a young man he operated a fruit and confectionary store in Brunswick. Later he became a log driver on the Androscoggin River. His father, Enoch, also in the lumber business, inspired young Joseph to start a mill business to manufacture box shooks.

From 1852 until 1864, Joseph Varney worked for Adam and Alfred Lemont. He bought the business, which employed more than fifty, and carried on the Lemont tradition of shipping the goods manufactured at the mills (such as lumber, timber, and house frames) from the adjacent shipyard to local towns and distant ports, such as New York and Boston. Although "Varney's Mill Road" was conceived with the birth of a road sign in the 1950s, replacing the spoken "Road to Down Street," research shows that there was more than one mill on this island.

Joseph Varney had four children by his first wife, Melinda J. Bishop of Brunswick, and eight children by his second wife, Julia A. Williams of Topsham. In 1894 his mills caught fire, causing $15,000 in damages. He retired the following year and died in Bath in 1900. The census of 1900 indicates that Julia Varney had moved to 1062 Washington Street in Bath.

Over the years, many local men worked at the mill, but the censuses of 1870 and 1880 show that workers who came from other countries, mainly Canada, boarded at the mill. Many interesting building foundations, some in good condition, remain at the site. Ship workers did not mix well with mill workers, so separate quarters were required. There is evidence of a well-preserved cistern; perhaps the bricks were burned at the south end of Line's Island where there is brick rubble today.

Part Four

Merrymeeting Bay—The Lake of New Somerset

From its summer camps for children to its flyway for migratory ducks, Merrymeeting Bay, its islands, and environs are rich in history, with Aaron Burr Jr., Benedict Arnold, and John Adams, among others, playing roles.

Merrymeeting Bay

Merrymeeting Bay, a delta which holds 9,550 acres of mostly fresh water, was polluted prior to 1970, mainly due to runoff from paper and leather mills, sewage, shipbuilding, and logging.[66] In the 1960s federal legislation was put into place to clean up the area for recreation and bird migration, and it once again has become a pristine spot with abundant fish and bald eagles.

For many years it was one of the world's most popular duck hunting spots; second to Chesapeake Bay, it is the largest flyway of migratory ducks and geese in the United States. According to Franklin Burroughs's book, *Confluence: Merrymeeting Bay*, this body of water has the distinction of being one of four places in the world where two rivers, from separate watersheds, share the same delta.

There are several theories as to how the bay acquired its name; colloquially, it would be "a place where people congregated." Another is the union of six rivers: Muddy, Abagadasset, Androscoggin, Kennebec, Cathance, and Eastern. Other titles were Chisapeak (Indian for "at the big part of the river"), and Nassouac or Naxoat, called so by a Jesuit priest, Father Gabriel Druilettes, meaning a halfway point between the Kennebec and the Androscoggin.[67] A most interesting interpretation is that the Indian sagamore Robin Hood, who resided near the Merrymeeting Bay area, may have practiced witchcraft, and, an assembly of witches was called a "merry meeting."[68]

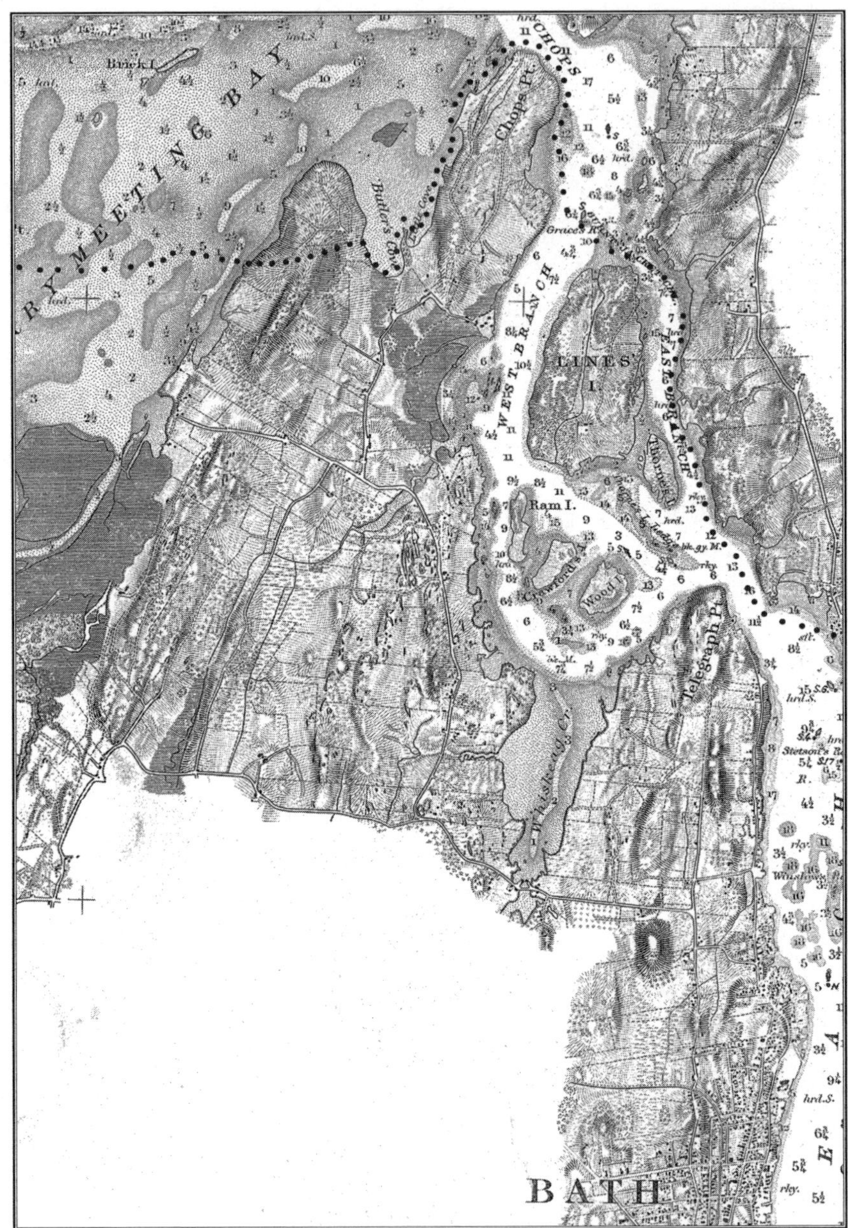

National Oceanic and Atmospheric Administration

The dotted lines show the Merrymeeting Bay area as discussed in this section.

Another name, Quabacook, according to Fannie Eckstorm, may mean head of a bay, or allude to the head of the salt water where the current begins on the Kennebec. In the early 1600s this bay was known as Purchas' Bay or Purchase's, named after Thomas Purchase, who owned adjacent land.

Merrymeeting was also called the Lake of New Somersett, with Somerset spelled several ways, including Summersett. Sir Ferdinando Gorges from Somersetshire County, England, briefly called his grant Somersetshire. One theory is that Somerset was named by Sir Richard Edgecomb upon his grant from Gorges, perhaps for a family homestead in England; or from a Scot-Irish (Ulster-Scot) settler named Andrew McFadden with fond memories of his in Bann Water, County Derry, Ireland. This is cited in several sources, including depositions.[69] In other Pejepscot papers it was called Swan Pond; Swan Alley referred to the western channel of the Kennebec, between Swan Island and the Richmond-Bowdoinham shore.[70]

Nancy Dearborn Lovetere Collection

Butler Cove, Merrymeeting Bay

Ida Sedgwick Proper, in her book, *Monhegan, The Cradle of New England*, quotes Joseph Williamson and the Massachusetts Historical Society notes of January 1888 as saying that Norsemen (Northmen) "entered a neighboring river, through which they were carried into a lake filled with salmon." Williamson, after viewing what might be Norse inscriptions on Manana Island, beside Monhegan, concluded that the lake was Merrymeeting Bay. Proper also hints that the people of Monhegan gave Samoset, an Indian from Norridgewock, his name with reference to Somersetshire or Somerset. His name appears on one deed as Somerset.

Christopher Levett, from Yorkshire, England, a member of the Council for New England, said this of Samoset: "Somerset, a sagamore, one that hath been found very faithful to the English, and hath saved the lives of many of our nation. Some from starving, other from killing."[71] Of course, Samoset was on the scene before the Scot-Irish immigrants and the proprietors, so it is up to the reader to decide if geography, witches, or homesickness bestowed the titles of the Lake of New Somerset and Merrymeeting Bay.

Butler Head Preserve

Butler Head Preserve consists of 135 public acres, which are under the auspices of the Bath Cemeteries, Parks and Recreation Department. This area was purchased by Ephraim Savage in 1714 and given to his daughter, Hannah, and her husband, John Butler. Butler Cove in Arrowsic is named for the same family, who moved there because of the Indian Wars. Butler is listed as an innkeeper and trader.

The Chops

The Chops, or Chopps, are located across from each other, in Bath and Woolwich, 200 yards apart. Job Lewis, a large landowner from Boston for whom Lewiston, Maine, is probably named, owned 1,000 acres in Woolwich and also land on the North Bath side of the Kennebec River. The Woolwich Pejepscot Proprietors built a fort,[72] which Job Lewis maintained, at the location of the present day Chops Point School. Lewis held one-eighth share of the Pejepscot Proprietors. This strategic location guarded the entry from the Kennebec River into Merrymeeting Bay and upward on the river.

The Maynes Ferry

The Maynes Ferry was the earliest known crossing in the Bath area. Patrons were transported by rowboat from the Chops area on the North Bath side to the Woolwich shore. The *1794 Plan of the Town of Woolwich*[73] by David Gilmore, surveyor, shows the distance between the two shores as 48 rods wide. The Maynes Ferry was most likely named for Joseph Mains, who established the ferry crossing in 1718, or possibly as early as 1690. The *Chace Map of 1858* shows four Mains families in this area. Henry O. Thayer states that in 1785, Joseph Mains kept a ferry at his Kennebec River landing. The most famous patron to use this service was John Adams who, in 1765, was traveling from Framingham, Massachusetts, on horseback to try a case at the Pownalborough Courthouse in present-day Dresden. Adams passed through Falmouth (now Portland), Brunswick, and North Bath to the Chops Point area to reach his ferry destination. There were no roads at the time, only blazed trails—a piece of wood was chopped off trees to serve as white markers in the dark forests.

Bowdoinham

Conflicting land claims arose with overlapping Indian deeds and English titles. Sir Ferdinando Gorges granted 8,000 acres on or around Merrymeeting Bay in 1637 to Sir Richard Edgecomb; an Edgecomb heir later defended the property transfer. James Bowdoin of Boston claimed that 3,200 acres were his by a grant from the Plymouth Proprietors and produced a quit-claim from the Indian Adagadusset.[74] Bowdoin ultimately won, and the towns of Bowdoin and Bowdoinham and Bowdoin College in Brunswick now bear his family name.

Bowdoinham, which lies on the west bank of the Kennebec River, was incorporated in 1762. Alexander Twait purchased the land from the Indians in 1656. During the first of the five Indian Wars, Indians killed or captured nine families living on the shore of Merrymeeting Bay. Thomas Gyles/Giles, who settled there in 1669, was killed in an attack on the family home in 1689. His young son, John, taken captive by the Maliseet Indians, lived in slavery from August 2, 1689, to June 13, 1698. His personal journal, which he kept during his captivity, left a record of his life over those nine years. He returned to the Merrymeeting area of Pejepscot (Brunswick) to live a life of civic responsibility as an army captain. In charge of building the new stone Fort George (formerly Fort Andross) in 1715, his company served there through the Indian Wars, 1723–24. Captain John Gyles, Esq., became the owner of the first lot of land in the town of Topsham.

Bowdoinham Village, originally called Cathance Landing, was settled in 1880. Its location was ideal for shipbuilding. More than 250 notable ships were built in Bowdoinham between 1768 and 1912.

Stone Chamber

This mysterious "cave" beneath towering power lines has always fascinated those passing by, especially local children as they biked along the dirt road to Butler Cove. Root cellar? Indian burial crypt? A Central Maine Power cache for dynamite used for power-line installation? A seventeenth-century jail? Perhaps the stone chamber was a receiving vault, used to hold bodies until the ground thawed enough to allow spring burials. The theories go on and on, but the real reason for its construction is unknown.

New England Antiquities Research Association, a group that has been studying stone structures for many years, has come to no conclusive purpose other than to say that there are several other similar chambers in Maine and the rest of New England, and eastern New York boasts several hundred as well. The more they are studied, the more the mystery deepens.

The chamber, with a large juniper growing on its top, faces southwest, uphill from swampy land, with inside measurements of approximately 8 by 14 feet. The opening is roughly 2 ½ feet wide. Partially underground and built into the hillside, large granite roof slabs show that the construction required considerable effort. Evidence of a metal pintle, or pintel (an upright bolt which serves as a pivot on which some sort of door must have been hung) and drill marks suggest the chamber is post-Colonial.

A farm occupied the land directly uphill from the chamber in the early twentieth century, and most likely before. There are several cellar holes in the area. One foundation is located about 150 yards from the chamber, across the dirt road. It runs parallel to the road, north-south, and measures about 40 by 18 feet. There is evidence of bricks in the southeast corner.

Summer Camps on the Water

Everyone who has enjoyed the Kennebec and the Androscoggin will attest to the sheer beauty of these glorious rivers, the perfect place for summer camps. The early 1900s saw construction of two large camps on the Kennebec, one for girls and one for boys. Not to slight adults, another camp for them was built on the Woolwich shore. Arthur R. Webster of Cincinnati, Ohio, owned and directed all three enterprises C. E. Baker, from Bath, was the resident manager for both children's camps.

The Boothbay Camp for Boys

Founded in 1912, the boys' camp was located on Thorne Island, where until recently one could find remnants of a dormitory, a dining hall, a baseball field, and tennis courts. The boys enjoyed competing against local boys, and swimming across the river and paddling upriver to the girls' camp, according to the camp newsletter, *The Pow Wow*. The camp operated for about twenty years. Charles McLane, in his book *Islands of the Mid-Maine Coast: Pemaquid Point to the Kennebec River*, states that the original owner had intended that the camp be named "Boothby" after an Indian chieftain; however, the camp brochures arrived with the misprint. Many camp provisions were mistakenly delivered to the town of Boothbay. The seven-acre island today sits in Woolwich waters and is privately owned.

Merrymeeting Camp

Merrymeeting Camp, where Chop Point School is today, opened in 1916 on 50 acres. The camp, on the Woolwich side of the Chops, marketed itself as a haven "for girls who enjoy the freedom of life in the out-of-doors. Health is abounding in the unrivaled air and sunshine of Maine." Some of the girls were sent to the camp to gain weight. A camp garden produced vegetables, and other supplies came from Bath, five miles downstream. The dining room was designed so that all windows faced the quadrants of the compass. The rising bell was heard at seven o'clock, followed by a swim at ten minutes after the hour. One popular event was a field trip to the White Mountains where campers stayed at the Madison Spring Hut and hiked the Presidential Range, sleeping over on Mount Washington. Automobile trips to Old Quebec followed the Benedict Arnold Trail.

Horseback riding, with both stock and English saddles, was popular; a camp brochure noted that the girls rode on deserted roads and trails through pine forests away from highways. Afternoons were devoted to letter writing, followed by vesper services in the evening. Motorboats took the campers to local churches on Sundays. Gymnastics, volleyball, basketball, baseball, tennis, folk dancing, arts and crafts, and archery were among the activities the girls enjoyed, with an emphasis on water sports. The camp owned rowboats, canoes, and a war canoe. A water carnival took place in July. With an allowance of 20 cents, each girl decorated the canoes and made costumes. By moonlight the campers glided before the judges' stand for prizes.

The campers' publication, *The Merrymeeting Moon*, exhibited poetry and activities. In the summer of 1931, one young girl by the name of Mary Jane Mains wrote:

The Tide
The Tide creeps up
On craggy rocks.
It comes slyly
Stealing drift-wood
And rock weed
From jagged masses
And creeps back

Girls were encouraged to bring to camp two pairs of blue serge bloomers, five middy blouses, high shoes, raincoat and rubbers, poncho or rubber blanket, galoshes, a steamer rug, and several simple summer frocks.

Brushwood

The adult camp, Brushwood, "a rustic camp for those who like such a life," had a northern view of the boys' camp. The Lodge, completed in 1929, consisted of a dining room, kitchen, bathroom, and six cabins. The main cabin had a sitting room with a fireplace, a screened-in porch, and five sleeping rooms.

Swan Island

Swan Island, a state-owned game preserve, is known as the Steve Powell Wildlife Management Area. This sanctuary at the head of Merrymeeting Bay is a temporary home to migrating waterfowl and meandering whitetail deer. At 1,755 acres, it is four miles long and about three-quarters of a mile wide. Little Swan Island, also known as Small Island and Calf Island, is close by, separated by The Narrows.

Like many islands over the years, Swan has had several names. The most commonly accepted meaning for "swan" is the Indian word *swango*, originally *sowangan* for bald eagle.[75] (An advertisement in 1859 touts Swan Island as having a spa, "Swango—The Only Eclectic Cure in This Country—Opposite Richmond, Me.") Other sources say it was named for migrating swans. The Pejepscot Proprietors called it Garden Isle; other names were Chisepeake and Perkins.

The island is rich in history. Indians had headquarters on Little Swan Island with a village on the south end near Maxwell Cove. Christopher Lawson bought the island from the Indians in 1614. Several members of the Popham Colony, in addition to Lawson, Captain John Smith, Aaron Burr, Benedict Arnold, and Henry Dearborn, are among the well-known people who visited.

Benedict Arnold

Benedict Arnold departed Cambridge, Massachusetts, on September 11, 1775, on a 350-mile expedition to Quebec. After navigating the narrow channel of the Chops, the American Revolutionary general and his troops, including Henry Dearborn, arrived at Swan Island, where Dearborn's ship ran aground. It is reported that Dearborn and Aaron Burr spent one night at the Gardiner-Dumaresq House, a saltbox on Swan Island built by Silvester Gardiner for his newly married daughter. On September 22, the company arrived at Colburn's shipyard in Gardinerstown (modern-day Pittston), where they were assigned bateaux, small, heavy flat-bottomed rowboats similar to canoes. A refreshing explanation for the usual "ill-fated" march to Quebec is illustrated by Stephen Clark in his book, *Following in Their Footsteps*. He contends that popular history of Arnold's march leaves us unaware of the many obstacles the inexperienced soldiers faced; namely, heavy, leaky boats, a late start in the season, a loss of food and supplies, and an underestimation of the elevation from Maine to Quebec. Eating dogs and the juice of boiled shoe leather says it all.

Aaron Burr Jr.

Aaron Burr Jr. was born in New Jersey, studied theology at Princeton University, and attended Tapping Reeve Law School in Litchfield, Connecticut, which was conducted by his brother-in-law. Burr accompanied Arnold to Quebec, a trip fictionalized by Kenneth Roberts in his book, *Arundel*. Dearborn, Arnold, and many other men kept journals, which were sources for the novel. Among Maine legends (which may have been Roberts's rhetoric) is Burr's love affair with the French-Indian maiden, Jacatawaw, of Swan Island. Jacatawaw accompanied Burr, Arnold, and Dearborn on the march to Quebec. Also joining the expedition were several dogs, and the only one of them that was not eventually eaten by the hungry, desperate men belonged to Burr. As Robert P. Tristram Coffin said, "the dogs were walking soup kitchens." Burr is also known for his duel with Alexander Hamilton.

General Henry Dearborn

General Henry Dearborn was born in 1751 in the Dearborn Homestead which still stands today in Hampton, New Hampshire.[76] He is a descendant of Godfrey Dearborn of Willoughby, Lincoln, England, father of all the Dearborns. The name was originally Dearebarne. He became a physician and surgeon, studying in Portsmouth, and practicing medicine at Nottingham Square, New Hampshire. Twice a widower, the first of his three marriages was to Mary Bartlett of Hampton, the second to Dorcas Osgood Marble of Andover, Massachusetts, and the third marriage was to Sarah (Bowdoin) Bowdoin of Boston, widow of her first cousin, the benefactor of Bowdoin College, James Bowdoin II, who was governor of Massachusetts in 1785–86.

In 1772 Dearborn organized a militia company and fought the battle of Lexington and Concord and the Battle of Bunker Hill in 1775. In September 1775 he joined Arnold on his march to Quebec. After becoming ill trudging through the forests and marshes of Maine, Dearborn was left behind on the Chaudiere River in Canada, recovering in time to be part of the capture in Quebec.

Nancy Dearborn Lovetere Collection

A portrait of General Henry Dearborn

Later Dearborn was appointed major of Colonel Alexander Scammel's First New Hampshire Regiment. He took part in the Battle of Monmouth, New Jersey, after spending the winter at Valley Forge. His regiment also took part in the force against the Iroquois in the Finger

Lakes Region of central New York. He and his men were under the command of George Washington, with Dearborn later joining Washington's staff as assistant.

In 1784 he and his family settled in Gardiner, Maine, then a district of Massachusetts. He became brigadier general, the first United States Marshal for the District of Maine, a census taker in 1790, and major general of the militia. Elected a member of Congress, he also served as Thomas Jefferson's secretary of war from 1800 until 1809.

With the War of 1812 looming, President Madison made Dearborn senior major general of the American Army for the territory extending from the Niagara River to the New England coast. The British defeated him in Detroit and Queenstown, New York, proving that the aging Dearborn was unable to plan defensive moves against the enemy. In 1813 he was placed in command of New York City. President Madison had nominated Dearborn to the position of secretary of war, but this choice created such a furor that Madison withdrew the nomination. Dearborn was honorably discharged in 1815. From 1822 to 1824 he served as minister to Portugal.

By his first wife he had two daughters. Sophia married Dudley Hobart, who was appointed by President Jefferson to the position of collector in the port of Bath. His second daughter, Pamela Augusta, married Allen Gilman. Dearborn's third daughter, Julia, by his second wife, married Joshua Wingate of the Portland Wingates. A Harvard graduate, Wingate served as Dearborn's assistant during his appointment as secretary of war. Wingate was appointed collector of customs in Bath, Maine, brigadier general of the militia, and a member of the committee that formed the Constitution of the State of Maine. Wingate also ran for governor twice.

Dearborn's first son by his second marriage was Henry Alexander Scammel Dearborn, who later became president of the Massachusetts Horticultural Society and founder of the Forest Hill Cemetery where Dearborn is buried.[77] Obviously impressed by his friend and fellow officer, Alexander Scammel, Dearborn named his firstborn son in his honor. His second son was George Raleigh Dearborn.

Dearborn died in 1829 at age seventy-eight in Roxbury, Massachusetts.

John Adams and the Pownalborough Courthouse

Before Maine became an independent state, distinguished lawyers from Boston traveled with judges to try cases. In 1765, John Adams, who would become the first vice president and second president of the United States, traveled the court circuit by horse and ferry to the Pownalborough Courthouse, one and a half miles north of Swan Island. This small colony was once called Frankfort Plantation. Pownalborough Courthouse was built within the fortification of Fort Shirley, ensuring safety from the French and Indians. The courthouse covered the territory of Wiscasset, Perkins, Alna, and Dresden. Built in 1761, the building consists of three stories, measuring 44 by 45 feet. Now owned by the Lincoln County

Nancy Dearborn Lovetere Collection

The backside of the Pownalborough Courthouse faces the Kennebec River.

Historical Association, the courthouse is listed in the National Register of Historical Places.

The remote setting of the Pownalborough Courthouse kept Adams from trying many cases there, opting for Falmouth (present-day Portland). A description of one journey is described in his autobiography, written in 1765.[78]

In the Spring of 1765, Major Noble of Boston had an Action at Pownalborough, on Kennebeck River. Mr. Thatcher, who had been his Council, recommended him to me, and I engaged in his cause, and undertook the journey. I was taken ill on the Road and had a very unpleasant Excursion. It is unnecessary to enlarge upon the fatigue and disgust of this journey. It was the only time in my Life, when I really suffered for want of Provision. From Falmouth in Casco Bay, to Pounalborough There was an entire Wilderness, except North Yarmouth, New Brunswick and Long Reach, at each of which places were a few Houses. In general it was a Wilderness, incumbered with the greatest number of Trees, of the largest Size, the tallest Height, I have ever seen. So great a Weight of Wood and timber has never fallen in my Way. Birches, Beaches, and a few Oaks, and all the Varieties of the Fir, i.e. Pines, Hemlocks, Spruces and Firs. I once asked Judge Cushing his Opinion of their hight upon an Avaradge, he said an hundred feet. I believe his estimation was not exaggerated. An Hemlock had been blown down across the Road. They had cutt out a logg as long as the road was wide. I measured the Butt at the Road and found it seven feet in Diameter, twenty one feet in circumference. We measured 90 feet from the Road to the first Limb, the Branches at Top were thick: We could measure no farther but estimated the Top to be about fifteen feet, from the Butt at the Road to the Root we did not measure: but the Tree must have been in the whole at least an hundred and twenty feet. The Roads, where a Wheel had never rolled from the Creation, were miry and founderous, incumbered with long Sloughs of Water. The Stumps of the Trees which had been cutt to make the road all remaining fresh, and the Roots crossing the path some above ground and some beneath so that my Horses feet would frequently get between the Roots and he would flounce and blunder, in danger of breaking his own Limbs as well as mine. This whole Country, then so rough, is now beautifully cultivated, Handsome Houses, Orchards, Fields of Grain and Grass, and the Roads as fine as any except the Turnpikes, in the State. I reached

Pownalborough alive, gained my Cause much to the Satisfaction of my Client and returned home. This Journey, painfull as it was, proved much for my Interest and Reputation, as it induced the Plymouth Company to engage me in all their Causes, which were numerous and called me annually to Falmouth Superior Court for ten years.

Between 1765 and 1775 John Adams's name appeared on the appellate court docket in Falmouth more than thirty times. He was often opposed by a fellow classmate at Harvard, David Sewall of Falmouth, and friend Jonathan Sewall of Boston. Intimate friendships existed between these men despite the different sides they took in the War for Independence.

Part Five

Bayshore Road to New Meadows—Wigwam Point
via Lovers Retreat

Indian carrying places, a failed canal between the New Meadows River and Merrymeeting Bay, African-American residents, and a journal-writing bridgekeeper are among the historical highlights of this section of North Bath.

Bayshore Road

At the end of North Bath Road, Bayshore Road leads in a westerly direction to the Androscoggin River and Merrymeeting Bay. Several small cottages and hunting camps have been replaced with year-round homes. Stoney (Stony) Island, which is shown as House Island on the *1718 Pejepscot Proprietors Map*, is close to shore; not too far south was the location of the Merrymeeting Bay Bridge. This map also shows possible Indian encampment symbols in this area. It is a natural spot for a Native American carry.

Many years ago a crude road led from this spot to where Whiskeag Road intersects with New Meadows Road, via Ham's Hill. It was probably called the "Cross Road," which is referenced in the 1880 census. The south end is Bridge Road. There is still a trail there that may have been

Courtesy of Barbara Marriner

Alonzo Fisher takes aim from a duck boat or gunning float.

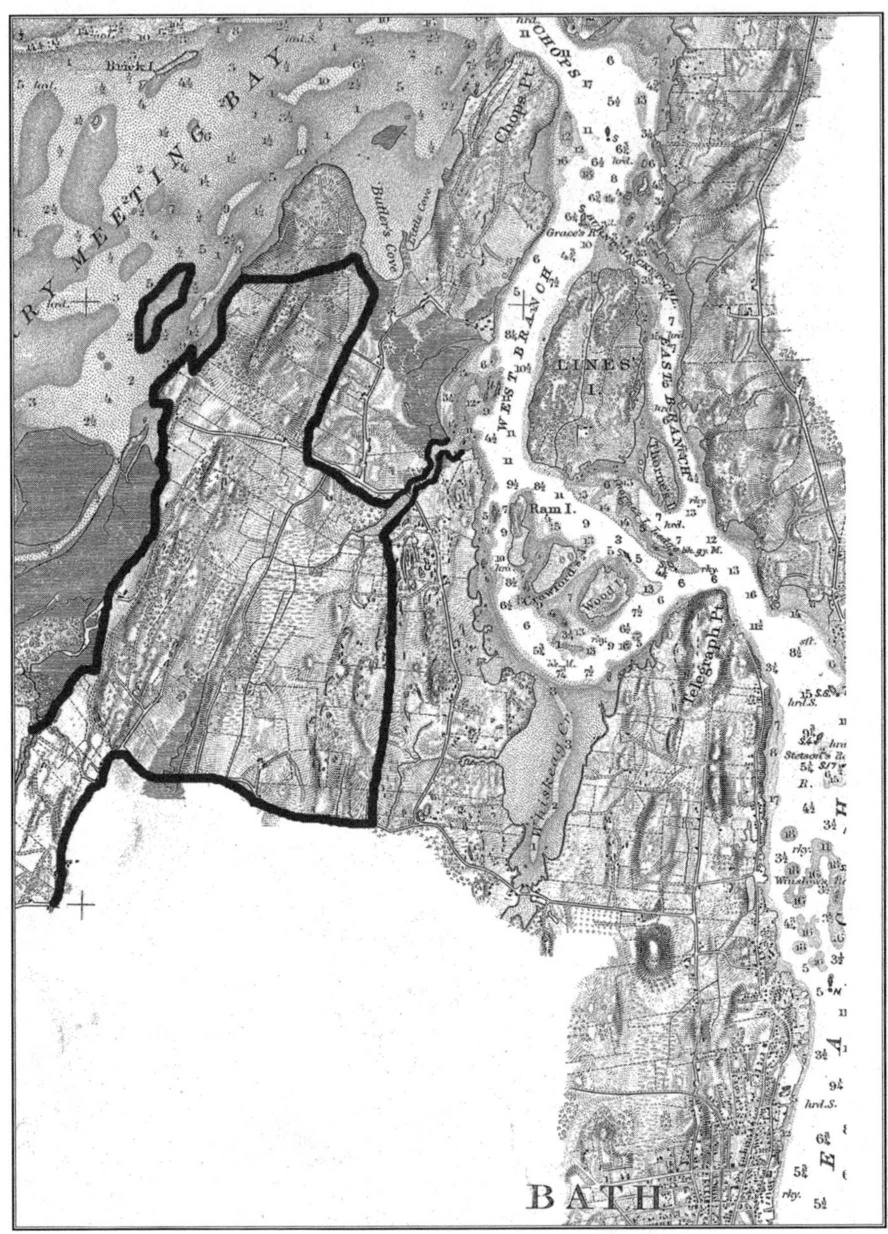

National Oceanic and Atmospheric Administration

Bayshore Road to New Meadows

Courtesy of Ray Nadeau

The Hawkes Farm on Bayshore Road

part of the stagecoach route. There were several old houses along this shore between New Meadows in Brunswick and the end of the Bayshore Road in North Bath. Today only cellar holes remain. The Harrison Cemetery, which is in poor condition, is the only reminder of life on the banks of the river. It has a beautiful westerly view of Stoney Island and the Topsham shore.

Ward Burial Ground

This site is located at the end of the Bay Shore Road on the right in a pine grove, not far from the shore of Merrymeeting Bay. The headstones are encircled by beautiful ground cover, and there is evidence of a white picket fence that once surrounded the cemetery.

Ward
1. James, d. May 29, 1862, age 88 yrs., 5 mos.
2. Robert, d. Jan 17, 1892, age 82 yrs., 8 mos. 25 days.
3. Mary, wife of Robert, d. Feb. 15, 1856, age 41 yrs., 9 mos.
4. Margaret, wife of Robert, d. Oct. 20, 1875, age 43 yrs., 10 mos.

5. Robert S., son of Robert and Mary, d. June 28, 1854, age 4 mos., 17 days.
6. Charles D., drowned May 18, 1862, age 22 yrs., 11 mos., 9 days.[79]

Crocker
7. Augusta A. (Ward), wife of William L., d. May 31, 1868, age 31 yrs.,
    6 mos.

Stone
8. Frank G., d. Sept 13, 1877, age 21 yrs., 7 mos.

Whittam Burial Ground

The remains, if any, of this burial ground are across the road from
Hawkes Greenhouse, about 200 yards into the woods.
1. Whittam, Albert T., son of Charles and Jane, d. Aug. 19, 1841, age 2
    yrs., 6 mos.

Ice Harvest on the Kennebec

Kennebec ice, shipped worldwide in the early 1900s, had a crystal-
clear reputation. Local resident Ardenne Haines was a twentieth-century
ice cutter, involved not in large corporate production but small cutting at
the Lily Pond in Bath and in Merrymeeting Bay. To secure his footing on
the ice, Haines wore crampons, or ice creepers, attached to his shoes.
After making a hole in the ice, he'd cut it with an iron saw with a long
handle. Harvesting was best during high tides because the ice blocks,
sometimes 16 inches thick by 2 feet wide, would float to the top of the
hole. After making a hole in the ice, an ice chisel was used to split the
blocks, and an iron ice pick attached to a twenty-foot pole was used to
push the ice along. Two men pulled the ice out of the water with tongs.
Horse-drawn sleds then brought the ice to an icehouse. Ramps and pulleys
hauled the ice to several levels in the building. Hay and sawdust spread on
each layer kept the ice frozen all summer.[80]

Fresh Meadow

Leaving Bayshore Road and heading south on Ridge Road, or Lovers Retreat Road, brings the traveler to a herd of buffalo grazing in a field that runs back east to the North Bath Road across from the Sagadahoc Rod, Gun & Skeet Club. Land divisions in this area commonly were long narrow strips of ownership, running from the river to the bay. The border of the buffalo pasture follows the Peterson Canal to the Crawford Burial Ground. This area appears on the *1718 Pejepscot Proprietors Map* and the *1764 Plymouth Company Map* as Fresh Meadow, a large meadow, with woods following the ridge to the intersection of the Bath Country Club and the Ham Burial Ground. It remains the same today.

In the 1900s Anna Campbell's cattle were led to this pasture from the present-day Hawkes Farm. In the photograph on page 101, the barn shown in the distance behind the golfers on the Bath Country Club green was part of the Crawford farm; it eventually became Lorin Eggleston's, owner of the old Sagadahoc Rod, Gun & Skeet Club property, and ownership was then passed on to Oscar Wright, who used the barn for hay storage.

John Lovetere Photo

Buffalo roam on and above Fresh Meadow.

The old pasture road can be seen on the map at the beginning of this chapter. Eggleston let Campbell use the field as well as the "summer barn" for milking her forty-five cows. This freed up the pasture for haying at the Campbell farm (Rich/Campbell/Hawkes).[81] The long ridge of evergreens through the Lovers Retreat or Ridge Road is apparent on the *1718 Pejepscot Proprietors Map* and the *1764 Plymouth Company Plan.*

The Manson/Wright Farm and the Bath Country Club

This property on Whiskeag Road, formerly East Brunswick Road, has deeds back to the Pejepscot Proprietors. Records show various succession, from Joseph Heath in 1719 to John Peterson; to John Ham, 1761–1836; to Robert P. Manson,[82] a shipmaster, 1836–75; to George K. Ingalls, 1875–77; and to Lewis E. Wright, 1877.

The deed was then conveyed to Frederick Wright,[83] who was married to Lorraine E. Stone Wright. Born in Woolwich in 1852, Frederick formed a partnership in the farm, known as the Elmwood Farm, with his cousin George F. Wright, son of Charles and Martha (Duley) of Woolwich. It then became the property of Arthur "Percy" Wright. Zita Bella Cameron[84] Wright, Percy's wife, was making strawberry ice cream in the backyard when she went into labor. Dr. Stott, a well-known physician in Bath, came out to the country to deliver the last baby born at the farmhouse, Charlotte Wright. A child playing with matches later burned down the barn. The Wright family was active in the Union Chapel in the Ireland section of North Bath.

The Hyde Windlass Company bought the farm in 1931. Hyde's president, Rodney E. Ross Sr., was also president of the newly formed Bath Country Club, later called Bath Golf Club, then back to Country Club again. The farmhouse was remodeled as a clubhouse, complete with wraparound porch. The nine-hole course, built in 1932, was designed by renowned golf architects Wayne Stiles and John Van Kleek. It was expanded to eighteen holes in 1994.

An annual guide, *Golf in Maine: The Season of 1947*,[85] gives a hole-by-hole description of the 3,223-yard, par-35 course.

First hole, 366 yards, orchard on right, brook crosses. Green trapped; second, 378, dogleg, up grade to elevated greens, trees along right of fairway; third, 433, tee in woods, ball played out through opening, dogleg, small pond in front of green, traps; fourth, 164, straightaway, traps at green; fifth, 417, dogleg, trap at left, green trapped; sixth, 432, dogleg, traps and trees, green trapped left and right; seventh, 150, straightaway, large trap along right side of green and small trap in front at left; eighth, 528, straightaway, woods and rough on right, green trapped; ninth, 355, straightaway, rough on left, green trapped.

Courtesy of Tom Perry

The Bath Country Club's nine-hole golf course was designed by Wayne Stiles and John Van Kleek.

Henderson Home and Barn

The Henderson Farm sits high on a hill on Whiskeag Road and remains in that family. As a stagecoach stop between Rockland and Portland, the two front rooms in the house served as a respite for travelers. Whispers over the years say that the home also served as a stop on the Underground Railroad.

Courtesy of Leona Henderson Libby

David Henderson's milk seal

David and Annie (Ames) Henderson were married in Bath in 1909. Moving here from Nova Scotia, David started a dairy and milk route in 1917, buying 98 acres and a gravel pit from Percy Wright. The attic roof of the house boasts ship's knees, wonderful hand-hewn tree trunks.

The Hendersons had five children, and several Henderson grandchildren and great-grandchildren remain in the Bath area.

Courtesy of Leona Henderson Libby

The Henderson home and barn

Courtesy of Leona Henderson Libby

Molly, the Henderson milk-route horse

New Meadows

The New Meadows region may have acquired its name from the Scot-Irish immigrants, or, as they are now defined, Ulster-Scots, who populated this area in the early 1700s.[86] The meadows were the lower salt marsh on which cattle fed before the upland fields were cleared. Wigwam Point, according to Fannie Eckstorm, means "the head of" *(wekw)* in Micmac; this often gets interpreted as *wigwam*. It was, however, an Indian carry.

Fort Andross / Fort George

Fort Andross was the first stone fort built in 1688 in Brunswick, Maine (Pejepscot), on the banks of the Androscoggin, a river[87] which had been named by the Indians as early as 1639. Sir Edmund Andros, governor of the Dominion of New England, built his fort as protection against the Indians. It was demolished in 1694, leaving the area unprotected against attack. The Pejepscot Proprietors bought the land in 1714 and established the town of Brunswick. The next year the stone fort was rebuilt under the direction of Captain John Gyles (Giles), and renamed Fort George after then King George I of England. Within the thick stone fort walls was a two-story house. The large population of Scot-Irish immigrants necessitated a public center. Even after the town was burned by Indians and rebuilt, the General Court of Massachusetts ordered the fort dismantled in 1736, much to the horror of the local citizenry. The property reverted to the Pejepscot Proprietors, who leased it out and later sold it for the development of businesses in 1761. By 1809, a cotton manufacturing mill was built that was later reorganized as Cabot Manufacturing Co. The old textile mill is today known again as Fort Andross.

Thomas Stevens

Thomas Stevens moved to New Meadows from North Yarmouth in 1675. His home is often mentioned as being above the dike, bridge, or the Peterson Canal. The upper section of the New Meadows River and the Lower Carrying Place, Stephen's or Steven's River and Steven's or Stephen's Carrying Place, were named for him. (See *1764 Plymouth Company Plan of Georgetown*.)

Captain James Thompson

Captain James Thompson moved to the New Meadows area in 1735, following his parents who settled there in 1727. He ran a general store, farmed, cobbled, and operated a ferry service.

Legend of Captain William Kidd

Local folklore has it that Captain William Kidd spent a winter on the New Meadows River back in the mid-1600s. According to "A Romance of New Meadows River, Founded on Fact," *Plymouth Church and Other Poems by Moses Owen*, a Bath poet, 1873, Kidd was being chased along the Maine coast. He scooted up the New Meadows River to Howard Point, where he went ashore with his crew to bury his cache of gold near a graveyard. Fifty years later, a member of Kidd's crew returned to New Meadows with a soiled map and found the treasure, which he shared with a local farmer, who to his final days kept "the pirate's time-worn plan." Legend says the gold was found in a rock hole on the eastern shore.

Roads, Ferries, and Bridges Across and Around New Meadows and Bath, 1718–1858

The following map is an amalgamation of several scarce sources.[88] The date reflected may be the year the road was constructed or when it was mentioned in various records. (Several routes were not added to this map as it is difficult to determine their exact paths.) Present-day High Street in Bath was the only route to Thorne Head before the north end of Washington Street extended that far. Although High Street dates back to 1718 as a "town road," it was not laid out until 1740.[89] Most roads grew from trails, acquiring different names over a period of many years, as well as changes in structure and direction. There were county roads and country roads. Passages over streams and brooks, often consisting of large rocks, were often too insignificant for notation. The width of the Peterson Canal, a continuation of Stevens (Stephens) River or the New Meadows River, is exaggerated to show its location as it ran under the Marsh and Muddy River bridges. While the placement of the old roads on the following map is an approximation, present-day Route 1 is illustrated to give the reader bearing.

The Old County Road

The Old County Road of 1718, also known as the Military Road, appears to be the oldest recorded. It connected the Robert Temple settlement on Merrymeeting Bay via the Maynes Ferry with Fort George in Brunswick and the Watts Fort in Arrowsic. It is possible that the Maynes Ferry was not at the location shown on this and Owen's map because the tidal current is very strong there; it most likely crossed a bit south, as shown on the *1795 Plan of the Town of Bath* by Dummer Sewall. In 1718, Brunswick built its end of the road, which led from Cooks Corner, and followed the shore of the Androscoggin River to the Bath Road at Ham's Cemetery.[90] The Old County Road took a southeasterly route on or near

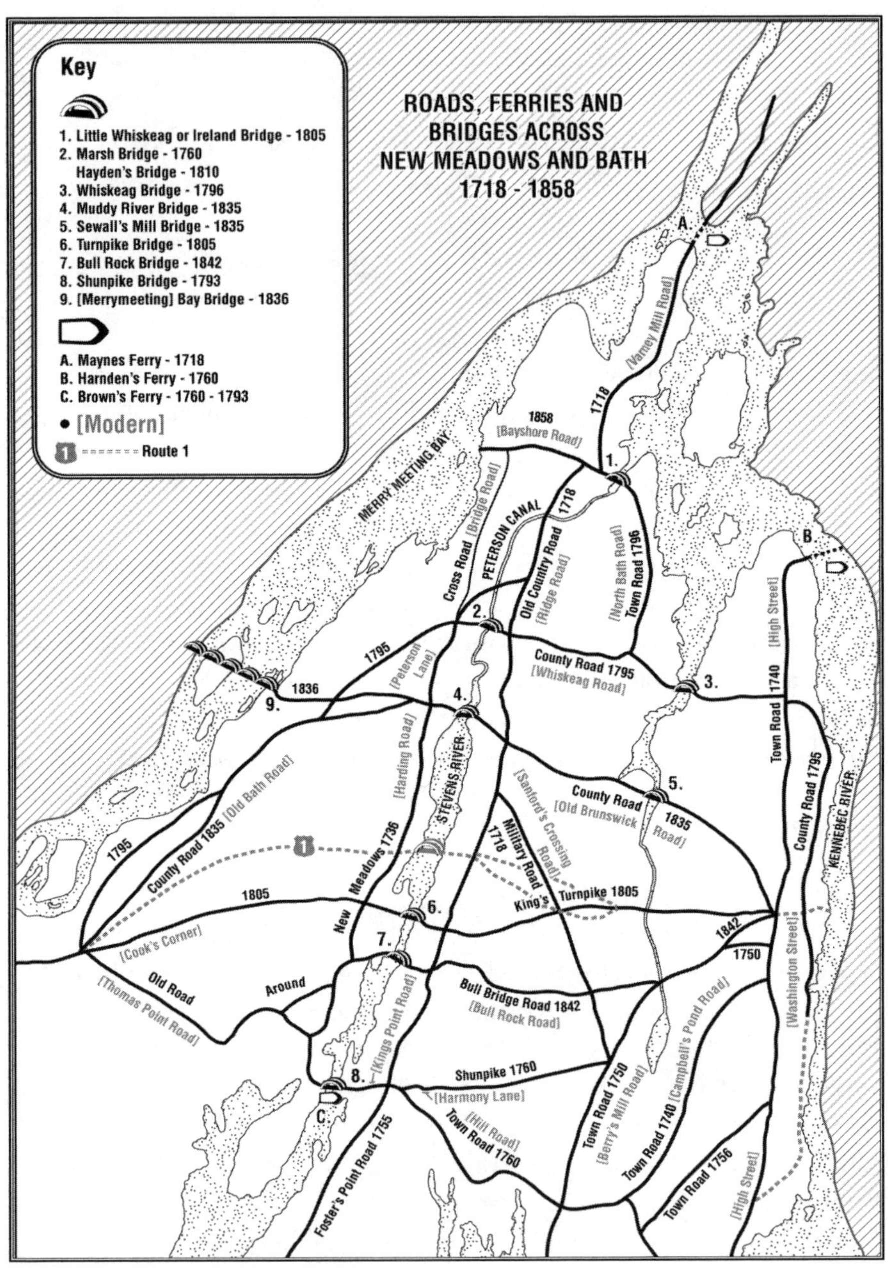
Key

1. Little Whiskeag or Ireland Bridge - 1805
2. Marsh Bridge - 1760
   Hayden's Bridge - 1810
3. Whiskeag Bridge - 1796
4. Muddy River Bridge - 1835
5. Sewall's Mill Bridge - 1835
6. Turnpike Bridge - 1805
7. Bull Rock Bridge - 1842
8. Shunpike Bridge - 1793
9. [Merrymeeting] Bay Bridge - 1836

A. Maynes Ferry - 1718
B. Harnden's Ferry - 1760
C. Brown's Ferry - 1760 - 1793

[Modern]
Route 1

ROADS, FERRIES AND
BRIDGES ACROSS
NEW MEADOWS AND BATH
1718 - 1858

MERRY MEETING BAY
1858
[Bayshore Road]
1718
[Varney Mill Road]
PETERSON CANAL
Cross Road [Bridge Road]
Old Country Road
[Ridge Road]
1718
[North Bath Road]
Town Road 1796
County Road 1795
[Whiskeag Road]
[High Street]
Town Road 1740
1795
[Peterson Lane]
1836
[Old Bath Road]
[Harding Road]
STEVENS RIVER
[Sanford's Crossing]
County Road
[Old Brunswick Road]
1835
County Road 1795
KENNEBEC RIVER
County Road 1835
1795
1805
New Meadows 1736
Military Road 1718
King's Turnpike 1805
1842
[Cook's Corner]
Old Road Around
[Thomas Point Road]
[Kings Point Road]
Bull Bridge Road 1842
[Bull Rock Road]
1750
[Washington Street]
Shunpike 1760
[Harmony Lane]
[Hill Road]
Town Road 1750
[Berry's Mill Road]
Town Road 1740 [Campbell's Pond Road]
Foster's Point Road 1755
Town Road 1760
Town Road 1756
[High Street]

the Sanford's Crossing Road in West Bath, and eventually linked with the Berry's Mill Road, shown on the map as the 1780 Town Road. Later this road was intersected by the County Road 1795 and the (New) County Road 1835. These both joined the Old Road Around New Meadows 1736, north of Hayden's Bridge.

The Shunpike

The most interesting road is the Shunpike, which led from Witch Spring Hill at Berry's Mill Road in West Bath to the crossing at Brown's Ferry. Recorded as a road in 1760, it acquired the name Shunpike when Governor William King built his turnpike in 1805; the Shunpike was used to avoid King's toll road. More than two hundred years later the west end of the Shunpike is Harmony Lane, across from the West Bath Town Hall on Foster's Point Road. The east end is located at Brown's Ferry Estates on the original Shunpike right of way, off Berry's Mill Road, where a portion of the old roadbed is being restored by a private developer. Perhaps someday the center portion of the Shunpike of 1760 will join each end of the original road.

The Old Road Around New Meadows

Before it was straightened in 1831,[91] the Old Road Around New Meadows crossed the Peterson Canal on the East Brunswick side at the end of the Stevens River near Bridge Road and the old Cavanaugh Farm, then ran up a steep hillside to join, at the north end of the woods, the Ridge Road or Lovers Retreat Road. "Thence by the ridge through Ireland to the Chops."[92] The new east-west direction took the road from the eighteenth tee at the Bath Country Club, down the hill past the Ham Cemetery, across the end of the canal/river, and up the hill to what is now the Bridge Road in East Brunswick. In 1906, this "bridge" was called "corduroy," a crossing ribbed with logs laid side by side across the swampy wetland, mainly for travel by horseback.[93]

Limits of the Highway Districts, No. 9

In 1825 the "Limits of the Highway Districts, No. 9" is described as: "The road from Ham's watering place to the Brunswick line and from the guideboard near Stephens River to the center of the bridge over Smelt

Brook." Guideboards (or signboards), which designated road directions, were popular as early as 1814.[94] It is possible that the base for the signage, which was at this intersection, is the concrete piece in the woods just off the road, or perhaps a contemporary version of it. This junction was also known as Crush's Corner, named after George Crush, who lived there.[95]

Several other roads that passed through New Meadows and Bath can still be partially traced on modern topographical maps. Most of these roads converged in Bath at one location, that of the Erudition School and the Meetinghouse, or North Church,[96] which stood kitty-corner to the Sagadahoc County Courthouse on the northeastern corner of High and Centre streets. The Shaw mansion, which became the Sedgwick Hotel, replaced the church. An office building stands there now.

Geography dictated the paths that Native Americans took, and these paths often became the route that most roads followed.

Indian Carrying Places

An Indian carry, or portage, is a stretch of land between two naviga-ble bodies of water over which a boat or canoe is carried. Two regional car-ries are The Upper Carrying Place and The Lower Carrying Place, or Upper Carry and Lower Carry.

The Upper Carry is above the falls at the bend of the Androscoggin River in Brunswick. The *1750*

Nancy Dearborn Lovetere Collection

The Bunganuc River, 1985

Kennebec Proprietors Map shows the Fort George symbol at the falls as well as a road-carry to Maquoit Bay initially following Maine Street. This road also split off to the Bunganuc[97] River (also called Bungungmungock Brook). *Johnston's 1754 Plan of Kennebeck and Sagadahok Rivers*[98] shows the carry illustrated by a symbol from the falls to Maquoit.

The Lower Carry, Stephen's (Steven's) Carrying Place, or Wigwam Point[99] is at the end of the New Meadows River or New Meadows Lake, north of the causeway. A slightly different symbol depicts the carry on the *Johnston Plan*, mentioned above as Steven's Carry Place.

At this point the carry goes up the hill in a northwesterly direction across Bridge Road and follows the large ledge to Merrymeeting Bay on the Androscoggin River. This detailed route is illustrated in the *1764 Plymouth Company Plan*. William C. Purington's book *Meadowsweet* mentions the Lower Carry as going from New Meadows to Whiskeag River (Kennebec). This logical but unpopular interpretation suggests that a canoe could be transported from the end of New Meadows in an easterly direction to the Kennebec, not Merrymeeting Bay as is more commonly written. At this point the traveler could go south on the Kennebec, whereas if he followed the carry to the north, he would be on the Androscoggin. Another nameless portage went from the Androscoggin River near Bayshore Road across the terrain about a mile to the Kennebec. This route is suggested on a map from the Davistown Museum.[100]

A third local portage runs between the head of Butler Cove and the Kennebec River, just above Little Whiskeag Creek. Fannie Eckstorm reiterates that the Chops in Merrymeeting Bay has a very strong current.[101] This carry eliminates a dangerous route. It is likely that all three portages were important.[102]

It seems that Wigwam Point was not considered an official carry, although Indians were seen there portaging canoes. This landing place of the Indians was once called Indian Town.

The Peterson Family

The concept of a canal connecting the north end of the New Meadows River with Merrymeeting Bay was ingenious; however, the two-hour difference of tides on either side was its downfall. Captain John Peterson, who moved to the New Meadows area from Duxbury, Massachusetts, about 1783, conceived of the idea of a canal to transport masts and lumber to Casco Bay, bypassing the Kennebec River and the ocean.

William E. Gerber, in his article for *The Best from American Canals*,[103] wrote this piece entitled "Twice-A-Day-Island," a great summary, in part, of the Peterson Canal.[104]

But not all traces of the canal are gone. Inspired by a reporter of long ago, this writer made his pilgrimage to the old canal and walked its frozen waters. There was, of course, no way to confirm that it was once three or four feet deep and it certainly no longer is. But in some places, the ice clearly exhibits the dimensions that history records; a width of 30 feet through much of its 2½ miles length, necking down to 20 feet at some points. Furthermore, Bath's peninsular status is still tenuous, at best. The entire end to end journey, except for perhaps half the length of a football field, can be made over the ice of the canal. Of course the walk is not as easy as it was 70 years ago. The northern section, between the North Bath and Lover's Retreat Roads, is still kept open by the flow of Welch's Creek (also known as Wittam's Creek). But from Lover's Retreat Road west and south to the headwaters of the New Meadows River, the channel is thick with impeding scrub growth. Approaching the former crossing of the Old Brunswick Road, marsh grasses obscure most traces of the canal edges, but south of this point, the route again becomes quite obvious.

What are the origins of the canal? When was it built; by whom and for what purpose? It hasn't made the news in a long, long time; in fact, the Bath Independent's *story of 1911 may have been the most recent significant news coverage. But a little digging produced the following: the first record of the canal concept is a petition to the General Court of the Commonwealth of Massachusetts for permission to cut a canal from the head of the New*

Courtesy of Richard O. Card

*The Peterson Canal, c. 1906, looking north to the present-day Hawkes Farm.
From a glass plate by J. F. Rollins.*

Meadows River into Merrymeeting Bay. It was dated January 1, 1786, and was signed by 98 citizens of Brunswick and Bath. (What a New Year's Party that must have been!) The purpose of the canal was to bring "Lumber and Masts directly into Casco Bay and to Falmouth without going to sea or running the hazard of going down that rapid torrent, the main Stream of the Kennebeck." The principal beneficiaries, of course, were to be the owners of the tidal mills along the New Meadows River. Timber local to the West Bath area was becoming scarce by this time and the canal would give the mills access to logs which even then were being floated down the Androscoggin and Kennebec Rivers into Merrymeeting Bay.

About four years later on March 5, 1790, the General Court passed an act authorizing the creation of a corporation to build the canal, listed the members of the corporation, and specified that no tolls would be required for public use. But on June 17th of the next year, a second act was passed amending the list of corporate members and making provisions for the collection of tolls. It read in part:"A canal from the head of the New Meadows River to Merrymeeting Bay . . . the New Meadows Canal . . . that the said canal shall be kept open for the passing of boats, rafts and other water crafts, and for all persons who may wish to pass or transact business therein, they paying the following toll; . . . every boat . . . of one ton, the sum of nine pence, and in the same proportion for vessels or boats of greater or less burthen not exceeding six shillings for any such vessel or boat. For every thousand feet of boards in rafts four pence half penny; and in the same proportion for all other kinds of lumber."

On March 22nd, 1793, the court passed an act recognizing that the canal had been opened " . . . from the New Meadows River to the waters of the river Kennebec, a little below Merrymeeting Bay, at a place called Welch's Creek, it having been found impracticable to open a canal directly to the Bay aforesaid, by reason of rocks and other obstructions." This act also empowered the proprietors to keep the canal open and to enjoy all rights and privileges. Based upon this act, it appears that the canal was probably completed the preceding year: i.e., in 1792.

One John Peterson must have been the driving force behind the canal or perhaps became its principal user. He built a dam across the upper cove, apparently in the vicinity of the present Maine Central Railroad Bridge, and established a gristmill at the eastern end and saw mills at the western end.

Eventually the New Meadows Canal became unofficially known as the Peterson Canal, and a road on the west side still bears his name.

The records don't tell us much about how the canal was operated. Among a number of people interviewed around the turn of the century, several insisted that the canal had never been completed and no logs had ever been transported through it. Others could recall their parents talking about going down to the locks but no conclusive evidence of locks or tidal gates has ever been found. It is not clear that anyone has ever seriously looked for them. There is a remnant of some kind of stone and mortar structure in the canal, near the north end but it is clearly not a lock and probably not a tide gate. One man, however, remembered his father telling how hard he had worked as a boy poling logs up through the canal. His father was born in 1795 and if he worked on the canal when he was only 10 years old, then the canal operated for at least 12 or 13 years. Of the various accounts, this one seems reasonably plausible. It is further substantiated by at least one other statement that under favorable conditions, two rafts of logs placed end to end, each raft composed of six large logs laid side by side, each log not less than 60 feet long, were easily floated through the canal.

Nevertheless, all evidence suggests that the canal was less than a resounding success. One problem concerned the difference in the times of high tide at each end of the canal. Typically, the canal could be used for only about three hours of each tide cycle. Other limiting factors seem to have been the insufficient depth to which the builders blasted through the ledge at the summit and the apparent lack of any flow control such as might be afforded by locks or tide gates.

Peterson and his wife, Sarah, built a home in 1783 on what is now the Adams Road in East Brunswick. Peterson used his complex as an inn and customhouse for packet boats coming up the New Meadows River. In addition to gristmills and sawmills, he had a store and shipyard across the road. The 268-ton *Nancy*, constructed in 1792, and *The Fair Lady*, were two of his vessels. Trade routes included the West Indies.

The home was later owned by the Francis Adams family. It was then passed on to relatives, the Conants, who made shore dinners famous at the original New Meadows Inn. The Trowbridge family bought the property, which included 300 acres, in 1904, and renovated it. The next owner, in 1917, was Edward Varney, who named the farm Meadowsweet, and left it to his daughter, Constance Varney Ring. This beautifully restored home is now owned by Constance Ring's son, C. Warren "Johnny" Ring.

After the failure of the canal in 1797, Peterson left New Meadows for what became known as the Peterson House at King's Dock, at 1463 Washington Street[105] in Bath. His new location was the site of the original Heath farm.

Today, the canal in some spots is reduced to a trickle of water through a thick mattress of sedge grasses, cattail, eulalia, and purple loosestrife.

Courtesy of C. W. "Johnny" Ring

Meadowsweet, after renovations that were completed in 1904

Captain Nehemiah Peterson

Nehemiah Peterson, the son of Nehemiah Sr. and Patricia (Dillingham) Peterson of Duxbury, Massachusetts, was born in 1765. Both he and his relative, John Peterson, were descendants of the *Mayflower* pilgrims John Alden and Priscilla Mullins.[106]

He left for the New Meadows area and married Lydia Larrabee in Brunswick on October 4, 1792. Nehemiah, as the story goes, discovered a stowaway on his ship, and the talented lad paid his fare by painting a portrait of the captain. This part of the Peterson family lived above the New Meadows Canal. The home there today, Riverside Farm, is the third Peterson-built structure; the first two were destroyed by fire. Peterson and his wife had six children: Benjamin, Hannah, Elisha, Rebecca, Nehemiah III, born in 1803, and Lydia. Nehemiah died in 1843 and is buried along with his wife at the Harding Cemetery, also known as the Thompson Brook Cemetery, located in East Brunswick on the Bath Road (U.S. Route 1) across from the Harding Plant.

The Ham Family

Tobias Ham Sr. was born in Newington, New Hampshire, on November 23, 1717. He was the son of John Ham, whose family immigrated from The Isle of Man. Tobias Ham later moved to New Meadows.

Ham Hill, on the Old Brunswick Road, is the large area at the top of the ridge that shares two side roads, Bridge Road and Peterson Lane, encompassing, in the opinion of the author, Stephen's Carrying Place. Ham, obtaining his land from the Kennebec Proprietors, owned the piece between Gutch and Heath tracts. Ham's Hill, Ham's Watering Place, Ham's Garrison, Ham's Hill School, Ham's Brook, and the Ham Cemetery are attributed to the Ham name. The part of the property with the Ham titles ran from the New Meadows River side down across the canal area and up the hill, opposite the eighteenth tee of the Bath Country Club, where the Ham Cemetery[107] is today. Ham was a shoemaker, farmer, and tanner who probably used these low-lying areas by the water for his tanning pits.[108]

Ham's Garrison was located on a ledge behind the Peterson barn, which became the Riverside Farm. A heavily traveled route by Native Americans between New Meadows and Brunswick (Pejepscot) necessitated the garrison. According to Wheeler's *History of Brunswick*, the garrison was probably built by tanner Joseph Smith, who settled at New Meadows in 1739. His son, Thomas, was killed by Indians in 1768 at age fourteen while tending cows near the tanning pits.

The Ham School was on the northwest side of the intersection of Bridge Road and Peterson Lane. Some local people recall attending the school, which is noted on the *1871 Brunswick and Harpswell Map* by F. W. Beers.[109] Along the path of Stephen's Carry are several cistern-like structures that Owen, in his *Plummer's History of Bath Maine*, refers to as possibly Ham's Watering Place. This would link the stagecoach stop at the Hamilton home, allegedly one of the oldest homes in Brunswick, with the original Peterson home and the Henderson farm.

Ham Burial Ground

Located west of the intersection of Ridge Road and Whiskeag Road, this secluded spot is across from the eighteenth tee of the Bath Country Club.

Ham
1. Theodore Ham, son of Benjamin and Martha (Morton) Ham, d. Mar 8, 1840, age 71. (Benjamin was the son of Tobias and Abigail Ham).
2. Sarah (Preble) Ham, wife of Theodore, d. Oct. 23, 1819, age 47.
3. Isaac, son of Theodore and Sarah Ham, d. Oct 14, 1805, age 1.
4. Rachel L., daughter of Theodore and Sarah Ham, d. 1867, age 67.
5. John, son of Tobias and Abigail Ham, d. Sept. 26, 1805, age 61.
6. Betsy, d. 1863, age 70.

Manson
7. Samuel, d. 1843, age 36.

Nancy Dearborn Lovetere Collection

The Ham cemetery in 2003

Rogers

8. Drummond, son of Nathanial and Nancy (Campbell) Rogers, d. Mar. 14, 1839, age 26.

Compiled by Lorelei Gustafson for The USGenWeb Project.

African-Americans on Merrymeeting Bay and the Brunswick Plains

The *Bath Daily Times*, Tuesday, August 18, 1885, reported: A CENTENARIAN DEAD. "Margaret Freeman, a colored lady at the north part of town in the vicinity of Merrymeeting Bay, died yesterday at the age of 104 years, 3 months and 10 days. She died of old age."

The *Bath Independent* on August 18, 1885: "Mrs. Margaret Freeman died approximately 100 years old. Her daughter married a local man and she lived with them in her last years." And on August 22, 1885: "Early in the week a Mrs. Freeman died in North Bath at the advanced age of 104 years and 3 months. The old lady had been quite smart up to her last sickness."

And so, in 1885, two local newspapers carried a typical two-line obituary commemorating the life of a black woman. African-Americans mixed easily within the New Meadows and northwest Bath communities.

In the 1850 United States Federal Census, of the 323 names reflected in the northwest rural part of Bath, 37 were designated as "Black." Maine's overall population that year was 99.8 percent white.[110] Color of skin was in the eye of the census taker, beholding the face of the head of household who answered his questions. "Some families were listed as 'negro' in one generation, 'mulatto' in the next and 'white' in subsequent generations."[111]

The New Meadows River did not always divide the towns as communally as it does today; in fact, this water highway encouraged socialization. An old road ran parallel to the Androscoggin River, an extension of Bridge Road[112] in East Brunswick. Ending at Merrymeeting Bay in North Bath, the route was scattered with African-American families such as Hill, Harrison, Garrison, and Freeman.[113] Most of these names are listed on the *1858 Chace Map*. This road intersected with Old Bath Road, which meandered through what was called the Brunswick Plains, home to Tobias Hill in 1821. A farmer, known as a great hog butcher, Hill blazed a bridle trail that became known as Toby's Turnpike, which led in a southerly direction from Cooks Corner at the Brunswick Plains to Gatchell's Pond. Hill also sold bayberry tallow to passersby.

Courtesy of Mary Jane Hill Cummings

James W. Hill, grandson of James F. Hill of North Bath, is at the center of this photograph, lying down. The woman in white is his sister, Evelyn (c. 1930–40).

Tobias's son, Sandy, settled on the Bath side of the New Meadows River. The home of his son, James F. Hill, is shown on the *Chace Map*. Located at the end of the Bayshore Road on Merrymeeting Bay, the Hills' home faced Topsham. The 1860 Census states that James F. Hill, thirty-six, lived there with his wife, Mary Jane, thirty-five, whose mother was Margaret Freeman. The James F. Hill family first appears in North Bath on the 1860 Census and last in 1880. Although a fire destroyed the Hill home many years ago, a magnificent, fragrant purple lilac tree still grows near the corner of the old foundation.

Harrison Burial Ground

Bath's only known African-American cemetery is located near the Brunswick-Bath boundary on the shore of the Androscoggin River on Merrymeeting Bay. Difficult to locate because of overgrown foliage, it is about a mile south from the end of Bayshore Road and a good hike if approached from the East Brunswick side of Bridge Road, whose northern end is listed as Cross Road in 1880. The headstones are in poor condition; a few unmarked fieldstones are there as well. United States Census records list the Harrisons as "Black" in 1850 and "Mulatto" in 1860.

Harrison
1. John, "Father," d. Jul. 12, 1876, age 76 yrs., 7 mos.
2. Lavina (Freeman), wife of John, "Mother," d. Feb. 25, 1872, age 68 yrs., 6 mos., 16 days.
3. John, b. Nov. 25, 1835, d. Jun. 28, 1891, age 56.

Curch[114]
4. Adriana, wife of John A., d. Oct. 31, 1855, age 22.
5. John H., son of John and Adriana, d. Mar. 20, 1855, age 9 mos., 5 days.

Compiled by Harold Brown, Helen McPhee, and Doris Rowland.

Chapel Yard Burial Ground

This burial ground is located on the old Bath Road in East Brunswick near the Chapel of Our Savior. Also known as the Heuston Cemetery, it is Brunswick's only African-American burial ground. Francis Heuston was a Revolutionary War veteran from Cape Cod and a well-respected farmer and seaman.

Davis
1. Levi Davis, d. 1889.
2. Rachel Davis, d. 1891.
3. Francis A., son of Levi and Rachel, d. 1852.
4. Gilbert P., son of Levi and Rachel, d. 1893.
5. Augustus A., son of Levi and Rachel, d. 1905.

Nancy Dearborn Lovetere Collection

The Chapel Yard or Heuston Burial Ground

Freeman

6. Samuel Freeman, d. circa 1850; one of the two fieldstones may be his marker.

Gardner

7. Marcellus R. Gardner, d. Sept. 9, 1883.
8. Francis Heuston, d. June 1, 1858, age 95.

Heuston

9. Pamelia W. Heuston, d. May 5, 1829, age 19 yrs., 10 mos.
10. Mahitable Heuston, d. August 25, 1851, age 70 yrs., 3 mos., 24 days.

Hill

11. Elizabeth Hill, wife of William Hill, died April 24, 1854, age 35 yrs., 7 mos.

Hopkins
12. Helen C. Hopkins, d. 1926.
13. Herbert, son of Aaron and Helen Hopkins, d. 1891.
14. Gilbert D., son of Aaron and Helen Hopkins, d. 1891.
15. Eddie M., son of Aaron and Helen Hopkins, d. 1903.
16. Austin A., son of Aaron and Helen Hopkins, d. 1954, not listed on monument; last person buried at this cemetery.

Jackson
17. Amy Ann Jackson, d. Sep. 13, 1904, age 85 yrs., 10 mos.
18. Oriana Jackson, d. Feb. 19, 1885, age 28.

Lewis
19. Ann Caroline Lewis, d. Oct. 1, 1851, age 10 yrs., 1 mo., 7 days.

Barbara Desmarais, webmaster of Brunswick, Maine, Cemeteries. Rootsweb host site.

Thomas Purchase

Thomas Purchase (Purchas) is one of the earliest known settlers at New Meadows, arriving from Devonshire, England, in 1628. A hunter, trapper, fisherman, and farmer, he traded with the Indians, having a successful post at the Androscoggin River Falls in Brunswick. Here he ran a sturgeon and salmon station, or fish house, with a London connection. Purchase's ownership of three home sites may have been made possible because of trade monopoly. His farm was near Bridge Road, just above the end of New Meadows River, which at one time was called Purchas' River. This was on the south side of the Old Canal, the Peterson Canal, at Wigwam Point. Purchase's name was also assigned to Lines Island as Purchas' Island and Merrymeeting Bay as Purchase's Bay.

Purchase's territory was between Mere Point, the Bunganuc River,[115] and the Sagadahoc River. His first marriage in 1631 at age fifty to Mary Gove may have been the reason he and his partner, George Way, were granted the Patent Right; Mary's cousin was said to be Christopher Gardner, an agent of Ferdinando Gorges. The land consisted of four square miles, or four miles square (confusion remains on this description) on the "Bishopscotte" River (Pejepscot) toward the sea. In 1639 Purchase granted all of the Pejepscot land to the Massachusetts Bay government; fear of the Indians or disappointment in the region's inability to create a government were likely reasons for this action.

One of the first regional attacks of King Philip's War[116] was at Purchase's home at New Meadows in 1675. As a sloop arrived at his storehouse to pick up corn, Indians attacked the crew. His son was at home but escaped. Purchase left New Meadows after the assault. His second marriage was to Elizabeth Williams of Essex, Massachusetts. He died in Salem, Massachusetts, in 1678 at age 101, leaving four children. His heirs sold his share of the patent to Richard Wharton.

The Bay Bridge and Samuel Foote

The bridge joining Topsham and East Brunswick was built in 1835. It crossed the Androscoggin and part of Merrymeeting Bay, with an anchor on Mustard Island (Baxter's,[117] Freyer's, Friar's). This connection provided a short route for farmers taking produce to Bath. Granite stones from the structure can still be seen on both sides, off Bay Bridge Road in Topsham and at Bay Bridge Landing on the East Brunswick side. An informative kiosk at the public landing describes its history in East Brunswick.

Martin Hall of Bowdoinham contracted the job at a cost of $20,000.[118] The city of Bath was an initial stockholder. Some of the other private investors were William King, Charles Clapp, Joseph Sewall, John Patten, George F. Patten, Daniel Marston, Oliver Moses, David Magoun, and William Richardson, all of Bath. William Purinton and William Randall of Topsham were shareholders, too.

The wooden bridge was 2,700 feet long with a 24-foot-wide deck. The pilings, with rocks around them for protection, were 20 feet apart. The pilings were later replaced with granite blocks.

The bridge was never a financial success. Bath had to borrow money for repairs when the bridge was just a year old. Floods, ice, and shifting river sand presented continuous problems. Over its sixty-year life span,

Courtesy of Millie Simpson Stewart

The Bay Bridge

the bridge cost more than one million dollars to repair and operate.

In 1864 the remaining private stockholders relinquished their shares, leaving Bath the sole owner. In 1875, one span washed out, making it unusable for three years. The Maine Legislature gave the bridge to Sagadahoc County in 1878. It was rebuilt, opening later that year. Some of the wooden spans were replaced with metal. The county operated the bridge until 1896, when several sections were washed out by floods and ice.

John Foster tended the bridge for ten years, followed by Samuel W. Foote of Bath, whose tenure was from 1851 until 1875. Lewis Thompson took over for five years; Thomas Nutter kept the bridge for nine years; and Lydia Young was the last keeper until the flood of 1896. The *Chace Map of 1858* shows a tollhouse on the Brunswick side.

The Foote Family

John Foote, born in 1739, married Martha Purrington. He may have been the son of John Foote of Amesbury, Massachusetts. He was granted land in Georgetown in 1777, which was most likely property in Bath, which ultimately became West Bath. A Thomas Foote had property in the same vicinity as John Foote; Holt suggests they may or may not have been related.[122]

John's son, Enoch,[123] was born June 5, 1792. Married twice, his children were Samuel W., born May 3, 1818, died 1900; and John, Julia, Harriet, Charles, Rachel, Ann Mary, and Sarah Maria.

Samuel W. Foote married Lucy R. Rogers of Topsham, daughter of Hugh and Isabella (Owen) Rogers. Their children were: Augusta J., Hugh

Rogers, Virginia M., Charles R., Samuel, John Alden, Fred E. (who married Annie Ward), and Katie Bell.[124]

Samuel Foote

Before Samuel W. Foote became a farmer and tollkeeper for the Merrymeeting Bay Bridge, he got his sea legs, as did many young men of that period, traveling to different ports for employment. At age twenty-six, he found himself in New Orleans. A letter, simply addressed to Samuel W. Foote, New Orleans, is coauthored by family members. After a brief salutation from his father, Enoch, his sister, Harriet, writes, in part:

"My dear brother Samuel, we are huddled up before the fire. Thomas brought me down to the bay bridge in the sleigh and I got home first rate. The neighbors are all well but some of them are rather mad about the new town which sets us off from the village. Ireland folks backed out and so the new word up here is the northern boundary line and most of Father's farm is in Bath and he will have to pay taxes in both towns and you know what a bother that will make. They think of calling the new town West Bath."

His brother writes a line or two, finishing the letter with: "Sarah says amen to it." West Bath became independent from Bath on February 14, 1844. Urban and rural differences were among the reasons for the separation.

After his travels, Foote bought land from his father less than a mile and a half from the Bay Bridge. He kept detailed, and for modern readers, illuminating, daybooks during his tenure from 1851 through 1875, and for many more years at his farm. His daily accounts were written with beautiful flowing penmanship, each entry beginning with the date, weather, and wind direction. "Thursday, Nov. 22, Thanksgiving Day. Blows a gale from the N.W. Went over to the salt river to haul out my boats; snowed about 6 inches last night—afternoon picking over my potatoes."

When he was not at the bridge, his farm duties seemed acceptably routine, with rare mention of illness, struggle, or frustration. "Wed., March 25 1891 Wind N.W. . . . I am sick today. What can I do."

Courtesy of John W. Voorhees

One of Samuel Foote's daybooks

Foote, with his five sons (Hugh, Charles, Samuel, John, and Fred), three daughters (Augusta, Virginia, and Katie Bell), and brother, Charles, raised crops for the market in Bath—barley, beans, corn, potatoes, pumpkins, turnips, cabbage, and apples. Detailed entries record his income for garden produce, fish—smelts, herring, and sea shad—and game—geese, black ducks, shildrakes, chickens, and turkeys.

His journals show that Foote was an industrious man. A gondola, boat, and a fish house required net repair, seine knitting, and weir- and sail-making. He repaired wagon wheels, built horse sleds, and fixed sled runners. He shoed his horses, cut wood, smoked hams, planted in the spring, and harvested in the fall. He built barns, a smokehouse, floats, boats, and fences; hauled manure and rockweed; and raked hay. He also brought animals to slaughter, his own and those of his folks. "Went over and weighed Mother's hog. 346 pounds."

Foote made daily trips to the busy mills of Varney, Lemont, Sewall, and Rogers with logs and trees felled for shingle shaving. His travels also took him to the Chops and New Meadows River, the "salt river." He crossed his bridge over the Androscoggin to visit the Rogerses, his wife's parents in Topsham. His daybooks mention Ham's Point, a cattle show in Topsham, Gatchell's Creek (Getchell), and taking smelt nets to Brick Island and the Ireland District in North Bath. Occasionally Foote "goes a gunning." "Sat., Dec. 22 1860 Wind NE Bill went to Ireland to get my smelt frame." "Sat., Dec. 31 1870 Wind S and quite warm. Rained some last night. The boys and I went to take up our weir and so ends the old year."

Foote's work on the failed Bay Bridge was never-ending. He was constantly repairing planks, posts, and footings; painting; and sweeping snow off the surface. Mustard Island, the land connection of this span, needed to be hayed.

For the Foote family, recreation was minimal. Several of the daybook entries mention optimal sledding conditions. On one occasion the children went down to Granite Wharf for a clambake. And, Foote mentions several times that the circus[119] crossed the bridge. Each day Foote's records are filled with chore descriptions, but Sundays' notations concerned weather and chapel attendance. Thanksgiving meant family visits to Topsham to see "Farther" or "Par" Rogers. Christmas was rarely mentioned; light work prevailed that day as well.

With humble acceptance of his life and a profound appreciation of family and health, Samuel Foote shows his spirituality in closing out the year:

"Fry, Dec 31, 1869 Wind S. Clear & warm. Sawing wood at the Door all Day. The old year has gone out very mild & warm and we are all alive & quite well and in hope the new year will be more Prosperous to us in health and the enjoyment of life which none but the Giver of all blessings can bestow on His sinful Children. And May he who rules the world guide & instruct us through the coming year, watch over & protect us from all harm for Thou are the ruler of the World."[120]

Samuel and Lucy Foote, including children Hugh and Katie Bell, and other family members, are buried at the New Rogers Cemetery in Topsham.[121] The *1858 Chace Map* shows S. Foote, on the Old Brunswick

Road in Bath, where the restored Foote home is today, complete with Fred Foote's carved initials preserved inside a closet door. The map also shows F. Foote nearby on the New Meadows Road in West Bath.

Deposition on Wigwam Point

The following 1763 Deposition on Wigwam Point is the testimony of a longtime resident concerning the ownership of property at Wigwam Point in North Bath. Taken at Pownalborough in preparation for a trial at Falmouth, it is a record of a typical boundary dispute of the time, with both plaintiffs and defendants familiar names among the people who lived, worked, and prospered here. It also exemplifies the connection between the early communities on the Kennebec River.

I, John Turp, of Georgetown in the County of Lincoln of lawful age testify that I have lived in Georgetown on Kennebec River for about thirty eight years; am well-acquainted with a Farm that is in the West Side of the Kennebec River and makes one side of the Chops at Merry Meeting Bay which Farmhouse formerly owned by Job Lewis et al: and now by Silvester Gardiner et al of Boston. And I well remember when Mr. Alexander Campbell lived on said Farm by lease from Lewis which was about twenty seven or twenty eight years ago: and I always understood by Campbell that the Southerly line of said Farm extended to Wigwam Point which is about half a Mile to the Southward of the head or Northernmost part of the Salt Marsh within the Bounds of Said Farm and about Thirty Years ago, I was informed by John Spooner, Esq. of Boston of one Mr. Treforth who lived in Georgetown by whom the Farm was claimed that the Southerly line of said Farm extended to Wigwam Point and the late Patrick Drummond et al of Georgetown aforesaid: has told me the same. And further testify and Declare that the said Wigwam Point is on Steven's River or Creek so called and a little to the Southward of the House where Mr. Elisha Baker now lives and a Small Creek and some Marsh runs partly around Wigwam Point which Point was the Place where the Indians usually landed and carried over to Merry Meeting Bay which I have often seen, as also Wigwam Point where the Indians dwelt and further say that Mr. Lewis above mentioned told me the

aforesaid: Point was called Wigwam Point and that it was the Southerly
Boundary his Farm and gave me Power of Atty. to take care of the same & see
that no persons cut Lumber thereon——Dated at Pownalborough the eleventh
day of May 1763——John S. Turpe Lincoln Cty May 11, 1763. Then the within
named John Turp personally appeared and being first duly cautioned & care-
fully examined made solomn oath that the written deposition by him
Subscribed contains the Truth, the whole Truth & nothing but the Truth being
taken to be used in a Case now pending between Joshua Purrinton of
Georgetown in the County of Lincoln Tanner and Samuel Thompson of
Brunswick in the County of Cumberland Yeoman; & Edward Welch & Thomas
Crawford Weavers & James Grace Husbandman all of Georgetown aforesaid
deposition: to be heard & try'd at the next Superior Court of Common Pleas to
be holden at Falmouth within & for the County of Cumberland on the third
Tuesday of May Ins: The said: John Turp being & living more then thirty miles
from Falmouth the place of Tryal, and the sd: Joshua Purrinton & Samuel
Thompson being duly notified but not present at the taking of Deposition.
Taken before me: I am Jon: Bowman
Copy examined by Stephen Longfellow

This deposition, found at the Suffolk, Massachusetts, County
Courthouse, describes a boundary dispute on land lying between the
Kennebec River and Merrymeeting Bay and New Meadows River, including the tip of Butler Head. The person deposed to make a statement as to
rightful ownership was John Tarp (Turp). He had lived in Bath
(Georgetown) on the Kennebec River for about thirty-eight years (since
1725), probably on the land where the Stone House is located, on the
Whiskeag Road in Bath. The deposition date is 1763; he was given power
of attorney to take care of the land to see that trees were not cut.

Tarp goes on to substantiate his position by naming tenants, owners,
or credible people who had testified to him as to the legal description and
boundaries of the land. In doing so he describes a farm on the west side of
the Kennebec, bordered by the Chops and Merrymeeting Bay. He says that
the farmhouse was owned by Job Lewis about 1725, leased by Alexander
Campbell about 1736, and at the present, 1763, owned by Silvester
Gardiner. He states that the south border of the land extended to Wigwam

Point at Steven's River or Creek. The late Patrick Drummond, Mr. Treforth, and John Spooner, Esq., reiterated the same information. He elaborates on his description of the southern border at New Meadows.

The deposition involved Joshua Purrinton, a tanner, of Georgetown (Bath), and Samuel Thompson, a yeoman[125] of Brunswick, against Edward Welch and Thomas Crawford, both weavers, and James Grace, husband-man, all of Georgetown (Bath). Welch, Crawford, and Grace all lived in the vicinity of Christopher Lawson's house. Crawford may have had a carding or weaving business at Little Whiskeag stream.

The plaintiffs were present at the deposition whereas the defendants were not, having been "duly notified." It is noted that the lawyer taking the deposition was Jonathan Bowman, friend of John Adams, a fellow classmate at Harvard in 1755.

Fannie Eckstorm, in her *Indian Place Names*, supposes that Wigwam Point is modern-day Howard's Point and Middle Bay in Brunswick. Logic dictates that an Indian would navigate the water as long as possible to eliminate a long carry. That is not to say that a carry did not exist from this point. However, why not go farther north than Howard's Point? It would be closer to the Merrymeeting Bay destination. As the deposition is rather vague in its description of the land in dispute, the author of *The Road to Down Street* encourages further investigation. The three old maps at the beginning of this book seem to place the deposition description in a more northerly position, closer to the Bath–East Brunswick corporate boundary, defining Stephen's Carry.

Another theory as to why Wigwam Point is at this location is that the deposition mentions it as being a little southward of Mr. Elisha Baker's lot, No. 55 in 1760, shown in *Wheeler's History of Brunswick, Harpswell and Topsham*, page 865. Another deposition mentions Baker's house not too far from a high ledge of rocks (*Sagadahoc and Kennebec: Collected Papers, Notes, Abstracts, Copies*, page 181). In 1750 the property becomes that of Joseph Smith, shown on a map in *Wheeler's History*. This map also shows Charles Casida's lot, which Wheeler mentions on Wigwam Point. This spot is as far on the upper stream as one could go even today.

Reverend Thayer's papers go on to substantiate this location by describing Smelt Brook as being a little north of Thomas Foote's house.

The Foote home stands today within view of where the author believes Smelt Brook and the falls are located, at the corner of the Ridge Road and the Old Brunswick Road. This brook is mentioned in 1825 as a "Limit of the Highway District."

Current maps clearly show the line separating Sagadahoc from Cumberland County. This corporate boundary, running northwest, ends at Stephen's Carry. The exact location of the boundary is still disputed. Some feel it begins near the middle of the wooded area of the Ridge Road in North Bath, at the remains of an old bridge over the old Peterson Canal. However, the perfectly straight boundary would be impractical as the original carry, as that route presents a very rugged zigzag or switchback course over very rocky ledge. It is possible that the end of the carry and the corporate boundary end are represented by the copper pin, which was placed on a ledge slightly below the high-water mark in Merrymeeting Bay. It is quite visible today. This pin was reported in an 1842 perambulation, a boundary survey done every seven years to see if the markers are still present. The boundary over the years has been moved back and forth. The beginning of the carry most likely started at the very end of the New Meadows River, with a short climb to the wooded area near the turnaround at Bridge Road, then up the hill beside a large ledge and then on down to the water's edge. The corporate boundary was made straight, and therefore the beginning of the boundary is probably not the official start of the carry.

About a quarter-mile away, during the excavation for the condominium complex called Springview, off the Ridge Road in Bath, shell middens were uncovered. The marsh, which runs beside the complex, is traceable for several miles, running parallel to the New Meadows River as it, too, becomes merely a stream. This was possibly a free-flowing waterway many hundreds of years ago before becoming a thick bed of cattails and other sedge grasses. It can be followed to the low area of the Bath Country Club and through to the low-lying terrain of the Peterson Canal.

Census Data

Driving Logs and Keeping House

The first United States Federal Census was taken in 1790 after the American Revolution. For privacy reasons, the census has a seventy-two-year statutory restriction (92 Stat. 915; Public Law 95-416; October 5, 1978). The census of 1940, for example, will be available in 2012. A fire in 1921 destroyed 99 percent of the census records for 1890. Census information prior to 1860 for the township of Bath, Maine, is listed under Lincoln County; the following years are listed under Sagadahoc County.

Census records for Bath from 1850 through 1930 are listed by wards and districts. The censuses included here cover the northwest rural part of Bath. Early censuses did not provide the specific location of the residences surveyed. Assuming that the census taker surveyed households neighborhood by neighborhood, censuses of 1850, 1860, and 1870 reflect an approximation of rural residents. Notation of streets and roads began in 1880.

The order in which a census was taken also varied; sometimes the enumerator would poll one side of the street before crossing to the other side. Others would go from each house, left to right. Streets and roads today may have different names: for example, what was once East Brunswick Road is now Whiskeag Road.

The districts listed below describe the parameters of neighborhoods in the northwest area of Bath. The censuses that follow fall within these districts:

District 6: Bath City, Ward 5, bounded north by railroad tracks, High Street north, ward line. East by the Kennebec River. South by ward line, Summer Street, Washington Street, Chestnut Street. West by Lincoln Street, Brunswick Road.

District 7: Bath City, Ward 6, bounded north by north ward line. East by the Kennebec River. South by the south ward line. North by Washington Street, Mechanic Street, High Street, and the Whiskeag Road. West by the Kennebec River, including several islands.

District 8: Bath City, Ward 7, bounded north by Merrymeeting Bay. East by city limits, ward line, Whiskeag Road, High Street, Mechanic Street, Washington Street. South by North Street, High Street, railroad tracks. West by City limits.

Many handwritten census entries are illegible, but the best effort has been made here to interpret the information. Names have been copied as they were written, even though a mistake may be evident. In a few instances when the name is familiar but written completely wrong, it has been corrected. An example would be "Foss" when the name should be "Voss." This error could lead to a dead-end genealogical search. Spellings of family names also may vary from census to census; for example, "Rook" in 1850, "Rouke" in 1860, and "Rooke" in 1910. The various spellings of this name have not been altered here, as it is evident that it could be the same family.

In genealogy research, a middle name is very important, as the first name is often repeated over many generations, not only from parents to children but from aunts, uncles, and grandparents. Often a child is known by his middle name to distinguish him from a parent with the same name, or because of family tradition. However, it should be noted that single initials are some of the most difficult items to transcribe from the handwritten census, so there may well be inconsistencies in the record, either from error by the original census taker or by transcription error.

Job descriptions, as well as their spellings, varied according to the year (labourer/laborer). Log driver, river driver, and craftsman can be similar or different occupations. The job description of "servant" sometimes referred to work for a private family, not within the family enumerated.

The age of a young child was often listed in early censuses with a fraction: for example, nine months is written as 9/12. Sometimes the census names are listed alphabetically. In a few instances when the sex of a person's name is questionable, an inserted brackets designate male or female. All people listed in the following censuses were born in Maine unless otherwise noted. The records were obtained from Ancestry.com.

Color or race was also questioned or noticed by the census taker. In the spaces where there is no racial designation, it is assumed the residents were white. In the 1850 and 1860 censuses, racial color was limited to "white, black, or mulatto." In the censuses of 1870 and 1880, "Chinese" and "Indian" were added. By the early twentieth century, the heading asked for just "color or race."

Following an individual from one census to another shows the progression of life. A young baby girl is listed as a fraction; then, "at school." Later she is listed as a wife, "keeping house." One census later she becomes a widow and is listed as "head of household." In another decade she is listed as "at home." And in ten more years, she is not listed at all.

1850 United States Federal Census

The 1850 census does not indicate the specific location of the residences surveyed. However, the census names include many of the well-known names from northwestern rural Bath. This census is considered the first modern census, as it lists the value of real estate, and all family members' names, ages, and places of birth.

It is interesting to note that of the 323 names collected here, 37 are designated as "black." Eleven percent of North Bath residents are black in 1850, a year when Maine's census reflects an overall population that is 99.8 percent white. In 1850, the census taker was asked to determine if the resident was "white, black, or mulatto." No other categories are included. In this census, only those who were not white were designated.

	Name/Age	Race	Profession	Real Estate Value	Place of Birth
1.	Samuel W. Foot, 31		Labourer	$400	
	Lucy H. Foot, 29				
	Julia A. Foot, 6				
	Martha V. Foot, 2				
	Charles R. Foot, 5/12				
2.	Briscilla Semor, 56	B			
	Lucretia Semor, 18	B			
	Eda Semor, 10	B			
	James Lee, 58	B	Marriner		Maryland
	Sarah Lee, 56	B			Maryland
	Priscilla Darling, 49	B			
	Eliza Darling, 26	B			
	Silvia Darling, 24	B			
	Samuel R. Darling, 19	B	Marriner		
	Fanny Darling, 18	B			
	William H. M. Darling, 13	B			
	Martha D. Darling, 11	B			
3.	Caleb Adams, 76	B	None		N Hampshire
	Stephen Hill, 30	B	Marriner		Maryland
	Caroline Hill, 18	B			
	James Hill, 1	B			

4.	James Ward, 76	Farmer	$400	
	Ruth Ward, 67			
5.	John Williams, 40	Marriner	$400	Madeira [Portugal]
	Condace Williams, 36			
	Rebecca R. Williams, 17			
	Narcissa W. Williams, 9			
	Joseph D. Williams, 7			
	Almond H. Williams, 2			
6.	Zaccheus Crooker, 72	Farmer	$4,000	
	Polly Crooker, 69			Massachusetts
	Sophrona Crooker, 48			
7.	Warren H. Crooker, 29	Farmer		
	Rachel J. Crooker, 26			
	Denison H. Crooker, 1			
	William Aiken, 14			Scotland
8.	Timothy S. Crooker, 27	Farmer		
	Lydia Crooker, 22			
	George W. Crooker, 1			
	John S. Crooker, 35	Marriner		
	Susan Crooker, 36			
	Louisa Crooker, 10			
	Ammi L. Crooker, 8 [m]			
	Susan J. Crooker, 7			
	Zaccheus Crooker 2nd, 3			
	John Crooker, 8/12			
	Eliza A. Winslow, 13			
9.	Isaiah Crooker, 42	Farmer	$1,000	
	Mary Crooker, 37			
	Angeline E. Crooker, 14			
	Charles W. Crooker, 12			
	Ellen A. Crooker, 10			
	Frances M. Crooker, 8			
	Edwin I. Crooker, 6			
	Jacob B. Crooker, 2			
	William Jaqueth, 24	Farmer		
10.	William Cornish, 28	Boarding House	$600	
	Belinda Cornish, 29			
	Dilbert D. Cornish, 7			
	James W. Cornish, 2			
	Esther Cornish, 54			

	Name	Occupation	Value	Birthplace
	John Cornish, 30	Millman		
	Caroline Getchell, 17			
	William Quinnan, 26	Fireman		
	John Munson, 20	Millman		
	Charles Thompson, 28	"		
	John Thompson, 30	"		
	Peter Pollard, 45	"		
	Joseph Holmes, 30	"		
	William Donnell 3d, 30	"		
	David B. Hodgkins, 22	"		
11.	Robert P. Manson, 41	Marriner	$3,000	
	Louisa J. Manson, 40			
	Ada J. Manson, 17			
	Vettory Manson, 13			
	Rufus Manson, 10			
	Ella Manson, 4			
	Amos Youngling, 26	Farmer		
12.	Isaac D. Cole, 40	Joiner	$800	Massachusetts
	Eliza Cole, 39			
	Isaac D. Cole, Jr., 16	Farmer		Massachusetts
	Charles B. Cole, 15	Farmer		Massachusetts
	Harriet E. Cole, 14			
	George W. Cole, 12			
	Lucy A. Cole, 11			
	Louisa Cole, 10			
	Caroline A. Cole, 8			
	Mary E. Cole, 3			
	James F. Cole, 1			
	Joseph Cole, 21	Farmer		Massachusetts
13.	Charles Whittam, 42	Raftsman	$500	
	Jane Whittam, 43			
	Charles E. Whittam, 23	Raftsman		
	Margaret J. Whittam, 18			
	Sarah E. Whittam, 17			
	Georgianna Whittam, 14			
14.	Owen A. Timmons, 33	Farmer	$1,000	
	Lucy Timmons, 33			
	Cosogine Timmons, 10			
	Anmoria Stinson, 28			
15.	James G. Crawford, 55	Farmer	$1,000	
	Rebecca Crawford, 42			

	James W. Crawford, 17	Clerk		
	Rebecca C. Crawford, 16			
	Margaret A. Crawford, 14			
	Hannah M. Crawford, 12			
	Lorenzo M. Crawford, 10			
	Thomas O. Crawford, 8			
	Adelia Crawford, 5			
	George Foster, 27	Laborer		
	Susan T. Foster, 30			
16.	Samuel F. Purington, 37	Farmer	$600	
	Susan Purington, 30			
17.	William Crawford, 67	Farmer	$2,000	
	Mary L. Crawford, 56			Massachusetts
	William H. Crawford, 26	Raftsman		
	Abby Crawford, 10			
	George W. Kelly, 6			
18.	Josiah D. Haley, 44	Farmer	$1,000	
	Mary Haley, 58			
	Mary F. Haley, 22			
	Catherine A. Haley, 17			
	John T. Haley, 14			
	Huldah G. Timmons, 29			
19.	Martha Timmons, 52		$500	
	Martha Ann Timmons, 18			
20.	John F. Roberts, 40	Raftsman	$500	
	Lydia Roberts, 44			
	Abigail Roberts, 13			
21.	Thomas Whittam, 34	Raftsman	$800	
	Abigail Whittam, 42			
	Asa P. Whittam, 8			
	James P. Whittam, 6			
	Abby J. Whittam, 5			
	Bethia Whittam, 3			
	Randolph Whittam, 2			
22.	Robert Ward, 40	Fisherman	$800	
	Elisa Ward, 35			
	Samuel O. Ward, 15			
	Augusta Ward, 15			
	Charles Ward, 11			

Thomas Ward, 9
George R. Ward, 6
Candace Ward, 3
Louisa Ward, 2

23. Jesse Briminjine, 30   Farmer $1,200
     Sarah Briminjine, 28
     Reliance Peters, 56 (f)
     Benjamin Peters, 30   Marriner
     John A. Peters, 21   Farmer
     James C. Peters, 18   Marriner
     Mary H. Peters, 24

24. George Crush, 37   Caulker $200   England
     Ellen Crush, 33
     George How, 21   Labourer

25. Hugh Rogers, 45   Millman $5,200
     Lydia Rogers, 41
     Charles M. Rogers, 20   Millman
     Martha J. Rogers, 19
     Nathaniel P. Rogers, 18   Farmer
     Isaac Rogers, 16   Farmer
     Augusta A. Rogers, 14
     George M. Rogers, 12
     Ellen P. Rogers, 10
     John H. Rogers, 6
     Abba L. Rogers, 9/12

26. Dominicus P. Campbell, 46   Cloth Dresser $700
     Adeline Campbell, 43
     Henry J. Campell, 17   Raftsman
     Alfred R. Campbell, 15
     Esyphana H. Campbell, 12
     Melvill C. Campbell, 8
     Elijah P. Campbell, 6
     Marcia A. Campbell, 4
     Issabella Oliver, 19

27. Nathan Covell, 81   Farmer   Massachusetts
     Caroline Covell, 40
     Ruth Dill, 44
     Rebecca C. Dill, 11
     James C. Dill, 9
     Julie B. Dill, 6
     Otis Mitchell, 24   Teamster

	Name, Age		Occupation	Value	Birthplace
	James Eisan, 30		Marriner		Nova Scotia
	Peter Griffin, 35		Marriner		Pennsylvania
28.	William T. Ham, 37		Farmer	$2,000	
	Rachel Ham, 50				
	Betsey Brown, 50				
	George House, 20		Farmer		
29.	James Jordan, 28		Farmer		
	Elisabeth Jordan, 26				
	James H. Jordan, 3				
	Hannah E. Jordan, 1				
30.	Henry W. Fields, 28		Trader		
	Almira H. Fields, 23				
	Augustus A. Fields, 2/12				
	Sarah Allen, 20				
	Lucretia Allen, 25	B			New York
31.	Ellison Brown, 61		Carpenter	$400	
	Elisabeth Brown, 55				
	Benjamin Brown, 19		Carpenter		
32.	John Harrison, 50	B	Farmer	$2,000	Baltimore
	Lavina Harrison, 46	B			
	George W. Harrison, 21	B	Marriner		
	Adrianna Harrison, 16	B			
	John Harrison, Jr., 14	B			
	Philena Harrison, 5	B			
	Albert Cobbinson, 30	B	Marriner		Pennsylvania
	Esther A. Cobbinson, 20	B			
	Henry Smith, 8	B			
	Sarah McDonald, 12	B			
	Benjamin Marston, 21		Fisherman		
	James North, 19		Fisherman		
	Robert Kincaid, 22		Fisherman		
33.	James McDonald, 24	B	Hack Driver	$100	
	Delia McDonald, 22	B			
34.	William Miller, 37		Boarding House		
	Julia Ann Miller, 39				
	Mary F. Miller, 9				
	George W. Miller, 7				
	Charles V. Miller, 6				
	Mary Lowell, 19				

	Sarah Pender, 65			
	Daniel Costine, 22		Marriner	
	Charles Jameson, 27		"	England
	Edward Trask, 12		"	
	Samuel Clary, 39		Clerk	
	John Cooney, 20		Labourer	Ireland
	William Soule, 22		Joiner	
	John W Swett, 23		"	
35.	Patrick Murphy, 30		Labourer	Ireland
	Bridget Murphy, 25			Ireland
	Michael Murphy, 2			Ireland
	Margaret Murphy, 4/12			
36.	Michael McCaib, 30		Labourer	Ireland
	Margaret McCaib, 28			Ireland
	John McCaib, 7			Ireland
	Bridget McCaib, 5			Ireland
	Patrick McCaib, 3			
	Mary McCaib, 1			
37.	Daniel F. Baker, 40		Cashier, Sagadahock Bank	
	Julia E. W. Baker, 31			
	Julia L. Baker, 6			
	Bridget Clark, 24			Ireland
38.	John Roberts, 40	B	Marriner	West Indies
	Hannah Roberts, 38	B		
	Emma J. Roberts, 10	B		
	Thankful Roberts, 7	B		
	John T. Roberts, 5	B		
	Rhoda Johnson, 22	B		
	John H. Johnson, 1	B		
39.	David Dudley, 47		Farmer	$500	
	Thankful B. Dudley, 42				Massachusetts
40.	Nathan Stilphin, 30		Carpenter	$100
	Ann Stilphin, 30			
	Julia Stilphin, 10			
	Margaret S. Stilphin, 9			
	Elvan W. Stilphin, 1			
	Tespa A. Riddle, 20			
41.	George R. Rook, 48		Farmer	$1,500
	Frances Rook, 48			

Ruth F. Rook, 18
James W. Rook, 16 — Farmer
Mary K. Rook, 8

42. Hylon Walker, 41 — Mason — $100
Maria G. Walker, 41
Henry J. Walker, 18 — Mason
Maria P. Walker, 10
Nancy J. Walker, 8
William H. Walker, 6
George S. Walker, 4
Alexander Blair, 32 — Labourer — Nova Scotia
Thomas Lumbard, 42 — "

43. Calvin G White, 25 — Gondola man — $400
Sabrina White, 26
Edward C. White, 5
Hannah M. White, 1/12
Elisabeth Stover, 30
Susannah Grows, 13

44. Benjamin F. Delano, 25 — Marriner
Rachel Delano, 21
Baby Delano, 1 [f]

45. John R. Buker, 28 — Carpenter — $600
Sarah Buker, 24
John R. Buker Jr., 4
Thomas Sturdevant, 22 — Farmer

46. Charles Wallender, 41 — Truckman — $500 — Sweden
Rebecca Wallender, 49
Abigail Roach, 85 — N Hampshire
Daniel Carter, 16 — Truckman — Nova Scotia

47. William Himes, 40 — Labourer — Ireland
Mary Himes, 45
Abby Himes, 15
Daniel Himes, 12
Henry Himes, 2

48. Cyrus Studley, 23 — Mason — Massachusetts
Malvira Studley, 22
Samuel O. Felker, 25 — Cabinet Maker
Alexander Duff, 26 — Blacksmith — Brit. Province
George Hawley, 28 — Carpenter — $100 — Brit. Province

49. Richard M. Barter, 33   Sailmaker
     Mary J. Barter, 30
     George Barter, 8
     Benjamin Barter, 6
     Franklin Barter, 4
     Richard M. Barter, Jr., 1

50. William Kelley, 27   Labourer
     Mary Jane Kelley, 24
     John Boobier, 25   Labourer
     Philenia Boobier, 23

51. Francis A. Lemont, 40   Marriner
     Emma Lemont, 34   England
     George H. Lemont, 28   Marriner

52. Ezekiel B. Drummond, 25   Marriner
     Susan D. Drummond, 20
     Baby Drummond, 8/12
     Elisabeth Campbell, 25   Pennsylvania

53. Asa Coombs, 33   Rigger
     Frances Coombes, 32   England

54. Jonathan Osgood, 81   None
     Sarah Osgood, 76
     Charlotte Chick, 33
     David Nutting, 31   Stable Keeper
     William O. Moody, 35   Merchant

1860 United States Federal Census

As with the 1850 census, the 1860 census included three options for "color": white, mulatto, or black. How someone was defined was at the discretion of the enumerator. Some families in this area that had been identified as black in 1850 were designated as "M" for mulatto in 1860. In another case, a person who was identified as black in 1850 is indicated as white (a blank box) in 1860.

The 1860 census asked whether any residents were "deaf and dumb, blind, insane, idiotic, pauper, or convict"; two residents in this portion of the 1860 census were noted as "idiotic."

	Name/Age	Race	Trade	Real Estate Value	Place of birth/ comments
1.	Joseph G. Stone, 45		Carpenter	$600/$0	
	Adaline Stone, 42				
	Josephene A. Stone, 12				Mass.
	John F. Stone, 7				
	Ada May Stone, 5				
	Freddie H. Stone, 1				
2.	George Jewett, 59		Farmer	$4,500/$500	
	Sarah Jewett, 43				Mass.
	Charles Jewett, 20		School Teacher		
	George F. Jewett, 19		Farm laborer		
	Frank E. Jewett, 16		Mariner		
	Edwin H. Jewett, 15				
	Hannah E. H. Jewett, 14				
	Frederick Jewett, 7				
	Nellie M. Jewett, 6				
3.	James Batchelder, 36		Joiner	$1,000/$200	
	Abbie Batchelder, 33				
	Willie R. Batchelder, 8				
	James E. Batchelder, 7				
	Georgeanna Batchelder, 1				
4.	B. T. Emery, 60		Farmer	$5,000/$200	
	Lucinda Emery, 48				
	Ann M. Emery, 20		Domestic		

	Charles D. Emery, 16		
	Briggs H. Emery, 14		
	Helen L. Emery, 11		
	B. Farnham Emery, 8		
	Ada F. Emery, 6		
	Charles T. Lord, 25	Tanner	$0/$500
5.	Isaac Rogers, 55	Mill Man	$1,050/$0
	Sarah A. Rogers, 18		
6.	Charles N. Rogers, 30	Mill Man	$2,000/$300
	Emely R. Rogers, 29		
7.	Hugh Rogers, 55	Lumber Mercht.	$6,200/$6,000
	Lydia C. Rogers, 51		
	Augusta S. Rogers, 23	School Teacher	
	George M. Rogers, 21	Mill Man	
	Ellen P. Rogers, 20	Domestic	
	John H. Rogers, 16		
	Abba L. Rogers, 10		
	Ada Rogers, 7		
8..	Saml F. Purington, 44	Farmer	$1,500/$300
	Susan Purington, 42		
	Samuel H. Purington, 10		
9.	Rachel Ham, 50	Domestic	$2,800/$500
	Betsey Brown, 60	Domestic	
10.	Samuel Edgecomb, 61	Farmer	$2,500/$500
	Elizabeth Edgecomb, 63		
	Silas W. Edgecomb, 32	Farmer	
	Mary E. Edgecomb, 27	Domestic	
	Lydia A. Edgecomb, 25	Milliner	
	Isabella J. C. Edgecomb, 20	Domestic	
	Scott Edgecomb, 7		
11.	George R. Edgecomb, 30	Mill man	
	Martha Edgecomb, 28		
	Alice Edgecomb, 1		
12.	John H. Farnham, 27	Carpenter	
	Martha A. Farnham, 28		
	Fred. E. Farnham, 4		
	Martha Timmings, 62		$250/$0

13. John F. Roberts, 49   Farmer $500/$100
     Lydia Roberts, 53
     Abigail Roberts, 23   Domestic

14. Alex. F. Boardman, 41   Trader   West Indies
     Silva J. Boardman, 30   Mass.
     Francis Boardman, 7
     Charles Boardman, 5
     Mina Boardman, 3
     Alonzo Haley, 22   Farm laborer
     Rosco Philbrook, 21   Farm laborer
     Maria Sewall, 21   M   Servant

15   John T. Haley, 24   Farmer $2,000/$300
     Rebecca Haley, 26
     Josephene Haley, 5
     Milton Haley, 9/12

16. O. A. Timmins, 43   Farmer $2,000/$500
     Lucy Timmins, 42
     Crosman Timmins, 20   Farmer
     Frank Timmins, 5

17. James Patridge, 43   day laborer $600/$0
     Nancy M. Patridge, 34
     Ann M. Patridge, 17
     Charles E. Patridge, 10
     Frank Patridge, 7

18. William Hodgkins, 39   Farmer $1,200/$300
     Frances M. Hodgkins, 41
     Owen A. Hodgkins, 10
     Clara A. Hodgkins, 6
     Edwin T. Hodgkins, 3
     Wilmot H. Hodgkins, 10/12

19. Frances Crawford, 70 $400/$0

20. James G. Crawford, 65   Farmer $1,500/$200
     Rebecca Crawford, 52
     Susan T. Foster, 41   Domestic
     James W. Crawford, 27   School Teacher
     Margaret A. Crawford, 24   Factory Girl
     Lorenzo Crawford, 20   Farmer
     Thomas O. Crawford, 17   Farmer
     Adelia Crawford, 15

21. Henry W. Little, 56   Day laborer
     Sarah Little, 49
     Mary L. Little, 14
     Almira J. Little, 12
     Wilber F. Little, 8

22. Wm. W. Varney, 25   River Driver $1,700/$1,100
     Rebecca C. Varney, 25
     Lunette Varney, 2
     Leola Varney, 6/12

23. Charles Whitham, 55   Farmer $800/$100
     Jane T. Whitham, 56
     Charles E. Whitham, 33   Farm laborer
     William P. Mitchell, 8

24. Benj. E. Peters, 40   Shipmaster $1,500/$2,800
     Mary Jane Peters, 30
     George H. Peters, 5
     Albert J. Peters, 3
     John A. Peters, 31   Farmer $0/$500
     Clara G. Peters, 21

25. John G. Rogers, 28   Farmer $3,300/$0
     Catherine S. Rogers, 32
     Charles S. Kelley, 8
     Rogers P. Kelley, 2
     Elizabeth S. Edgecomb, 40   Domestic
     Joel Edgecomb, 29   Farmer

26. Isaac Sylvester, 67   Farmer $1,200/$500
     Catherine Sylvester, 66
     Elizabeth Sylvester, 88   Mass.

27. Isaiah Crooker, 53   Cooper $1,000/$500
     Mary Crooker, 47
     Charles W. Crooker, 22   Carpenter
     Ellen A. Crooker, 20   Upholsterer
     Frances M. Crooker, 18
     Edwin J. Crooker, 16   Farmer
     Jacob V. Crooker, 12
     Marietta Crooker, 4

28. Albert Smith, 30   Blacksmith $1,000/$200
     Susan E. Smith, 28

Ada F. Smith, 8

29.	Timothy S. Crooker, 38 Augusta Crooker, 26 George W. P. Crooker, 11 Earnest C. Crooker, 9 Grace D. Crooker, 6 Albert S. Crooker, 4 Infant Crooker, 2/12	Cooper	$1,500/$500	
30.	Warren H. Crooker, 39 Rachel Crooker, 34 Dennison Crooker, 12 Sarah J. Crooker, 9 Elsie M. Crooker, 8 Frank W. Crooker, 5 Tudor F. Crooker, 10/12	Cooper	$1,500/$500	
31.	Joseph Varney, 36 Malinda J. Varney, 31 Marylinda Varney, 9 Joseph M. Varney, 7 Hattie K. Varney, 1	Lumber Mercht.	$3,000/$500	
32.	Wm. H. Chambers, 35 Harriet A. Chambers, 25 Mary I. Chambers, 3 Susan M. Chambers, 2	Millman		Nova Scotia Nova Scotia
33.	John Eaton, 39 Ann Eaton, 41 Daniel P. Eaton, 11	Millman		
34.	James B. Ward, 34 Lydia B. Ward, 30 Emma F. Ward, 9 Albert S. Ward, 5	Millman		
35.	John J. Dunning, 44 Elizabeth Dunning, 45 Mary E. Dunning, 15 Hannah Dunning, 13 Lawrence Driscoll, 45 John Driscoll, 17	Carpenter Millman	$600/$100	 Ireland Ireland
36.	Caleb Ridley, 34	Shingle Weaver		

Ruth A. Ridley, 29
Caroline E. Ridley, 9
Lucy E. Ridley, 7
Henry H. Ridley, 2

37. Samuel C. Morse, 36   Carpenter $1,500/$300
     Amanda Morse, 34
     Charles W. Morse, 12
     Clarisa A. Morse, 8
     George H. Morse, 5
     Margaret Eaton, 55

38   Mary Edgecomb, 68   Domestic

39. Saml W. Rogers, 58   Farmer $12,000/$400
     Lucinda Rogers, 51
     Alden Rogers, 25   Farmer
     Alpheus Rogers, 22   Machinist
     Emma L. Rogers, 18
     Sarah J. Owen, 43   Domestic

40. John Williams, 50   Mariner $800/$0   Madeira, Portugal
     Candace Williams, 46
     Narcissa W. Williams, 19   Domestic
     Joseph D. Williams, 16   Mariner
     Amon Williams, 12

41. James Ward, 86   Farmer $800/$250
     Ruth Ward, 76
     Zachariah Longly, 52   Farmer
     Narcissa S. Longly, 43

42. Wm. Rogers, 47   Farmer $800/$0
     Hannah P. Rogers, 40
     Thomas Rogers, 19   Farmer
     Elizabeth A. Rogers, 17
     Arabella A. Rogers, 15
     James W. Rogers, 13
     George W. Rogers, 10
     Jesse R. Rogers, 6
     Frederick Rogers, 6/12

43. Thomas Whitham, 44   Farmer $500/$100
     Abigail Whitham, 51
     Asa P. Whitham, 17
     James C. Whitham, 16

Abbie J. Whitham, 14
Bethiah Whitham, 13
Randolph Whitham, 11
William H. Whitham, 8

44. George R. Rouke, 58   Farmer $800/$50
     Fanny G. Rouke, 58
     Ruth F. Rouke, 27
     James W. Rouke, 25
     Mary K. Rouke, 17

45. Robert Ward, 50   Farmer $800/$150
     Margaret Ward, 30
     Samuel O. Ward, 25   Fisherman
     Charles Ward, 21
     Thomas Ward, 18
     George Ward, 15
     Candace Ward, 13
     Louisa Ward, 11
     Mary Ward, 9
     Lorena Stone, 7
     Frank Stone, 4
     Fanny Ward, 2

46. James F. Hill, 36   M   Farmer $800/$100
     Mary J. Hill, 35   M
     Aravesta S. Hill, 6   M
     Alfred A. Hill, 4   M
     Philena Hill, 2   M

47. John Harrison, 60   M   Farmer $2,000/$150   Maryland
     Levina Harrison, 56   M
     John Harrison, 24   M   Mariner
     Philena Harrison, 16   M
     F. Chandler Gardner, 16 M

48. Jacob Edgerley, 68   Farmer $2,800/$200
     Harriet Edgerley, 58
     Emerly Edgerley, 41   Domestic
     John M. Edgerley, 40   Farmer
     Loren B. Edgerley, 33   Shoemaker
     William Edgerley, 31   Farmer
     Almena Edgerley, 28   Factory Girl
     Charles Edgerley, 23   idiotic
     Richard Edgerley, 20   Clerk

49.	R. P. Manson, 52		Ship Master	$5,000/$6,000	
	Louisa Manson, 52				
	Veturia Manson, 22				
	Ella Manson, 14				
	Ada Manson, 9				
	Alfred Maxwell, 38		Farmer		
	John Wyman, 16		Farmer		
	Frank Lowell, 11				
	Adeline Carroll, 40	M			
50	Precilla Semore, 63	M		$200/$0	
	Lucretia Semore, 25	M	Domestic		
	Edith Semore, 21		Domestic		
51.	James Lemont, 54		Farmer	$2,000/$350	
	Lydia J. Lemont, 47				
	Abigail Lemont, 74				
	Mary Lemont, 26				idiotic
	Derius Parks, 14				
52.	George Crush, 48		Calker	$150/$400	
53.	Isaac White, 36		Joiner	$1,500/$150	
	Clara White, 36				
	Emma J. White, 5				
	Albertine White, 10				
54.	Geo. F. Manson, 50		Ship Master	$6,000/$14,000	
	Elizabeth Manson, 25				France
	George F. Manson, 1				France
	Jane Beck, 23				England
55.	Lydia Jewell, 55				

1870 United States Federal Census

This is the first census that asks for those who are Chinese or Indian (Native American) to be identified in the color column. An interest in the residents' heritage provided a column for a simple check mark to indicate "foreign-born" parentage. This is helpful to identify naturalized citizens and immigrant relatives. Another column entitled "Constitutional Relations" applied to U. S. male citizens twenty-one years and older. They were asked to check the column if their "right to vote was denied on other grounds than rebellion or other crime."

	Name/Age	Race	Profession	Property/ Personal Value	Place of Birth
1.	George Jewett, 69		Farmer	$4,000/$1,000	
	Sarah Jewett, 52		Keeps house		Mass.
	Hannah E. Jewett, 24		at home		
	Ford A. Jewett, 18				
	Nellie M. Jewett, 16		at home		
2.	Benjamin F. Emery, 71		Farmer	$2,100/$500	
	Lucinda W. Emery, 58		Keeping house		
	Ada F. Emery, 16		At home		
3.	John E. Hersey, 34		Ship Carpenter	$300	
	Hannah C. Hersey, 34		Keeping house		
	Frank A. Hersey, 14				
	Wm. H. Hersey, 9				
	Anthony C. Hersey, 2				
4.	Wm. H. Mitchell, 49		Rigger	$300	
	Sarah Mitchell, 51		Keeping house		England
	John H. Mitchell, 17		works in Ice house		
	Chas. O. Mitchell, 15				
	Ann E. Mitchell, 11				
5.	Harriet B. Wisewell, 55		Tailoress		
6.	Washington Gilbert, 54		Attorney at Law	$4,000/$2,000	
	Jane P. Gilbert, 52		Keeping house	$1,000	
	Margaret J. Gilbert, 19		at home		
	Clara D. Gilbert, 17				

7.	Thomas L. Reed, 40	Dentist	$800/$300	
	Delia A. Reed, 37	Keeping house		
	Jeremiah Reed, 75	retired Mariner		
	Nancy M. Reed, 77			
8.	Frank J. Hastings, 23	works on farm	$250	
	Helen M. Hastings, 23	Keeping house		
	Anne Hastings, 3			
	Henry Northby, 18	Works on Farm		
9.	Isaac Rogers, 35	Saw mill man	$2,000/$3,000	
	Sarah A. Rogers, 28	Keeping house		
	Emery B. Cushing, 33	Dentist	$300	
	Dorianna A. Cushing, 31			
10.	Chas. T. Lord, 36	Tanner	$1,500/$300	
	Ellen P. Lord, 30	Keeping house	$1,000	
	Mabel E. Lord, 9			
	Anne R. Lord, 5			
	Clara L. Lord, 2			
	Fred H. Lord, 1/12			
	Lottie M. Emery, 19	domestic		
11.	Henry W. Lemont, 24	Calker	$500	
	Sarah E. Lemont, 22	Keeping house		
	David W. Lemont, 6/12			
12.	Oliver E. Silsby, 27	Farmer	$500	New York
	E. Amanda Silsby, 31	Keeping house		
	Minnie Silsby, 12			
	Charles A. Silsby, 10			
13.	James Lemont, 65	Farmer	$3,000/$1,200	
	Lydia J. Lemont, 57	Keeping house	$300	
	Octavia J. Mitchell, 32	domestic		
	Edwin Austin, 16	works on Farm		
14.	Joseph Varney, 46	Prop Stm Lumb Mill	$10,000/$8,000	
	Julie A. Varney, 31	Keeping house		
	Mary L. Varney, 19	At home		
	Joseph M. Varney, 18			
	Harriet K. Varney, 12			
	Carrie H. Varney, 5			
	Nellie M. Varney, 3			
	Clara A. Varney, 1			

15.	Frances Young, 40	Keep Board. house	/ $500	Nova Scotia
	Arthur S. Young, 14			
	Charles Furbush, 20	Millman		
	Charles Douglass, 24	Millman		
	Fuller Sprague, 18	Millman		
	Enoch Coburn, 33	Millman		
	A. Jackson Travers, 20	Millman		
	Courtney Varney, 40	Millman		
	George Byran, 25	Millman		
	Albert Wright, 18	Millman		
	Wm. H. Tobey, 22	Millman		
	Eugene Morin, 19	Millman		Canada
	Louis Gamache, 23	Millman		Canada
16.	Wm. H. Chambers, 47	Millman		Nova Scotia
	Everline R. Chambers, 34	Keeping house		
	Harriet M. Chambers, 5			
	Wm. H. Chambers, 3			
	Jeannie Chambers, 10/12			
17.	James P. Witham, 26	Millman		
	Emma E. Witham, 18	Keeping house		
18.	Ruel J. Jewett, 34	Millman		
	Mary Frances Jewett, 24	Keeping house		
	Anne Jewett, 5			
	Reuel Jewett, 2			
19.	James Varney, 52	Mill man		
	Harriet B. Varney, 30	Keeping house		
	Elsinora Varney, 3			
	Kingsbury M. Varney, 1			
20.	Andrew J. Stilkey, 39	Millman		
	Clara Stilkey, 22	Keeping house		
	Ella Stilkey, 4			
	Chas. O. Temple, 33	Millman		Mass.
	Abbie Temple, 24	Keeping house		
21.	Paul Chadbourn, 21	Millman		Canada
	Mary Chadbourn, 21	Keeping house		Canada
	Joseph W. Chadbourn, 4/12			
22.	Samuel W. Rogers, 68	Farmer	$6,000/$3,000	
	Alden O. Rogers, 35	Farmer	/$1,000	

	Sarah E. Rogers, 28	Keeping house	
	Wiley F. Rogers, 3		
	Francis J. Merryman, 31	Master Mariner	/$2,000
	Emma L. Merryman, 29		
	Sarah J. Newall, 56	domestic	
	Marie A. Grouse, 53	domestic	
23.	Wm. W. Varney, 35	works Log driving	$700/$300
	Rebecca C. Varney, 35	Keeping house	
	Leola Varney, 10		
	Margaret L. Varney, 8		
	Howard E. Varney, 6		
	Lizzie M. Varney, 3		
24.	Samuel C. Morse, 48	Ship Carpenter	$800/$300
	Amanda J. Morse, 45	Keeping house	
	Clara A. Morse, 17	Teacher in Pub. Schl.	
	Geo. H. Morse, 15		
	John H. Morse, 5		
	Margaret M. Eaton, 66		/$1500
25.	Warren H. Crooker, 50	Cooper & Farmer	$2,500/$1,000
	Rachel J. Crooker, 46	Keeping house	
	Dennison H. Crooker, 21	Cooper & Farmer	
	Sarah J. Crooker, 19	work in Upholst. shop	
	Elsie M. Crooker, 18	At home	
	Frank W. Crooker, 15		
	Polly Crooker, 89		Mass.
26.	Thomas J. Gray, 22	works in Saw Mill	
	Harriet A. Gray, 23	Keeping house	
27.	Mary Edgecomb, 78	Keeping house	
28.	Timothy S. Crooker, 48	Farmer & Cooper	$2,500/$1,000
	Augusta C. Crooker, 35	Keeping house	
	George W. Crooker, 21	works Log driving	
	Ernest C. Crooker, 18	Seaman	
	Grace G. Crooker, 16		
	Albert S. Crooker, 14		
	Jennie H. Crooker, 10		
	Lewis W. Crooker, 8		
	Joseph D. Crooker, 6		
	Otis M. Crooker, 4		
29.	Isaiah Crooker, 62	Farmer & Cooper	$2,000/$1,000

	Mary B. Crooker, 58	Keeping house	
30.	Isaac Sylvester, 77	Farmer	$1,300/$800
	Esther Percy, 33	Keeping house	
31.	John G. Rogers, 38	Farmer	$1,000/$1,000
	Catharine S. Rogers, 42	Keeping house	
	Owen E. Rogers, 1		
	Chas. S. Kelley, 18	works on Farm	/$500
32.	Elizabeth Edgecomb, 50	Keeping house	$1,000/$300
	Joel Edgecomb, 40	works on Farm	/$400
	Rogers P. Kelley, 12		/$500
33.	Benj. E. Peters, 50	M. Mariner	$2,000/$300
	Mary J. Peters, 40	Keeping house	
	George H. Peters, 16	At home	
	James C. Peters, 38	Calker	
34	Charles Whitham, 63	Log driver	$500/$300
	Jane T. Whitham, 64	Keeping house	
	Fred Mitchell, 14		
35	Asa P. Whittam, 27	Log driver	$600/
	Emma F. Whittam, 19	Keeping house	
36	Owen A. Timmins, 53	Farmer	$1,500/$500
	Lucy Timmins, 53	Keeping house	
37	John T. Haley, 35	Farmer	$1,200/$400
	Rebecca R. Haley, 36	Keeping house	
	Josephine A. Haley, 14		
	Milton R. Haley, 9		
	Mary F. Haley, 76		
38	Rebecca Crawford, 62	Keeping house	$2,000/$500
	F. Adelia Crawford, 25	At home	
	Susan T. Fostis, 51		
	James A. Varney, 13		
39	William Hodgkins, 49	Log driver	$2,000/$1,000
	Frances M. Hodgkins, 49	Keeping house	
	Owen A. Hodgkins, 19	Log driver	
	Clara A. Hodgkins, 17		
	Edwin T. Hodgkins, 14		
	Wilmot H. Hodgkins, 11		

Fannie Crawford, 80

40	James Patridge, 51	Log driver	$500/
	Charles E. Patridge, 25	Log driver	
	Frank Patridge, 18	Log driver	
	Ann M. Walch, 27	Keeping house	
	Willard Patridge, 7		
	Charles Walch, 5		
	Ednor E. Walch, 6/12		
41	Chas. G. Wright, 46	Farmer	$4,500/$500
	Martha J. Wright, 43	Keeping house	
	Chas. L. Wright, 21	works on Farm	
	George F. Wright, 14		
	Ann Mary Wright, 11		
	Jane A. Wright, 9		
	Lizzie F. Wright, 6		
	Wm. H. Wright, 4		
	Carrie E. Wright, 3/12		
	Sarah B. Carlton, 58		
	Alice Carlton, 13		
42	John H. Farnham, 37	Ship Carpenter	
	Martha A. Farnham, 38	Keeping house	$300/
	Fred E. Farnham, 14		
	Lillian M. Farnham, 5		
	John F. Roberts, 59	Farmer	$600/
	Abbie E. Roberts, 33	Keeping house	
43	Samuel Edgecomb, 71	Farmer	$2,000/$1,000
	Elizabeth S. Edgecomb, 73		
	Silas W. Edgecomb, 41	works on Farm	$200/
	Lydia A. Edgecomb, 33	At home	
	Isabella J. Edgecomb, 30	At home	
	Mary E. S. Paine, 38		$1,500/$1,000
	Ella M. Paine, 8		
44	Lydia C. Rogers, 61	Keeping house	$3,000/$4,000
	John H. Rogers, 25	Saw Mill broker	$1,000/$1,000
	Abbie L. Rogers, 20	Teacher Pub. schl.	/$1,000
	Ada Rogers, 17	Invalid	
	Edward Bacheller, 17	Works on Farm	
45	Chas. N. Rogers, 40	Saw mill owner	$3,000/$2,000
	Emily R. Rogers, 39	Keeping house	
	Alice E. Rogers, 7		

Warren P. Rogers, 1

46	Sam'l F. Purington, 51		Farmer	$900/$250	
	Susan Purington, 49		Keeping house		
	Henry Marsh, 11				Louisiana

47	William Edgerley, 41		Farmer	$3,500/$500	
	Clara Edgerley, 31		Keeping house		
	Ada Edgerley, 1				
	Harriet Edgerley, 68				

48	Geo. K. Ingalls, 30		Farmer	$4,500/$3,000	
	Mary E. Ingalls, 26		Keeping house		Ohio
	Mary A. V. Ingalls, 5				
	Mavil A. D. Ingalls, 3				Virginia
	Geo. J. H. Ingalls, 8/12				Virginia
	Warner Bailey, 13	B	domestic		Virginia

| 49 | George Crush, 57 | | Calker | $300/ | England |
| | Isabella McDonald, 42 | | Keeping house | | |

| 50 | Ephraim Freeman, 69 | B | Laborer | | |
| | Priscilla Freeman, 74 | B | Keeping house | $500/ | |

51	Daniel H. Wakefield, 24		Saw mill man		
	Mariam T. Wakefield, 23		Keeping house		
	George Henry Wakefield, 1				

52	Thomas T. Whittam, 54		Farmer	$1,000/$300	
	Abagail K. Whittam, 61		Keeping house		
	Bertha Whittam, 23		At home		
	Randolph Whittam, 22		Log driver		
	William Whittam, 19		Log driver		
	Nellie Whittam, 3				

53	Samuel O. Ward, 35		Laborer	$500/	
	Clara G. Ward, 31		Keeping house		
	Robert S. Ward, 6				
	Wm. Payne Ward, 4				
	George T. Ward, 2				

54	William Rogers, 57		Farmer	$1,200/$500	
	Hannah P. Rogers, 50		Keeping house		
	Arabella R. Rogers, 24		At home		
	Geo. W. Rogers, 20		works on Farm		
	Jessie R. Rogers, 18		works on Farm		

Fred Rogers, 10

55   Robert Ward, 60   Farmer $1,000/$1,500
Margaret Ward, 39   Keeping house
Fannie R. Ward, 13
Charles Ward, 8
Anne Ward, 2
Infant not named Ward, 3/12
Frank Stone, 14

56   George R. Rooke, 68   Farmer $1,000/$1,000
Fannie G. Rooke, 68   Keeping house
James W. Rooke, 35   works on Farm   /$500

57   James F. Hill, 47   B   Farmer & Fisherman $800/
Mary Jane Hill, 45   B   Keeping house
Aravesta S. Hill, 17   B
Alfred A. Hill, 14   B
Mary P. Hill, 12   B
Llewellyn B. Hill, 8   B
Charlotte B. Hill, 6   B
Roscoe L. Hill, 3   B
Roswell H. Hill, 3   B
Lydia Hill, 91   B

58   John Harrison, 70   B   Farmer $1,500/$500   Maryland
Lavina Harrison, 66   B   Keeping house
Wm. Swain, 26   B   Seaman
Lena Swain, 25   B
Orrie St. C. Swain, 11/12 B
Waldron Marr, 65   works on Farm

1880 UNITED STATES FEDERAL CENSUS

The 1880 census is the first to specify the relationship between household members, which is a great help to genealogists. It is also the first census to specify the street location of each household, although there are not yet street numbers for each house in the Bath census.

The 1880 census for this part of Bath begins to show the impact of immigration and industrialization on the community. The Abbott family kept a boardinghouse on the "Country road from Whisgeag Mills to Varney's Mill"; sixteen men lived there and worked at the sawmill. Thirteen were from Canada, and it is clear that the enumerator in 1880 did not know French or ask the boarders to spell their names, as the last names listed seem to be spelled phonetically. (See Tibbo, for example, which is likely to have been Thibeault.) Beginning in 1870, Franco-Americans from Canada were the backbone of the workforce in the mills and factories of New England.

Name/Age	Race	Relation	Occupation	Place of Birth
Whisgeag Street [Whiskeag Road today]				
1. Geo. W. Brooks, 42		Head	Farmer	
Abbie J. Brooks, 44		Wife	Keeping House	
Nellie G. Brooks, 18		Daughter	At School	
Mabel V. Brooks, 18		Daughter	At School	
Florence G. Brooks, 6		Daughter		
2. Chas. T. Lord, 45		Head	Tanner	
Ellen P. Lord, 39		Wife	Keeping House	
Mabel E. Lord, 18		Daughter	At Home	
Annie R. Lord, 15		Daughter	At School	
Clara L. Lord, 12		Daughter	At School	
Fred H. Lord, 10		Son	At School	
Arthur M. Lord, 6		Son		
Nellie Lord, 5		Daughter		
Lydia Lord, 2		Daughter		
3. Isaac Rogers, 45		Head	Manuf. of Lumber	
Sarah A. Rogers, 38		Wife	Keeping House	

4.	Saml. T. Edgecomb, 46	Head	Night Watchman	
	Jane Edgecomb, 37	Wife	Keeping House	
	Eda F. Edgecomb, 6	Daughter		Massachusetts

Country Road from Whisgeag Mills to Varney's Mill

5.	Chas. N. Rogers, 50	Head	Farmer	
	Emily R. Rogers, 49	Wife	Keeping House	
	Alice E. Rogers, 17	Daughter	At School	
	Warren P. Rogers, 11	Son	At School	
6.	Lydia Rogers, 70	Head		
	Ada Rogers, 26	Daughter	At School	
	Charles H. Rogers, 20	G'd Son	Farm Laborer	
	Abbie Burns, 30	Daughter		
	Fred E. Burns, 4	G'd Son		
	Harry Burns, 1	G'd Son		
	Caroline Rogers, 36	Daughter		
7.	Saml. F. Purington, 60	Head	Farmer	
	Susan Purington, 61	Wife	Keeping House	
8.	Geo. K. Ingalls, 39	Head	Farmer	
	Mary E. Ingalls, 37	Wife	Keeping House	Ohio
	Mary A. V. Ingalls, 14	Daughter	At School	
	Mabel A. D. Ingalls, 12	Daughter	At School	Virginia
	Geo. J. H. Ingalls, 9	Son		Virginia
	Maud M. H. Ingalls, 8	Daughter		
	Eugene E. W. Ingalls, 1	Son		
9.	Saml. Edgecombe, 81	Head	Farmer	
	Lydia Edgecombe, 44	Daughter	Keeping House	
	Mary Payne, 48	Daughter	At Home	
	Ella M. Payne, 18	Grand-daughter	At School	
	Christopher Carter, 42	Son in Law	Master Mariner	
	Margaret E. Carter, 42	Daughter (wife / Christopher)	At Home	
	Abbie F. Carter, 12	Grand-daughter		
	Jessie C. Carter, 8	Grand-daughter		England
	Isabella E. Carter, 6	Grand-daughter		
10.	Martha Farnham, 48	Head	Keeping House	
	Fred E. Farnham, 24	Son	House Joiner	
	Lillian N. Farnham, 15	Daughter	At School	
	John F. Roberts, 68	Head	Farm Labour	
	Abbie Roberts, 43	Daughter	Keeping House	

11. Charles G. Wright, 54   Head   Farmer
     Martha Wright, 52   Wife   Keeping House
     Charles L. Wright, 31   Son   River Driver
     James R. Wright, 29   Son   At Home
     Herbert Wright, 14   Son   At School
     Carrie Wright, 10   Daughter   At School
     Mattie Wright, 5   Granddaughter
     Lulu Wright, 4   Granddaughter

12. Geo. F. Wright, 24   Head   Farmer
     Lulu A. Wright, 22   Wife   Keeping House
     Louisa Wright, 4   Daughter

13. William W. Varney, 45   Head   Raftsman
     Rebecca Varney, 45   Wife   Keeping House
     Margie L. Varney, 18   Daughter   At Home
     Howard E. Varney, 15   Son   At School
     Lizzie M. Varney, 13   Daughter   At School

14. Edwin Hodgkins, 24   Head   Raftsman
     Jennie Hodgkins, 19   Wife   Keeping House

15. Edwin Brown, 21   Head   Cooper
     Leola Brown, 20   Wife   Keeping House

16. James R. Wright, 26   Head   River Driver
     Julia Wright, 24   Wife   Keeping House
     Zadia Wright, 4   Daughter
     Arthur Wright, 2   Son

17. George Ward, 36   Head   Laborer
     Abbie Ward, 34   Wife
     Luella M. Ward, 2   Daughter
     Frank E. Ward, 6/12   Son

18. Asa P. Whitam, 37   Head   River Driver
     Emma F. Whitam, 29   Wife   Keeping House
     Winfield S. Whitam, 9   Son
     Fred F. Whitam, 2   Son

19. Mary Peters, 50   Head   Keeping House
     Geo. H. Peters, 25   Son   Machinist
     James C. Peters, 48   Brother-in-law Farmer

20. Charles H. Abbott, 40   Head   works in steam saw mill
     Melvena W. Abbott, 42   Wife   Keeps Boarding House

	Name, Age	Relation	Occupation	Birthplace
	John Donnell, 45	Boarder	works in Saw Mill	Canada
	Owen Driscoll, 50	Boarder	Watchman	Ireland
	M. Nemore, 22	Boarder	Works in Saw Mill	Canada
	M. Normand, 28	Boarder	Works in Saw Mill	Canada
	N. Nemure, 30	Boarder	Works in Saw Mill	Canada
	M. Boswell, 32	Boarder	Works in Saw Mill	Canada
	A. Nemure, 25	Boarder	Works in Saw Mill	Canada
	A. Tibbo, 50	Boarder	Works in Saw Mill	Canada
	A. Tibbo Jr., 21	Boarder	Works in Saw Mill	Canada
	A. Petroy, 40	Boarder	Works in Saw Mill	Canada
	L. Strout, 22	Boarder	Works in Saw Mill	
	C. Toronto Jr., 26	Boarder	Works in Saw Mill	Canada
	C. Toronto, 46	Boarder	Works in Saw Mill	Canada
	James Varney, 23	Boarder	Works in Saw Mill	
	David Le Forta, 30	Boarder	Works in Saw Mill	Canada
	F. Boswell, 28	Boarder	Works in Saw Mill	Canada
21.	Joseph Varney, 56	Head	Manufacture of Lumber	
	Julia A. Varney, 41	Wife	Keeping House	
	Carrie H. Varney, 15	Daughter	At School	
	Nellie M. Varney, 13	Daughter	At School	
	Clara Varney, 11	Daughter	At School	
	Alice Varney, 1	Daughter		
22.	Saml. C. Morse, 58	Head	Ship Carpenter	
	Amanda J. Morse, 55	Wife	Keeping House	
	John H. Morse, 16	Son	At School	
	Joel Edgecombe, 49	Boarder	Farm Labour	
23.	Chas. W. Crooker, 42	Head	Cooper	
	Addie Crooker, 32	Wife	Keeping House	
	William Crooker, 13	Son	At School	
	George Crooker, 11	Son	At School	
24.	Saml. W. Rogers, 78	Head	Farmer	
	Huldah Rogers, 59	Wife	Keeping House	
	Eveline R. Maynes, 70	Sister		
	William S. Tabor, 19	Boarder	Farm Laborer	New Brunswick
25.	James Varney, 60	Head	works in Saw Mill	
	Hattie Varney, 39	Wife	Keeping House	
	Elsie Varney, 12	Daughter	At School	
	Kingsbury M. Varney, 11	Son	At School	
	John H. Varney, 3	Son		
	Wylie W. Varney, 1	Son		

26.	Warren Crooker, 60	Head	Farmer	
	Rachel J. Crooker, 55	Wife	Keeping House	
	Charles Crooker, 9	relationship not noted		
	Margaret Eaton, 75	Head	Keeping House	
27.	Frank W. Crooker, 24	Head	Farm Laborer	
	Josie Crooker, 21	Wife	Keeping House	
	Warren G. Crooker, 4/12	Son		
	Kate Joy, 20	Sister-in-law	Works in Laundry	
28.	Isiah Crooker, 72	Head	Cooper	
	Mary D. Crooker, 68	Wife	Keeping House	
	Joseph Prescott, 16	Boarder	Farm Laborer	
29.	Catherine Voss, 51	Head	carries on a Farm	Holstein, Germany
	William H. Whittam, 28	Son-in-law	Works in Saw Mill	
	Mary C. F. Whittam, 23	Daughter	At home	
	Harry W. Whittam, 2/12	Grandson		
	Fred C. Voss, 15	Son	At School	
30.	Hiram Cornish, 36	Head	Farmer & Cooper	
	Ellen Cornish, 40	Wife	Keeping House	
	Edwin I. Cornish, 13	Son	At School	
	Mary A. Cornish, 6	Daughter		
	Frank H. Cornish, 2	Son		
31.	John G. Rogers, 48	Head	Farmer	
	Catherine S. Rogers, 52	Wife	Keeping House	
	Owen E. Rogers, 11	Son	At School	
	John G. Bodwell, 17	Servant	Farm Labour	
32.	Saml. Ward, 45	Head	Labour	
	Clara Ward, 41	Wife	Keeping house	
	Robert S. Ward, 16	Son	At School	
	William P. Ward, 14	Son	At School	
	Geo. T. Ward, 12	Son	At School	
	Edith Ward, 9	Daughter		
	Ernest A. Ward, 7	Son		
	Bessie Ward, 9/12	Daughter		

Cross Road to Bay Shore

33.	Jesse Rogers, 24	Head	Farmer
	Fred Rogers, 20	Brother	Farmer
34.	James Rook, 45	Head	Farmer
	George Rook, 77	Father	At Home

	Fanny Rook, 77		Mother (Wife of George Rook)	
			Keeping House	
35.	Robert Ward, 70		Head	Farmer
	Charles Ward, 17		Son	Labour
	Annie Ward, 11		Daughter	At School
	Grace Ward, 10		Daughter	At School
36.	James F. Hill, 56	Mu	Head	Farmer
	Mary Jane Hill, 55	Mu	Wife	Keeping House
	Alfred A. Hill, 24	Mu	Son	Labour
	Llewellen F. Hill, 18	Mu	Son	Labour
	Charlotte B. Hill, 16	Mu	Daughter	At School
	Roscoe L. Hill, 13	Mu	Son	At School
	Roswell H. Hill, 13	Mu	Son	At School

Road from Ireland School House to Brunswick Road

37.	Albert S. Ward, 25	Head	Laborer	
	Annie M. Ward, 21	Wife	Keeping House	
38.	Thos. T. Whittam, 64	Head	Farmer	
	Abigail Whittam, 71	Wife	Keeping House	
	Nellie Whittam, 13	Granddaughter	At School	
39.	William T. Dunton, 39	Head	Farmer	
	Mary A. Dunton, 32	Wife	Keeping House	
	Hattie A. Dunton, 10	Daughter	At School	
	Wilmington Dunton, 9	Son		
	Edward Kennedy, 24	Boarder	Farm Laborer	Massachusetts
40.	Alden Rogers, 42	Head	Farmer	
	Sarah E. Rogers, 38	Wife	Keeping House	
	Wylie F. Rogers, 13	Son	At School	
41.	Lucretia Garrison, 50	B	Head	Keeping House
42.	George Crush, 67	Head	Labour	England
43.	William Edgerly, 50	Head	Farmer	
	Zelda Edgerly, 30	Wife	Keeping House	
	Harriet Edgerly, 11	Daughter	At School	
	Jason Edgerly, 7	Son		
	Grace Edgerly, 3	Daughter		
44.	Frederick Wright, 27	Head	Farmer	
	Ella F. Wright, 27	Wife	Keeping House	

| 45. | Fred A. Willis, 34 | Head | Farmer |
| | Louisa M. Willis, 29 | Wife | Keeping House |

Brunswick Road

46.	Saml. W. Foote, 62	Head	Farmer
	Lucy H. Foote, 58	Wife	Keeping House
	Julia A. Foote, 33	Daughter	Dressmaker
	Virginia M. Foote, 31	Daughter	works in ____ factory
	Charles R. Foote, 29	Son	Mariner
	Saml. W. Foote Jr., 27	Son	Mariner
	John A. Foote, 22	Son	Mariner
	Fred E. Foote, 17	Son	Farm laborer

47.	Henry B. Rowell, 48	Head	Market Gardener
	Emily Rowell, 47	Wife	Keeping House
	Clara M. Rowell, 22	Daughter	Tailoress
	Emma J. Rowell, 20	Daughter	Tailoress
	Mary E. Rowell, 18	Daughter	At Home
	George H. Rowell, 15	Son	At Home
	Lucy K. Rowell, 13	Daughter	At School
	Florence E. Rowell, 7	Daughter	
	Rose E. Rowell, 5	Daughter	

High Street

48.	Washington Gilbert, 64	Head	Probate Judge	
	Jane P. Gilbert, 64	Wife	Keeping House	
	Margaret J. Gilbert, 27	Daughter	Music Teacher	
	Clara D. Gilbert, 26	Daughter	School Teacher	
	Mary Conley, 20	Servant	Domestic Servant	New Hampshire

1900 United States Federal Census

The 1900 census is, in many ways, a genealogical treasure trove. It is the first to devote three columns to citizenship: year of immigration, number of years in the United States, and naturalization status. This is useful in investigating ships' passenger lists. In addition, the 1900 census is the only one to ask for the month and year of each person's birth.

In the section of the census dedicated to home ownership information, the word *mortgage* appears for the first time. There is a column for the occupation, trade, or profession of each listed person ten years old or older, and a place where the number of months unemployed in the last year can be noted.

The transcript below includes, for the most part, only the basic information captured in previous censuses. Consider it an introduction to a wealth of additional information available in the full census for 1900.

Name, Age	Race	Relation	Profession/ Birth Place	Year immigrated
Brunswick Road				
1. Cyrus Aderton, 64		Head	Spar maker	
Harriet M. Aderton, 51		Wife		
Agnes J. Aderton, 35		Daughter		
Florence M. Rich, 20		Daughter		
Eugene E. Aderton, 17		Son	[illegible]	
Isabel C. Aderton, 14		Grand daughter	At school	
2. William H. Sewall, 58		Head		
Emily C. Sewall, 63		Sister		
Julia E. G. Stinson, 55		Housekeeper	Housekeeper	
3. Fred P. Rounds, 54		Head	Ship crpntr/Missouri	
Jenette T. Rounds, 46		Wife	Canada (Eng)	1863
Margaret B. Rounds, 19		Daughter	Seamstress/Mass.	
Harold F. Rounds, 17		Son		
4. Alec Johnson, 54		Head	Ship carp./Canada (Eng)	1884
Mrs. Alec Johnson, 43		Wife	Canada (Fr)	1884
Oscar R. Johnson, 15		Son	At school	
James O. Johnson, 9		Son	At school	

5.	Gilbert P. Powers, 63	Head	On railroad
	Augusta E. Powers, 52	Wife	
	Allen C. Powers, 31	Son	Flagman, R.R.
	Gilbert A. Powers, 28	Son	Conductor
	Annie E. Powers, 22	Daughter	
	Ammon K. Powers, 22	Son	Section hand
	Frank P. Powers, 17	Son	Grocery clerk

North Bath Road

6.	Emery M. Wing, 41	Head	Farmer	
	Mary A. Wing, 75	Mother		
	Julia M. Wing, 31	Sister		
	Earl E. Wing, 18	Servant	Farm hand	
	Albert Henderson, 18	Servant	Farm hand/Canada (Eng)	1892

| 7. | Isaac Rogers, 65 | Head | |
| | Sarah A. Rogers, 58 | Wife | |

8.	Fred G. Proctor, 33	Head	House joiner
	Lottie L. Proctor, 28	Wife	
	Bertha M. Proctor, 12	Daughter	At school

9.	Charles H. Rogers, 39	Head	House joiner
	Nellie G. Rogers, 38	Wife	
	Walter M. Rogers, 11	Son	At school
	Mildred F. Rogers, 10	Daughter	At school
	Edwin A. Rogers, 6	Son	At school
	Mable E. Rogers, 2	Daughter	
	Ada Rogers, 47	Aunt	
	Abbie J. Brooks, 64	Boarder	

10.	Elmer Edgcomb, 38	Head	Ship carpenter
	Nellie M. Edgcomb, 33	Wife	
	Carrie E. Edgcomb, 14	Daughter	At school
	Lena M. Edgcomb, 11	Daughter	At school

11.	Frederick Wright, 47	Head		
	Lorraine E. Wright, 46	Wife		
	Mary A. Wright, 18	Daughter		
	Arthur P. Wright, 14	Son	At school	
	Harrison N. Wright, 11	Son		
	Amial Arsenault, 24	Farm Hand	Farm laborer/Canada (Fr)	1899

| 12. | George K. Ingalls, 59 | Head | Farmer |
| | Mary E. Ingalls, 57 | Wife | Ohio |

	Agnes K. Ingalls, 34	Daughter	Straw-work trimming
	Mable A. D. Ingalls, 32	Daughter	Straw-work trimming/Virginia
	Eugene E. W. Ingalls, 21	Son	Agent for brush & mfs
	Josephine E. E. Ingalls, 18	Daughter	At school
13.	Mary E. Paine, 67	Head	
	Lydia A. Edgecomb, 64	Sister	
14.	Martha Farnham, 68	Head	
15.	Abbie Roberts, 63	Head	
16.	Chas. G. Wright, 78	Head	Farmer
17.	Chas. L. Wright, 51	Head	Day laborer
	Ellen S. Wright, 47	Wife	
	Effie C. Wright, 14	Daughter	At school
18.	George Wright, 44	Head	Farmer
	Amanda L. Wright, 42	Wife	
	Eva J. Wright, 18	Daughter	
	Lucy E. Wright, 16	Daughter	At school
	Mason E. Wright, 13	Son	At school
	Oscar F. Wright, 10	Son	At school
	Zetta M. Wright, 9	Daughter	At school
	Ferne D. Wright, 4	Daughter	
19.	Chas. S. Winslow, 64	Head	Farmer
	Flora Winslow, 40	Wife	Massachusetts
	Warren Winslow, 27	Son	Mill hand
20.	George R. Ward, 56	Head	Farmer
	Abbie J. Ward, 53	Wife	
	Luella M. Ward, 22	Daughter	
	Frank E. Ward, 20	Son	Book keeper
	Sydna H. Ward, 17	Son	Farm hand
21.	Edwin A. Russell, 25	Head	House carpenter
	Mary A. Russell, 27	Wife	Rhode Island
	Edna A. Russell, 1	Daughter	
22.	James R. Wright, 49	Head	Ship carpenter
	Lillie M. Wright, 17	Daughter	
	Rosa B. Wright, 14	Daughter	At school
	Florence R. Wright, 13	Daughter	At school
	Walter S. Wright, 10	Son	At school

	Albion P. Wright, 8	Son	At school
	Ralph E. Wright, 7	Son	At school
	Ethel G. Wright, 5	Daughter	At school
	Helen A. Wright, 3	Daughter	
23.	Fred M. Mitchell, 47	Head	
	Carrie E. Mitchell, 30	Wife	
	Laura A. Mitchell, 10	Daughter	At school
	Ruth B. Mitchell, 5	Daughter	
24.	Saml. Morse, 78	Head	
	John H. Morse, 35	Son	Farmer
	Clara L. Morse, 33	Daughter-in-law	
	Doris Morse, 1/12	Granddaughter	
	Sam A. Morse, 16	Grandson	At school/California
25.	Herbert C. Wright, 33	Head	Farmer
	Addie M. Wright, 36	Wife	
	Ralph E. Wright, 6	Son	At school
26.	Will H. Crooker, 32	Head	Laborer sawmill
	Lena M. Crooker, 29	Wife	
	Lester H. Crooker, 5	Son	
	Carl B. Crooker, 4	Son	
	Thomasine L. Crooker, 2	Daughter	
27.	Warren H. Crooker, 80	Head	Farmer
	Emma W. Crooker, 72	Wife	
	Aubery Smith, 48	Farm Hand	Farm hand
28.	Frank Amis, 49	Head	Lumber millman
	Ella M. Amis, 49	Wife	
29.	Chas. W. Crooker, 62	Head	Farmer
	Adrianna Crooker, 52	Wife	
	George E. Crooker, 31	Son	Laborer saw mill
	Frederick W. Lindsay, 26	Boarder	Laborer saw mill
30.	Robert R. Donnell, 26	Head	Farmer
	Grace L. Donnell, 23	Wife	
	Guy E. Donnell, 3	Son	
	Harry W. Donnell, 1	Son	
	Olive M. Donnell, 4/12	Daughter	
31.	Alden P. Rogers, 65	Head	Farmer
	Sarah E. Rogers, 58	Wife	

	George A. Rogers, 19		Son	Farm hand
32.	Eddie G. Ball, 58 [f]	B	Head	
	Sam'l. H. Morrison, 27	B	Boarder	Day laborer
33.	James Deering, 49	B	Head	Day laborer/Canada (Eng)
	Eleanor C. Deering, 40	B	Wife	
	Eva M. Deering, 22	B	Daughter	Massachusetts
34.	Fred A. Willis, 53		Head	Farmer
	Louise M. Willis, 51		Wife	
	Harry G. Barrett, 14		Ward	At school
35.	Sam'l. O. Ward, 65		Head	Farmer
	Clara G. Ward, 61		Wife	
	Edith M. Ward, 29		Daughter	
	Bessie G. Ward, 20		Daughter	
36.	James B. Ward, 34		Head	Boiler maker
	Lydia B. Ward, 70		Wife	
37.	James C. Peters, 67		Head	
	Mary J. Peters, 70		s-in-law	
38.	Owen E. Rogers, 31		Head	Farmer
	Lillian M. Rogers, 35		Wife	
	Catherine S. Rogers, 72		Mother	
	Sarah A. Edgecomb, 77		Boarder	Washington, DC
	Elery Whittemore, 20		Farm Hand	Farm hand
39.	Earnest A. Ward, 27		Head	Farm hand
	Ellen M. Ward, 24		Wife	
	Lucy G. Ward, 7/12		Daughter	
40.	Elmer Rich, 38		Head	Farmer
	Rose E. Rich, 35		Wife	
	Fred P. Rich, 8		Son	At school
	David E. Rich, 5		Son	At school
	Ruben E. Rich, 1		Son	
	John L. Parker, 24		Farm Hand	Farm hand/Canada (Eng) 1896

Brunswick Road

41.	Sarah E. Lemont, 52	Head	
	D. Wylie Lemont, 30	Son	machinist
	Marcia M. Lemont, 29	Daughter-in-law	

42.	Sam'l. Foote, 82	Head	Farmer
	Lucy H. Foote, 78	Wife	
	Julia A. Foote, 53	Daughter	
	Jennie M. Foote, 50	Daughter	
	John A. Foote, 42	Son	Ship joiner
	Eleanor F. Foote, 11	Granddaughter	At school
	Maya P. Foote, 9	Granddaughter	At school

North Bath Road
[Includes Varney Mill Road, although this is not noted on the census]

43.	Chas. T. Lord, 65	Head	Farmer
	Ellen T. Lord, 50	Wife	
	Arthur M. Lord, 26	Son	Electrician
	Lydia A. Lord, 22	Daughter	

44.	Hiram C. Cornish, 56	Head	Farmer
	Ellen A. Cornish, 60	Wife	
	Frank H. Cornish, 22	Son	Farm hand

45.	Wm. H. Whittam, 48	Head	Farmer
	Mary T. Whittam, 43	Wife	
	Harry W. Whittam, 20	Son	laborer sawmill
	Winnifred Whittam, 7	Daughter	At school
	Clarence T. Whittam, 11	Son	At school
	Lillian A. Whittam, 5	Daughter	At school
	Iola R. Whittam, 1	Daughter	
	Catherine C. Voss, 71	Mother-in-law	Germany	1856
	Proctor A. Hagan, 40	Boarder	Sea captain

46.	James Rook, 66	Head	Farmer
	George W. Rook, 13	Son	Farm hand
	Fannie G. Rook, 10	Daughter	
	Margaret L. Rook, 8	Daughter	At school
	Affie J. Rook, 5	Daughter	

47.	Randolf F. Whittam, 51	Head	Day laborer
	Emily B. Whittam, 40	Wife	England
	Alton S. Whittam, 20	Son	Day laborer
	Ida M. Whittam, 14	Daughter	
	Doris A. Whittam, 2	Daughter	

Brunswick Road

48.	Henry Rowell, 69	Head	Farmer
	Emily Rowell, 68	Wife	
	Clara M. Foote, 42	Daughter	Servant
	Harry Foote, 17	Grandson	Draftsman (apprentice)

Chas. H. Foote, 15	Grandson		
Cora Foote, 14	Granddaughter	At school	
Eddie Foote, 10	Granddaughter	At school	

49.	Mary A. Dunton, 53	Head	Farmer	
	Wellington F. Dunton, 29	Son	Farm hand	
	Joseph Arsenault, 22	Servant	Farm hand/Canada (Fr)	1899
	Alfred Arsenault, 22	Servant	Farm hand/Canada (Fr)	1900

1910 United States Federal Census

Prior to 1910, the census asked for the street or road of residence. In this census, the urban word *avenue* is added. For those looking for genealogical information, the 1910 census includes the number of years of the present marriage, and for women, the number of children born and the number still living. Residents are asked to identify if they are a survivor of the Union or Confederate Army or Navy. Other columns asked whether a person was blind (both eyes), deaf, or dumb.

Unfortunately, the microfilm of the 1910 census for this area is of poor quality; the transcription below occasionally relies on comparing information from this census to the names and spellings in other censuses. Please consider this data accordingly.

Brunswick Road R.F.D. 1

1.	Emily Rowell, 78	Head	Farmer	
	Rose E. Rowell, 34	Daughter	Servant in private home	
2.	John A. Foote, 52	Head	House Joiner	
	Myra P. Foote, 19	Daughter	At school	
	Augusta J. Foote, 65	Sister	Milliner	
	Virginia M. Foote, 62	Sister	Milliner	
	Ida F. Dart, 62	Servant	Servant	Mass.
3.	Robert W. Donnell, 36	Head	Grocer	
	Grace L. Donnell, 34	Wife		
	Guy E. Donnell, 12	Son	At School	
	Henry W. Donnell, 11	Son	"	
	Olive M. Donnell, 10	Daughter	"	
	Alonzo S. Donnell, 6	Son	"	
	Irwin F. Donnell, 5	Son		

North Bath R.F.D. 1

4.	Frederick Wright, 57	Head	Farmer	
	Loraine E. Wright, 56	Wife		
	Harry N. Wright, 22	Son	Farmer	
	Elizabeth Wright, 19	Daughter-in-law		
	Ralph Mank, 16	Boarder	Farm laborer	
5.	Pierce A. Wright, 24	Head	Farmer	
	Lulu E. Wright, 21	Wife		
	Dorothy L. Wright, 2	Daughter		Minnesota

	Name, Age		Relationship	Occupation	Birthplace
	Evelyn M. Wright, 5/12		Daughter		Minnesota
6.	Fred A. Willis, 58		Head	Farmer	
	Thomas P. Richardson, 36		Boarder	Farm laborer	
	Myra L. Richardson, 35		Wife		
7.	George W. Rooke, 23		Head	Farmer	
	Mary Haines, 26		Sister		
	Maggie L. Rooke, 18		Sister	Servant in private home	
	Affie J. Rooke, 15		Sister	Servant in private home	
8.	Samuel O. Ward, 70		Head	Farmer	
	Bessie G. Palmer, 30		Daughter		
9.	Elmer J. Rich, 48		Head	Farmer	
	Rosa E. Rich, 45		Wife		
	Fred P. Rich, 18		Son	Farm laborer	
	David E. Rich, 15		Son	At school	
	Reuben E. Rich, 12		Son	At school	
	Lydia M. Martin, 85		Grand mother		
10	Wellington F. Dunton, 38		Farmer		
	Hattie A. Dunton, 40		Sister		
	Charles Rietero, 18		Boarder	Farm laborer	
11.	Sara E. Rogers, 68		Head	Farmer	
	Wylie F. Rogers, 44		Son	Machinist, Bath Iron Works	
	Lilly M. Rogers, 37		Daughter- in-law		
	George A. Rogers, 28		Son	House joiner	
	Rose B. Rogers, 24		Daughter- in-law		
	Clarence A. Rogers, 11		Grandson		
12.	Louise H. Hill, 46	B	Head		
	Richard R. Garrison, 40	B	Boarder	Laborer, Odd Jobs	
13.	James A. Deering, 50	B	Head	Peddler	
	Eleanor C. Deering, 50	B	Wife		
	Eva M. Johnson, 31	B	Daughter		Mass.
	James L. Johnson, 1-6/12	B	Grandson		
14.	Sarah Rogers, 64		Head		
	Mary W. Judkins, 20		Boarder		Mass.
15.	Arthur M. Lord, 36		Head	Machinist, Hyde Windlass	Mass.
	Annie L. Lord, 25		Wife		
	Ellen L. Lord, 7		Daughter	At school	

	Marion E. Lord, 4	Daughter		
	Elsie M. Lord, 2	Daughter		
16.	Charles H. Rogers, 49	Head	House joiner	
	Nellie G. Rogers, 48	Wife		
	Walter M. Rogers, 21	Son	Lumber mill man	
	Mildred F. Rogers, 20	Daughter	At school	
	Edward A. Rogers, 16	Son	At school	
	Mabel E. Roger, 12	Daughter	At school	
17.	William Plummer, 61	Head	Farmer	
	Harry A. Plummer, 32	Son	Grocery salesman	
	Ferdinan Plummer, 89	Mother		
	Mary A. Hawthorne, 48	Servant	Farm laborer	Spain
	Ellmer M. Hawthorne, 9	Boarder	At school	
18.	John M. Loring, 41	Head	Farmer	
	Priscilla J. Loring, 41	Wife		Canada Eng
	Milton W. Loring, 14	Son	At school	
	Mary E. Loring, 11	Daughter	At school	
	John M. Loring, Jr., 3	Son		
19.	George K. Ingalls, 69	Head	Farmer	
	Mabel A. D. Ingalls, 42	Daughter		Virginia
	Eugene E. W. Ingalls, 31	Son	Boat builder	
20.	Lydia A. Edgecomb, 74	Head		
	Mary E. Paine, 77	Sister		
	Alton P. Wright, 18	Boarder	Machinist	
21.	Abbie S. Roberts, 72	Head		
22.	Arthur W. Brawn, 36	Head	Machinist	
	Winifred H. Brawn, 37	Wife		
	Fred S. Brawn, 14	Son	At school	
	Herbert A. Brawn, 12	Son	"	
	Mildred L. Brawn, 8	Daughter	"	
	Grace E. Brawn, 6	Daughter	"	
	Margaret Brawn, 2	Daughter		
	Arthur A. Brawn, 1	Son		
23.	George F. Wright, 54	Head	Farmer	
	Amanda L. Wright, 52	Wife		
	Oscar F. Wright, 19	Son	Farm laborer	
	Jennie D. Wright, 14	Daughter	At school	

24.	Ernest A. Wood, 48	Head	Riveter	England
	Elizabeth G. Wood, 46	Wife	X	England
	Ernest A. Wood, Jr., 17	Son	At school	
	Herbert Wood, 15	Son	At school	
	Elise Wood, 13	Daughter	At school	
	Lillian C. Wood, 9	Daughter	At school	
	Edna B. Wood, 6	Daughter	At school	
25.	George R. Ward, 66	Head	Farmer	
	Abbie J. Ward, 64	Wife		
	Frank E. Ward, 30	Son	Cemetery nurseryman	
	Sidney H. Ward, 27	Son	"	
26.	Charles B. Winslow, 74	Head	Farmer	
	Flora B. Winslow, 50	Wife		Mass.
27.	Charles W. Crooker, 38	Head	Barber	
	Margaret M. Crooker, 31	Wife		Can (Eng)
28.	James R. Wright, 58	Head	House Carpenter	
	Lilly M. Wright, 41	Daughter		
	Florence R. Wright, 23	Daughter		
	Walter S. Wright, 20	Son		
	Ralph E. Wright, 16	Son	At school	
	Ethel G. Wright, 15	Daughter	At school	
	Helena A. Wright, 13	Daughter	At school	
29.	Emil G. Lawson, 41	Head	Machinist	Sweden
	Selma A. Lawson, 36	Wife	"	Sweden
	Annie K. Lawson, 13	Daughter	At school	Mass.
	John T. Lawson, 10	Son	At school	Mass.
	Signe A. Lawson, 8	Daughter	At school	
	Elmar E. Lawson, 8/12	Son		
30.	Ernest A. Ward, 37	Head	Farmer	
	Ellen M. Ward, 33	Wife		
	Lucy G. Ward, 10	Daughter		
	Mildred D. Ward, 6	Daughter		
	Arthur J. Ward, 4	Son		
31.	Charles O Johnson, 48	Head	Blacksmith	Sweden
	Hulda M. Johnson, 47	Wife		Sweden
	Edith M. Johnson, 14	Daughter	At School	Mass.
	Rosa C. Johnson, 8	Daughter	At School	Maine
	Edward C. Johnson, 6	Son	At School	Maine

32. George H. Peters, 56   Head   Farmer
     James C. Peters, 77   Father
     Mary L. Tuttle, 67   Servant   Servant

33. Owen E. Rogers, 41   Head   Farmer
     Lillian S. Rogers, 45   Wife
     Arthur M. Berry, 19   Servant   Farm laborer
     Abbie M. Whitney, 22   Boarder   Teacher

34. Hiram C. Cornish, 74   Head   Farmer
     Ellen A. Cornish, 74   Wife
     Augusta S. Maddock, 23 [m]   Boarder   Farm laborer   Can (Eng)
     Addie R. Parker, 23   Boarder   Mass.
     Mary R. Haines, 49   Servant   Servant

35. Joseph Stoehr, 41   Head   Salesman
     Mary A. Stoehr, 38   Wife

36. William H. Whittam, 58   Head   Mill man
     Mary G. Whittam, 53   Wife
     Henry W. Whittam, 30   Son   Laborer, odd jobs
     Clarence F. Whittam, 21   Son   "
     Winnifred M. Whittam, 19   Daughter   Servant, private home
     Lillian A. Whittam, 15   Daughter   At school
     Iola R. Whittam, 11   Daughter   At school
     Catherine F. Voss, 81   Mother-in-law   Germany

37. Charles W. Crooker, 72   Head   Farmer
     Addie W. Crooker, 62   Wife
     William Crooker, 42   Son   Mill man
     George E. Crooker, 41   Son   "
     Lester H. Crooker, 15   Grandson   At school
     Abbie Cornish, 87   Mother-in-law

38. Frank M. Arris, 58   Head   House joiner
     Ella Arris, 59   Wife

Shore Road

39. Fred M. Mitchell, 51   Head   Cemetery nurseryman
     Carrie E. Mitchell, 47   Wife
     Laura A. Mitchell, 20   Daughter
     Ruth B. Mitchell, 15   Daughter   At school
     Alfred Ward, 54   Boarder   Iron Works laborer

40. John V. Morse, 45   Head   Farmer
     Clara L. Morse, 42   Wife

	Margery L. Morse, 6	Daughter	At school	
41.	William H. Crooker, 43	Head	Mill man (saw mill)	
	Lena M. Crooker, 39	Wife		
	Carl B. Crooker, 14	Son	At school	
	Thomas L. Crooker, 12	Son	At school	
	Lawrence W. Crooker, 2			
42.	Herbert C. Wright, 45	Head	Farmer	
	Addie M. Wright, 44	Wife		
	Ralph E. Wright, 16	Son	Farm laborer	
	Charles G. Wright, 87	Father		
	Williams Laffows, 20	Boarder	Farm laborer	England
	Fred Armandal, 20	Boarder	Farm laborer	Canada (Eng)
43.	Elmira P. Lord, 69	Head		
	Ella M. Lord, 33	Daughter		
	Gertrude E. Lord, 29	Daughter		
44.	Emery Wing, 45	Head	Farmer	
	Earl E. Wing, 28	Brother	Farm laborer	
	Lydia S. Sampson, 50	Servant		

1920 United States Federal Census

This census pays particular attention to "nativity" and "mother tongue" as well as the year of naturalization for new U. S. citizens, making it easier to trace foreign-born ancestors. Columns were provided for the place of birth and language spoken. It is apparent that more women are working outside the home in this census. It is also easy to see how the community has been affected by immigration and the boom in shipbuilding during the war. More families than in the past have at least one member who was not born in Maine, and more families, even in the rural parts of Bath, are employed in shipbuilding.

	Name, Age	Relation	Occupation	Birth Place
Brunswick Road				
1.	Parker E. Lewis, 37	Head	Supt. Elec. Railroad	
	Isabell S. Lewis, 13	Daughter		
	Priscilla P. Lewis, 8	Daughter		
2.	Eugene E. Aderton, 38	Head	Iron ship laborer	
	Jessie B. Aderton, 38	Wife		
	Josephine Aderton, 15	Daughter		
	Scot E. Aderton, 12	Daughter		
3.	Wiliam H. Sewall, 77	Head	Farmer	
4.	William G. Grover, 56	Head	Foreman, Ice Cutter	
	Isabell T. Grover, 46	Wife		Canada (Eng)
	Walter G. Grover, 28	Son	Carpenter, iron ships	
5.	James Doyle, 72	Head	Laborer, box factory	Canada (Irish)
6.	John S. Doyle, 48	Head	Carpenter, iron ships	Canada (Irish)
	Maud L. Doyle, 41	Wife		
	Nellie M. Doyle, 18	Daughter		
	John E. Doyle, 15	Son		
	James F. Doyle, 13	Son		
	Charles B. Doyle, 10	Son		
7.	Margaret B. Rounds, 39	Head	Factory stitcher	Massachusetts
	Harold F. Rounds, 37	Brother	Ship carpenter	

8. Charles McCausland, 60 — Head — House carpenter
    Johannah McCausland, 58 — Wife — — Nova Scotia
    Leon McCausland, 25 — Son — shipfitter
    Mary Dort, 69 — Mother-in-law — — Nova Scotia

9. Earl Mandigo, 30 — Head — shipfitter — Quebec
    Isabelle Mandigo, 29 — Wife — — Massachusetts

10. John Loring, 31 — Head — Shipfitter — Massachusetts
    Rillah Loring, 30 — Wife — — Massachusetts

11. Michael Rawley, 63 — Head — Shipyard laborer
    Clara Rawley, 66 — Wife

12. Walter Dean, 20 — Head — Machinist, shipyard
    Anelise Dean, 18 — Wife

13. Robert Gaddis, 34 — Head — Steam engineer, shipyard — Massachusetts
    Amelia Gaddis, 29 — Wife — — Vermont

14. Nellie Card, 53 — Head
    Alphonso Burnham, 38 — Son — Caulker, shipyard
    Elizabeth Burnham, 33 — Daughter-in-law
    Vivia Burnham, 5 — Grand daughter
    Madeline Davis, 15 — Lodger
    Raymond Davis, 9 — Lodger

15. Eldridge Wallace, 78 — Head
    Julia Wallace, 75 — Wife

16. Jay Dodge, 27 — Head — Marine engineer
    Gladys Dodge, 23 — Wife
    Kenneth Dodge, 6 — Son
    Dorothy Dodge, 4-4/12 — Daughter
    Virginia Dodge, 1-8/12 — Daughter

North Bath Road

17. John M. Loring, 50 — Head — Farmer
    Priscilla J. Loring, 50 — Wife — — Canada (Eng)
    Elizabeth M. Loring, 21 — Daughter
    Malcolm J. Loring, 13 — Son
    Henrietta C. Loring, 8 — Daughter

18. Mary E. Payne, 87 — Head — — Massachusetts
    Ella P. Kendall, 57 — Daughter
    Alton P. Wright, 28 — Boarder — Clerk, shipyard

19.	Loring J. Eggleston, 57	Head	Dairy Farmer	N.Y
	Nora A. Eggleston, 45	Wife		Illinois
	Loraine J. Eggleston, 17	Daughter		N.Y.
	Allan A. Eggleston, 14	Son		N.Y.
	Dudley J. Paine, 62	Hired man	Farm labor	N.Y.
20.	George F. Wright, 62	Head	Farmer	
21.	Eugene E. Ingalls, 41	Head	Farmer	
	Elma L. Ingalls, 41	Wife		Virginia
	Eugene G. Ingalls, 7	Son		
	Albert L. Ingalls, 5	Son		
	Raymond J. Ingalls, 1	Son		
22.	George R. Ward, 76	Head	Retired riverman	
	Abbie J. Ward, 74	Wife		
	Luella M. Ward, 42	Daughter		
	Frank E. Ward, 40	Son	Foreman, City of Bath	
	Sidney H. Ward, 36	Son	Fisherman	
	Pearl E. Donnell, 6	Boarder		
23.	George O. Rideout, 43	Head	Boiler maker, shipyard	
	Olivia M. Rideout, 42	Wife		Massachusetts
	John C. Rideout, 16	Son		Massachusetts
	Myrtle C. Rideout, 13	Daughter		Massachusetts
24.	Earl E. Wing, 38	Head	Farmer	
	Adeline D. Wing, 33	Wife		Canada (Eng.)
25.	Owen E. Roger, 51	Head	Farmer	
	Lillian M. Rogers, 55	Head		
	Mary E. Philbrook, 31	Boarder	Teacher, public school	
26.	William H. Whittam, 68	Head	General laborer	
	Mary C. Whittam, 63	Wife		
	George Harness, 29	Boarder [son-in-law]	Riveter, shipyard	Canada (Eng.)
	Winifred M. Harness, 39	Daughter		
	Bernice Harness, 8	Grand daughter		
	Eleanor Harness, 6	Grand daughter		
	Catherine Harness, 4	Grand daughter		
	Wilburt Harness, 3-6/12	Grand son		
27.	Elmer J. Rich, 58	Head	Farmer	
	Rose E. Rich, 56	Wife		
	David G. Rich, 25	Son	Farmer	

	Edith G. Rich, 24	Daughter [in-law]	Nurse, private home	Canada (Eng.)
	Amasa W. Ring [m], 81	Boarder	Joiner, boat	
28.	Ernest A. Ward, 47	Head	Carpenter, shipyard	
	Mabel E. Ward, 43	Wife		
	Lucy G. Ward, 20	Daughter	Stenographer	
	Mildred Ward 16	Daughter		
	Arthur Ward, 14	Son		
29.	Mary A. Johnson, 56	Head		Sweden
	Edward C. Johnson, 18	Son	Riveter, shipyard	
	Flora B. Winslow, 62	Boarder		

North Bath Ridge Road

30.	Wellington F. Dunton, 48	Head	Farmer, dairy farm	
	Edith M. Dunton, 43	Wife		New Hamp.
	Frank O. Dunton, 9	Son		
	Wilfred E. Dunton, 8	Son		
	Mary A. Dunton, 4-8/12	Daughter		
	Harold E. Dunton, 2-4/12	Son		
	Hattie E. Dunton, 50	Sister		
	George A. Allen, 37	Hired man	Farmer, dairy farm	
31.	William A. Murphy, 30	Head	Shipyard carpenter	Canada (Eng.)
	Mary J. Murphy, 29	Wife		N. J
	Marie Murphy, 6	Daughter		N. J.
	William F. Murphy, 4-8/12	Son		N. J.
	Rita C. Murphy, 3	Daughter		N. J.
32.	Frederick Wright, 67	Head	Farmer	
	Harry N. Wright, 30	Son	Farmer	
	Lizzie Wright, 33	Daughter-in-law		
	Sophia G. Wright, 7	Grand daughter		
	Harry Donnell, 21	Hired man	Hired man, dairy farm	
33.	Robert W. Donnell, 47	Head	Clerk in Grain Store	
	Guy E. Donnell, 22	Son	Machinist, shipyard	
	Olive M. Donnell, 20	Daughter	Housework, private home	
	James Donnell, 18	Son	General laborer	
	Alonzo S. Donnell 16	Son	General laborer	
	Irving F. Donnell, 15	Son		
	Walter Donnell, 14	Son		
	Mildred Donnell, 5	Daughter		
	Lillian G. Donnell, 9			
	Robert F. Donnell, 6			
	Elsie W. Donnell, 4-8/12			

Harry Bullard, 32	Boarder	Erector at shipyard	Mass.

Brunswick Road

34. Thomas Leask, 29	Head	Ship fitter	Virginia
Ethel M. Leask, 28			
Thomas W. Leask, 7			
William H. Leask, 5			
Robert S. Leask, 3			
Glendon Leask, 1			

35. John A. Foote, 60	Head	Pattern maker, shipyard	
Virginia M. Foote, 67	Sister	House keeper, private home	
Ida F. Dart, 63	Boarder		Massachusetts
Charles A. Foote, 69	Brother	House Painter	
Charles Ward, 54	Hired man	General laborer	
Ralph W. Wright, 21	Lodger	General laborer	

East Brunswick Road

36. David S. Henderson, 31	Head	Farmer	Canada (Eng.)
Annie A. Henderson, 32	Wife		
Stanley D. Henderson, 7	Son		
Vincent A. Henderson, 6	Son		
Eva M. Henderson, 2-6/12	Daughter		
Doris H. Henderson, 7/12	Daughter		

37. David Walsh, 38	Head	Farmer	Canada (Eng)
May E. Walsh, 34	Wife		
Clifford E. Walsh, 14	Son		
Clifford Belanger, 74	Father-in-law	Retired farmer	Canada (Fr)
Rena J. Walsh, 18	Niece		Canada (Fr)

Whiskeag Road

38. George M. Rogers, 81	Head		
Hannah A. Rogers, 77	Wife		
Rose G Rogers, 34	Daughter		
Eta A Bloom, 56	Niece		New Jersey

North Bath Road

39. Samuel Morse, 36	Head	Paymaster, shipyard	Washington
Mildred Morse, 30	Wife		
Austin Morse, 7	Son		
Carroll E. Morse, 2-6/12	Son		

40. Augusta A. Rogers, 79	Head		

41. Herbert W. Rogers, 36	Head	Joiner, shipyard	

	Name	Relation	Occupation	Birthplace
	Fannie Rogers, 35	Wife		
	Lillian G. Rogers, 14	Son		
	N. Emery Rogers, 10	Son		
	Adeline A. Rogers, 8	Daughter		
	Virginia B. Rogers, 5	Daughter		
42.	Alice Rogers, 56	Head		
43.	Clarence Baker, 22	Head	Machinist, shipyard	
	Gertrude E. Baker, 23	Wife		
	Irving C. Baker, 9/12	Son		
44.	Charles H. Rogers, 59	Head	House joiner	
	Nellie G. Rogers, 58	Wife		
45.	Walter M. Rogers, 30	Head	Machinist, garage	
	Laura A. Rogers, 23	Wife		
	Marguerite E. Rogers, 2	Daughter		
	Melvin A. Rogers, 2/12	Son		
46.	Louis Bredeau, 69	Head	General laborer	Canada (Fr)
	Judith Bredeau, 54	Wife		Canada (Fr)
	John L. Bredeau, 39	Son	General laborer	Canada (Fr)
	Mathilda Bredeau, 41	Daughter-in-law		Canada (Fr)
	Amana Bredeau, 5	Grandaughter		N.H.
47.	Arthur Sewall, 32	Head	Dairy farmer	
	Laura B. Sewall, 32	Wife		N.Y.
	Mary Sewall, 2-6/12	Daughter		
	Ina B. Savage, 65	Hired woman	House work	
48.	Payson G. Reed, 47	Head	Laborer, dairy farm	
	Emma P. Reed. 33	Wife		
	Annie I. Reed, 17	Daughter		
	Fred W. Reed, 16	Son	Laborer, dairy farm	
	Charles W. Reed, 10	Son		
49.	William S. Thurston, 27	Head	Pool room manager	
	Ida E. Thurston, 33	Wife		Canada (Fr)
	Grace G. Thurston, 9/12	Daughter		
50.	Harry A. Plummer, 41	Head	Dairy farmer	
	Ferdinand Plummer, 79	Uncle	Ret. Engineer	
	Rose M. Lord, 50	Housekeeper	House work	
	Thomas Gleason, 69	Hired man	Dairy farm labor	Massachusetts

51. Everett E. Cornish, 60   Head   House joiner
     Elizabeth F. Cornish, 55   Wife
     Herbert C. Cornish, 32   Son   Foreman rigger, shipyard
     Maud E. Cornish, 23   Daughter in law
     Basil H. Cornish, 3/12   Grand son

52. Ella A. Arras, 70   Head

53. George A. Arey, 52   Head   Machinist, shipyard
     Linnie B. Arey, 44   Wife
     Marjory E. Farnham, 27   Daughter
     Kathleen J. Farnham, 5   Grand daughter
     Barbara P. Farnham, 3-9/12   Grand daughter
     Helda L. Farnham, 9/12   Grand daughter
     Herbert B. Arey, 20   Son   Machinist, shipyard
     Florence Arey, 11   Daughter

54. Allan H. Arey, 24   Head   Machinist, shipyard
     Pearl F. Arey, 21   Wife

55. George W. Arey, 22   Head   Machinist, shipyard
     Sarah W. Arey, 24   Wife   Massachusetts
     Wilbur L. Arey, 1-6/12   Son

56. John H. Morse, 55   Head   Fruit Farmer
     Clara L. Morse, 52   Wife
     Margery L. Morse, 16   Daughter

57. Martin Bergquist, 36   Head   Laborer, shipyard   Sweden
     Katherine Bergquist, 35   Wife

58. Ralph L. F. Palmer, 40   Head   Dairy farmer
     Bessie B. Palmer, 40   Wife
     Ralph R. Palmer, 15   Son
     Lawrence W. Palmer, 13   Son
     Lewis E. Palmer, 11   Son

59. Harry W. Whittam, 37   Head   Painter, shipyard
     Fannie G. Whittam, 30   Wife

60. George W. Rook, 33   Head   Dairy Farmer
     Margaret L. Rook, 26   Sister
     Frazier J. Haines, 15   Nephew
     Royden D. Haines, 15   Nephew
     Earl F. Haines, 13   Nephew

1930 United States Federal Census

The 1930 census asked residents if they were college-educated. Was their homestead a farm? Did they own a radio set? What was their age at "first marriage" and the "marital condition"? Spinner, salesman, and riveter were listed as examples of occupation choices. Industry or business examples included: cotton mill, dry goods store, shipyard, and public school. The value of a home or monthly rental fee was required.

Name, Age	Relation	Occupation	Home Value /Rent Paid	Place of Birth
Brunswick Road				
1. Harold F. Rounds, 47	Head	Laborer	$1,200	
Margaret B. Rounds, 49	Sister	Stitcher		Mass
2. John S. Doyle, 56	Head	Carpenter	$1,500	Can (Eng)
Maud L. Doyle, 50	Wife			
John E. Doyle, 25	Son	Helper, Iron shipyard		
Chas B. Doyle	Son			
3. James Doyle, 81	Head	Caretaker & gardener	$2,000	Can (Eng)
4. Albert M. Pinkham, 34	Head	Helper shipyard	$12	
Josephine Pinkham, 29	Wife	Stitcher, sheet factory		Mass
5. George W. Larrabee, 24	Head	Pttrn mkr, iron shpyrd	$2,800	
Mae F. Larrrabee, 23	Wife			
George W. Larrabee, Jr, 8/12	Son			
Charles Foose, 48	F-in-law	Sea Capt. "Unlimited"		Ohio
6. Frank H. Beals, 63	Head	Asst. Supt. elctrc railwy	$2,800	
Ida M. Beals, 60	Wife			
Parker E. Lewis, 47	Roomer	Supt electric railway		
7. Walter O. Donnell, 21	Head	Farmer	$2,500	
Raymond R. Donnell, 18	Brother	Farmer		
8. David S. Henderson, 42	Head	Farmer	$5,000	Can (Eng)
Annie H. Henderson, 42	Wife			
Stanley D. Henderson, 17	Son			
Vincent A. Henderson, 16	Son			
Eva M. Henderson, 12	Daughter			

	Name, Age	Relationship	Occupation	Value	Birthplace
	Doris N. Henderson, 10	Daughter			
	Lena E. Henderson, 5	Daughter			
9.	Wellington F. Dunton, 59	Head	Dairy farmer	$4,000	
	Edith M. Dunton, 54	Wife			New Hamp
	Frank O. Dunton, 19	Son			
	Mary A. Dunton, 14	Daughter			
	Harold E. Dunton, 12	Son			
10.	John A. Foote, 72	Head	Farmer	$3,000	
	Ida Dart, 79	Cousin			Mass
11.	Gardiner D. Rogers, 39	Head	Slsmn, h/w store	$3,500	
	Susan H. Rogers, 35	Wife			
	Doris V. Jordan, 19	Niece	Office stenographer		
12.	Bates E. Stover, 48	Head	Star Route (rural) mail carrier	$3,000	
	Nella S. Stover, 43	Wife			
	Eben G. Stover, 19	Son	Stevedore, coal docks		
	Courtney E. Stover, 18	Son			Mass
	Marjorie V. Stover, 16	Daughter			Vermont
	Rosamond S. Stover, 14	Daughter			Vermont
	Francis W. Stover, 11	Son			Vermont
	Carleton C. Stover, 8	Son			Vermont
	Gloria M. Stover, 6	Daughter			Vermont
	Carol A. Stover, 1/12	Daughter			
	Mary J. Goodwin, 83	Mother in law			Mass
13.	Alphonso Burnham, 47	Head	Iceman	$1,000	
	Elizabeth E. Burnham, 43	Wife			
	Viva M. Burnham, 16	Daughter			
	Barbara R. Burnham, 2	Daughter			
	Raymond P. Davis, 20	Step-son	Laborer, machine shop		
14.	Nellie M. Card, 64	Head		$1,500	
	Madeline M. Curran, 25	Grand daughter			
	Beverly A. Curran, 1-3/12	Great grand daughter			
15.	Albion H. Johnson, 56	Head	Iceman	$3,000	
	Mary J. Johnson, 42	Wife			
	Albion H. Johnson Jr., 18	Son			
	Carleton G. Johnson, 8	Son			
	Lucy Jones, 11	Boarder			
16.	Frank P. Benjamin, 67	Head	Laborer, lumber	$100	

17. Joseph Johnson, 55	Head	Farmer	$5,000	Sweden
Rose E. Johnson, 54	Wife			
18. Doris E. Jordan, 19	Head	Office clerk	$10	
19. Albion S. Bartlett, 22	Head	Welder, shipyard	$16	
Frances F. Bartlett, 21	Wife			

Whiskeag Road

20. Ernest C. Perkins, 42	Head	Farm helper	Free	
Lena Z. Perkins, 38	Wife			Mass.
Ernest B. Perkins, 15	Son			Mass.
Thelma C. Perkins, 13	Daughter			Mass.
Elwood J. Perkins, 12	Son			Mass.
Ashley M. Perkins, 10	Son			Mass.
21. Arthur W. Sewall, 42	Head	V.P. Bank	$10,000	
Laura B. Sewall, 42	Wife			Iowa
Mary Sewall, 13	Daughter			
William D. Sewall, 9	Son			
Lena Ogden, 21	Servant	Housework		
Olive H. Andros, 72	Servant	Cook		
22. Samuel A. Morse, 46	Head	Paymaster, Mchnry plnt	$2,500	California
Mildred F. Morse, 40				
Samuel A. Morse, Jr., 17	Son			
Carroll E. Morse, 12	Son			
Robert W. Morse, 9	Son			
23. John S. Bishop, 56	Head	Joiner, shipyard	$20	
Lillian E. Bishop, 45	Wife			
Dora M. Bishop, 17	Daughter			
Alice A. Bishop, 15	Daughter			
Glenwood Sukeforth, 23	Boarder	Erector, shipyard		
24. Herbert W. Rogers, 46	Head	Foreman, shipyard	$4,000	
Fannie A. Rogers, 45	Wife			
Emery W. Rogers, 20	Son	Electrician, shipyard		
Adeline A. Rogers, 18	Daughter			
Virginia B. Rogers, 16	Daughter			

North Bath Road

25. Harry A. Plummer, 63	Head	Farming	$4,500	
Minnie M. Crosby, 56	Servant	Housework		New Jers

Shirley J. Foote, 5	Boarder			
Charles Ward, 70	Boarder	Farm helper		
26. John M. Loring, 60	Head	Frmr/schl bus driver	$3,000	
Priscilla J. Loring, 60	Wife			Can (Eng)
John M. Loring, Jr. 23	Son			
Henrietta Loring, 18	Daughter			
Merline Harvey, 5 (m)	Boarder			Mass.
27. Walter M. Rogers, 41	Head	Service man, garage	$2,000	
Laura A. Rogers, 33	Wife			
Marguerite E. Rogers, 12	Daughter			
Melvin E. Rogers, 10	Son			
Donald H. Rogers, 5	Son			
Velma S. Rogers, 1	Daughter			
Doris E. Oliver, 25	Servant	Housework		
28. Charles H. Rogers, 69	Head	Carpenter & builder	$3,000	
Nellie G. Rogers, 68	Wife			
Edwin A. Rogers, 37	Son	Carpenter		
29. David E. Rich, 35	Head	Farmer	$3,500	
Edith G. Rich, 34	Wife	Nurse		Can (Eng)
David E. Rich, Jr., 9	Son			
Margaret L. Rich, 5	Daughter			
Elmer D. Rich, 68	Father			
Rose E. Rich, 63	Mother			

Whiskeag Road

30. Fred E. Blake, 55	Head	Cook, Boarding house	$1,500	New Hamp
Fannie M. Blake, 52	Wife	Cook, Boarding house		New Hamp
Doris A. Blake, 24	Daughter			
Frank T. Blake, 21	Son	Fireman, gas plant		
Lawrence L. Blake, 17	Son			
Earl E. Blake, 15	Son			
Gladys E. Blake, 12	Daughter			
31. George F. Wright, 72	Head		$4,000	
Oscar F. Wright, 39	Son	Farmer		
Hazel E. Wright, 31	Dtr-in-law			
Chester A. Wright, 5	Grand son			
32. Eugene E. Ingalls, 50	Head	Farmer	$500	
Alma J. Ingalls, 50	Wife			Virginia
Eugene G. Ingalls, 17	Son			
Albert L. Ingalls, 14	Son			

	Name	Relation	Occupation	Value	Origin
	Raymond J. Ingalls, 11	Son			
	Virginia C. Ingalls, 9	Daughter			
33.	George R. Ward, 86	Head	Operator (farm)	$1,500	
	Luella M. Ward, 52	Daughter			
	Frank E. Ward, 50	Son	Cemetery helper		
	Sidney H. Ward, 47	Son	Cemetery helper		
34.	John J. Fitzpatrick, 60	Head	Farmer	$800	Can (Eng)
	Alice M. Carr, 52	Housekpr	Housework		
35.	Harry W. Whittam, 49	Head	Painter, shipyard	$900	
	Fanny G. Whittam, 43	Wife			
	Herman F. Whittam, 5	Son			
36.	Earl E. Wing, 49	Head	Farmer	$4,000	
	Adeline B. Wing, 43	Wife			Can (Eng)
	L. Patricia Wing, 7	Daughter			
	Estelle G. Dyer 71	Aunt			
37.	Owen E. Rogers, 61	Head	Farmer	$7,000	
	Lillian M. Rogers, 65	Wife			
	Albert S. Ward, 74	Boarder			
	Alice E. Rogers, 66	Boarder			
	Arthur J. Brown, 21	Hired man	Farm helper		
38.	George E. Crooker, 60	Head	Farmer	$2,500	
	Hattie M. Crooker, 39	Wife			
	Hazel L. Crooker, 9	Daughter			
39.	Ella M. Arras, 78	Head		$500	
40.	Edwin O. Chandler, 51	Head	Farmer	$2,000	
	Jessie Chandler, 44	Wife			Can (Eng)
	Edwin O. Chandler, Jr., 21	Son	Helper, farm		
	Margaret D. Chandler, 23	Dtr-in-law			
	Robert E. Chandler, 3	Grand son			
41.	John H. Morse, 65	Head	Farmer	$2,000	
	Clara L. Morse, 62	Wife			
	Marjorie L. Morse, 26	Daughter	Grocery store clerk		
42.	Albion C. Brown, 71	Head		Free	
	Emma Brown, 68				
43.	Charles V. Broden, 65	Head	Farmer	$1,500	Sweden

		Hilda M. Broden, 68	Wife			Sweden
44.		Ernest A. Ward, 57	Head	Farmer	$2,500	
		Mabel E. Ward, 53	Wife			
		Lucy G. Ward, 30	Daughter	Bookkeeper, store		
		Arthur J. Ward, 24	Son	Electrician, shipyard		
45.		Ralph L. Palmer, 59	Head	Farmer	$1,600	Sweden
		Bessie G. Palmer, 50	Wife			
		Ralph R. Palmer, 25	Son			
		Lawrence W. Palmer, 28	Son			
		Lewis E. Palmer, 21	Son	Laborer, shipyard		
46.		George W. Rooke, 43	Head	Farmer	$2,000	
		Mary A. Haynes, 41	Sister			
		Margaret L. Rooke, 36	Sister	Nurse		

Endnotes

1   Southeast of London on the Thames River, there is a suburb in the Borough of Greenwich called Woolwich, which includes a Fiddler's Reach and a Long Reach. The Thames also takes two turns at this point, which are very similar to the turns or "elbows" in the Kennebec River in Arrowsic-Bath. And, could Doubling Point be a corruption of Dublin, an Irish settlement, or perhaps just Yankee vernacular?

2   Fannie Hardy Eckstorm was born in Brewer, Maine, in 1865; she spent many days traveling with her father, living with the Indians and woodsmen of Maine. Her book, written in 1941 for the University of Maine, entitled, *Indian Place Names of the Penobscot Valley and the Maine Coast*, puts to rest any colloquial meanings as she analyzes each word or phrase by defining its reference to Latin and other languages.

3   Not to be confused with the name Kennebec, an entirely different word, which means "level water, long, and quiet." Sagadahoc, the lower part of the Kennebec River from Bath to the ocean, means "mouth of the river."

4   Henry Otis Thayer, *Sagadahoc and Kennebec: Collected Papers, Notes, Abstracts, Copies*, Maine Historical Society Collection 3046.

5   Carol B. Smith Fisher, "Who Really Named Maine?," *Bangor Daily News*, February 26, 2002.

6   The original measurement was later found to be much less.

7   Maine Province and Court Records 2:223.

8   According to S. H. Whitney, in his book, *The Kennebec Valley* (Augusta, Maine: Sprague, Burleigh & Flint, 1887), "Elder" Gutch and Christopher Lawson were both settled in Bath as early as 1640.

9   *Old Map of Bath, Maine. Part of What was Formerly Long Reach District.* Drawn by T. M. Fowler.

10   westcountrygenealogy.com/wincanton/colonizers.htm.

11   Ibid.

12   Thayer, *Sagadahoc and Kennebec Collected Papers, Notes, Abstract, Copies*, 167.

13   Ibid.

14   Rootsweb.com.

15   James Phinney Baxter, *Documentary History of the State of Maine*, Vol. XXIII. (Maine Historical Society, Portland, Maine, 1916) 206–207.

16   Ibid.

17   The five Indian Wars were conflicts for territorial controls in North America, with England and France vying for Native American support. The Indians, for the most part, allied with the French. The wars following King Philip's War were: King William's War (1689–97); Queen Anne's War (1702–13); King George's War (1744–48); and the French and Indian War (1754–63).

18   Title 13, Chapter 83, Cemetery Corporation: Maine Statute 1101-A.

19   Levi P. Lemont, *1400 Historical Dates of the Town and City of Bath and Georgetown from 1604 to 1874.* (Bath, Maine: Published by author, 1874.)

20   See Merrymeeting Bay section, which explains direction of the portage at the Chops.

21   Grape Island is Sandy Island today.

22   Eckstorm, *Indian Places Names of the Penobscot Valley and the Maine Coast.*

23   *John North, Plan of a Tract of Land Lying Fifteen English Miles on Each Side of Kennebec River . . .3d. Feby. 1750/1, Ms. Copy, 1785*, George J. Mitchell Dept. of Special Collections & Archives, Bowdoin College Library, Brunswick, Maine.

24   The original map is at the Maine Historical Society, Portland.

25   Wood Island is now Woods, Ram was also Haley's, and Thorne on the *1858 Chace Map* is assigned to Wood and not at the location we know today, a little southwest of Lines. Crawford was also known as Sheep.

26   Henry W. Owen, *History of Bath* (Bath, Maine: The Times Co., 1936).

27   William D. Williamson, *History of the State of Maine*, Baxter Manuscripts Vol. XXII (Hallowell, Maine: Glazier, Masters & Smith, 1839).

28   *Sentinel Times*, Bath, Maine, 1914.

29   Charles Knowles Bolton, *Scotch Irish Pioneers in Ulster and America* (Boston: Bacon and Brown, 1910).

30   The 1861 England Census lists a Daniel Wilkinson, sixteen, born in Barnet, Middlesex, England, living on "miscellaneous ships at sea or abroad." His home was on the vessel *Alexton*, which listed the "Rating of the Men and Boys of the Crew." He was listed as "Boy." Those with him were: George Preston, thirty-two (Master) and William Samuels (Mate), nineteen. (It is speculative that this is the Daniel Wilkinson who was hanged at Maine State Prison.) The 1880 U.S. Census lists a Daniel Wilkinson, age thirty-three, born in England, with the occupation of

"seaman." The list of "household members" included thirteen men and one woman who were fellow prisoners in Wiscasset, Maine.

31   Sewall Woods, an 88-acre preserve, was an acquisition of The Lower Kennebec Land Trust. It is located across the road from the Stone House, former residence of William D. Sewall. He and his heirs provided much of the land (with 2,300 feet of water frontage on Whiskeag Creek).

32   A granite quarry on the property suggests the stone was local.

33   Probably called the Upper Ferry to distinguish it from the ferry location in downtown Bath. A Dummer Sewall map in 1795 shows a West and South Ferry in this northern location.

34   From interviews with Timer Savage.

35   Thayer, *Sagadahoc and Kennebec: Collected Papers, Notes, Abstracts, Copies*.

36   Ibid.

37   This style was also used for transportation to Varney's Island, according to an old deed. Samuel Foote also mentions his gondola in his daybooks.

38   Records have spelled this name several ways: Purrington, Puddington, Perrington, and Purinton, to name a few. The headstone names are spelled with two *r*'s. The U.S. Census records of 1790 and 1850 list his name as Joshua Purington. Family information is found in Alfred Holt's *Bath Families in the 19th Century*, a handwritten manuscript, housed in the Sagadahoc History and Genealogy Room at the Patten Free Library in Bath. Holt's source was *The Purinton-Purington Families in America,* from the Maine State Library. *The Genealogical Dictionary of Maine and New Hampshire* by Sybil Noyes, Charles T. Libby, and Walter G. Davis (Baltimore: The Genealogical Publishing Co., Inc., 1972) says that Purington is the only spelling of this name found in early New England records.

39   Edgecombe is spelled with and without an *e* at the end depending upon the family member. Pendleton's brother, John, who built homes farther up the road, tended to spell his name without the *e*.

40   Gen. Samuel Thompson is noted as a defendant in the Wigwam Point Deposition. He had the distinction of having a town named for him, "Thompsonboro," but he was so contentious that the residents renamed the area Lisbon. Many of his family members settled at New Meadows on the East Brunswick side.

41   13 July 1892 diary entry of Ella P. Kendall, in possession of Lorelei Gustafson.

42   In 1938 the SRG&S Club united with all the county gun clubs, including
      Brunswick, to form an organization known as the Merrymeeting Bay
      Clubs Association. It joined the National Skeet Association in 1961.

43   Thayer, *Sagadahoc and Kennebec: Collected Papers, Notes, Abstracts, Copies*, 150.

44   Original blueprint at the City of Bath Assessor's Office.

45   In possession of Eldie Johnston.

46   William A. Baker, *Maritime History of Bath, Maine and the Kennebec River
      Regions* (Maine Maritime Museum, 1973), lists several ships by the name
      of *Hiram*; one built in Bath in 1797 and one in Bowdoinham in 1806. The
      Florida was built in Bath in 1808. John Crawford's brother, Captain
      Thomas Crawford, was lost at sea in 1811.

47   Captain Thomas Timmins, brother-in-law to John and Thomas Crawford,
      died at sea around Christmas in 1832; he starved on the brig of which he
      was Master. (From notes of Lorelei Gustafson)

48   The New Meadows River was sometimes called Muddy River, not to be
      confused with the small river by the same name, which empties into
      Merrymeeting Bay in Topsham.

49   Sagadahoc County Registry of Deeds. (Lincoln County West, Vol. 15)

50   John Mann, *Ulster-Scots on the Coast of Maine* (St. Andrews Society, 2006).

51   Patrick and James Drummond were listed as farmers on Merrymeeting
      Bay in 1736.

52   U.S. GenWeb.

53   Samuel was also married to Huldah Grace Timmons (Timmins, or
      Timmens), another noteworthy family.

54   From interviews with Harry Higgins.

55   Timmons and Timmens used interchangeably throughout this research.

56   Diary in possession of Joyce K. Bibber.

57   Dennison Harding Crooker, born c. 1849, died March 10, 1886, while
      serving as an engineer on a Long Island tugboat named *John Marks*. Frank
      Warren Crooker, born 1855, died the same day while working as a fire-
      man with his brother. (From Holt, *Bath Families in the 19th Century*)

58   Names of various teachers are listed in Bath City Directories at the
      Sagadahoc History and Genealogy Room at the Patten Free Library and
      the Maine Maritime Museum; they are also listed in *Owen's History of Bath*,
      p. 407.

59   National Archives and Records Administration, Washington, D.C.

60   According to wingfamily.org, Deborah joined the "ten men of Saugus"
      with three of her sons in 1637, upon receiving a grant from the Crown to

the Sandwich property. The family today maintains the 360-year-old Wing Fort House in Sandwich, the oldest home in North America with continuous ownership by the same family.

61   A prominent Puritan preacher in England and the Netherlands with published sermons.

62   They sailed on the ship *William and Francis*.

63   Wing's Pond was renamed Pocasset Lake in 1838.

64   Although Zacheus's son, Isaiah, was credited in his 1887 obituary as having built the only brick home in North Bath with bricks he had burned, the date above the door is 1800. Isaiah was not born until 1807. The first two Isaiahs died in 1796 and 1795. According to Lincoln County Deed Vol.1 16:220, a John Stockbridge recorded a deed for this house on March 26, 1800. Zacheus and Polly Merritt named a son born in 1815 John Stockbridge.

65   John was part owner of the mill at "Whisgig" Creek.

66   Friends of Merrymeeting Bay, friendsofmerrymeetingbay.org.

67   Eckstorm, *Indian Place Names of the Penobscot Valley and the Maine Coast*.

68   Emerson W. Baker and James Kences, "Maine, Indian Land Speculation, and the Essex County Witchcraft Outbreak of 1692," *Maine History*, Vol. 40, No. 3, Fall 2001, 159–189.

69   Henry Otis Thayer, *Transient Town of Cork, Collections and Proceedings of the Maine Historical Society, Series 2*, Vol. 4, pp. 240–265; George A. Wheeler and Henry W. Wheeler, *History of Brunswick, Topsham and Harpswell* (Boston: Alfred Mudge & Son, 1878).

70   Charles Edwin Allen, *History of Dresden, Maine* (Maine: Kennebec Journal Print Shop, 1931), p. 94.

71   Christopher Levett, "A Voyage into New England, Begun in 1623 and Ended in 1624, Preformed [sic] by Christopher Levett, His Majesty's Woodward of Somersetshire, and one of the Council of New England." Collections and Proceedings of the Maine Historical Society 2:73–109.

72   The fort measured 50 feet square with timbers 12 feet high.

73   Found at the Sagadahoc Registry of Deeds and the Woolwich Historical Society.

74   *1750 Kennebec Proprietors Map* shows the Bowdoin name on several lots.

75   Eckstorm, *Indian Place Names of the Penobscot Valley and the Maine Coast*.

76   The home on 73 Exeter Road was constructed in 1648 for Godfrey Dearborn; it is believed to be the oldest frame dwelling in New Hampshire.

77   Henry Dearborn was buried in a tomb in Mount Auburn Cemetery in
       Cambridge; his remains were moved to Forest Hills Cemetery in Boston
       as a result of his son's position.

78   John Adams autobiography, part 1, "John Adams," through 1776, sheet 9
       of 53 [electronic edition]. *Adams Family Papers: An Electronic Archive.*
       Massachusetts Historical Society, masshis.org/digitaladams.

79   The daybooks of Samuel Foote mention the death of Charles Ward by
       drowning. Note that James Ward died eleven days later.

80   Fisher Mitchell Elementary School Fourth Graders, *Voices From Our
       Agricultural Past, The Countryside of Bath, Maine* (privately printed, 1999).

81   Interviews with Ray Nadeau.

82   Ham, Manson graves at the Ham Burial Ground.

83   Frederick died in Hollywood, California, in 1932. He is buried in Oak
       Grove Cemetery, Bath.

84   Zita Bella Cameron was born in Wellington, Prince Edward Island, and
       came to Bath when she was eighteen. Lewis's mother, Marianne
       Greenleaf, was related to the poet John Greenleaf Whittier, whose por-
       trait hung in Zita's living room. (From interviews with Carol Bartel)

85   Published by Harry C. Webber, Bath, Maine. Courtesy of the Patten Free
       Library, Bath.

86   According to the *Genealogical Dictionary of Maine and New Hampshire,*
       Newmeadows was an early name of a settlement on both sides of that
       river between Harpswell and Georgetown.

87   Fannie Eckstorm interprets *Androscoggin* to mean a place to prepare and
       cure migratory fish such as alewives, but also salmon, shad, and bass.

88   Owen, *History of Bath*; Lemont, *1400 Historical Dates of the Town and City of
       Bath and Georgetown from 1604 to 1874*; Wheeler, *History of Brunswick,
       Topsham and Harpswell*; maps of F. W. DesBarres, Dummer Sewall, and J.
       Chace Jr.; and various censuses.

89   Owen, *History of Bath, Maine,* page 357.

90   Ibid., p. 361.

91   Lemont, *Historical Dates of the Town and City of Bath and Georgetown from
       1604 to 1874*, 41.

92   Ibid., 40–41.

93   William C. Purington, *Meadowsweet* (Brunswick, Maine: C. W. Ring,
       ______).

94   Wheeler, *History of Brunswick, Topsham and Harpswell*, Maine, 541.

95   William C. Purington, *A Look into West Bath's Past* (privately printed by author, 1976). Crush appears in several censuses.

96   The Paul Revere bell from the North Church of 1804 proudly peals from the Davenport Memorial City Hall in Bath today.

97   Fannie Eckstorm says that the varied spelling of this stream suggests *a boundary brook*; one is found in Maine, Massachusetts, and Connecticut.

98   Map at Maine Historical Society.

99   Author's opinion.

100   Davistown Museum, Liberty, Maine.

101   See *1718 Pejepscot Proprietors Map*.

102   It is interesting to note that the Peterson Canal was originally intended to follow the same northwesterly direction to the Androscoggin River, but ledge prevented this course, which was changed to Little Whiskeag Creek in a northeasterly direction.

103   William E. Gerber, "Twice a Day Island," *The Best from American Canals*, Number II (York, PA: American Canal and Transportation Center, 1984) 11.

104   Some historians are often confused by the canal location; in 1901 George L. Vose, a professor at Bowdoin College, read a dissertation entitled *The Old Canal at New Meadow and Kennebec River* (Bath, ME: Bath Enterprise, 1901). He references several authors in his description of the canal. What he and others may not have considered is that the name Whiskeag Creek also, or more importantly, refers to the smaller Whiskeag Creek in North Bath.

105   Col. Dummer Sewall halted work by the king's carpenters on masts for the Royal Navy in 1775, subsequent to the Revolution. The *1774 Sproule Chart* shows *Mast Dock*.

106   Soule Family online, various sites.

107   Other Ham family members are buried at another Ham Cemetery, on the Old Brunswick Road in East Brunswick, behind what was the Bonnie Borok Farm, now Bay Bridge Estates. This burial property was once owned by the City of Bath. Attempts have been made to restore the badly vandalized graveyard.

108   The hides of various animals, usually cows, pigs, goats, and sheep, were soaked in large containers with lime. Later the fat and hair were scraped off. The hides were returned to the solution for several months and then in and out of the vats for more months. Tannic acid from various tree barks, along with other acidic agents, was added to preserve the hide. A

neutral agent was then added to stop the acid process. This required more
months of soaking before the hides were removed and processed with oils
for leather production.

109   Author's collection.

110   census.gov/population/www/documentation/twps0076.html.

111   H. H. Price and Gerald E. Talbot, *Maine's Visible Black History* (Gardiner,
ME: Tilbury House Publishers, 2006).

112   The census of 1880 mentions a "Cross Road" in this location where the
Hill Family lived.

113   Brunswick's only African-American cemetery, Chapel Burial Ground, is
located on the Old Bath Road on the former Francis Heuston farm. The
Harrison Burial Ground is predominantly African-American.

114   Compiler Harold Brown's notes say "Curch"; however, the worn
headstones may read "Church," as census records as well as Holt's biogra-
phies list an "Adrianna" Harrison married to a James Church of Norwich,
Connecticut. Brown's records say "John," not James Curch. Other children of John Harrison, who is listed as a farmer from Baltimore,
Maryland, and Lavina were: George, born in 1829; John Jr., born about
1835; and Philena, born 1844–45.

115   Mere Point, according to William D. Spencer's *Pioneers on Maine Rivers*
(Baltimore: Genealogical Publishing Co. Inc., 1973), was called Mare
Point where Purchase raised colts. Wheeler's *History of Brunswick, Topsham
and Harpswell* speculates that before the Pejepscot Proprietors claim, a
man named John Mare settled in this region; another thought is that
French settlers, who were never documented as having lived there, named
it "Sea Point," which would account for "Mer."

116   King Philip, of the Wampanoags, son of Massasoit, who befriended the
Pilgrims, led the war between the English settlers and the Pokanoket.

117   Named for the Rev. Joseph Baxter, missionary to the Indians, according to
Wheeler's History of Brunswick. Mustard Island is now owned by The Nature
Conservancy.

118   Other sources say $12,000.

119   Rate for a circus elephant was one dollar; top carriage and four-wheel
cart, twenty-five cents; two-wheel shay, fifteen cents; farmer's team, ten
cents; sheep or swine, three cents each, and people on foot, three cents.

120   Samuel W. Foote's daybooks and Foote family correspondence in possession of John W. Voorhees.

121   The New Rogers Cemetery is on Cathance Road, off Route 24 North
      (Middlesex Road) in Topsham.
122   Holt, *Bath Families in the 19th Century*.
123   Enoch with two wives, Julia Ann Hunter Foote and Rachael A. Shaw
      Foote, and three of his children, Charles Alden, Rachel S., and Sarah M.,
      are buried in the White Cemetery located behind the West Bath School on
      the New Meadows Road.
124   Holt, *Bath Families in the 19th Century*.
125   A yeoman in English society was a middle-class farmer who owned a
      small amount of land, which he cultivated. This was a step above a hus-
      bandman or farmer but lower in status than a gentleman.

Bibliography

Books

* Denotes essential references

*Allen, Charles Edwin. *History of Dresden, Maine*. Augusta, ME: Bertram E. Packard, 1931.

Attwood, Stanley Bearce. *The Length and Breadth of Maine*. Augusta, ME: Kennebec Journal Print Shop, 1953.

Baker, William Avery. *A Maritime History of Bath, Maine and the Kennebec River Region*. Bath, ME: Marine Research Society of Bath, 1973.

Ballard, Rev. Edward. *Memorial Volume of the Popham Celebration*. Portland, ME: Bailey & Noyes, 1863.

Bibber, Joyce K. *Bath and West Bath*. Dover, NH: H. Arcadia Publishing, 1995.

Bolton, Charles Knowles. *Scotch Irish Pioneers in Ulster and America*. Boston: Bacon and Brown, 1910.

Bourque, Bruce J. *Twelve Thousand Years: American Indians in Maine*. Lincoln: University of Nebraska Press, 2001.

Burroughs, Franklin. *Confluence: Merrymeeting Bay*. Gardiner, ME: Tilbury House Publishers, 2006.

Chadbourne, Ava Harrie. *Maine Place Names, Cumberland and Sagadahoc Counties*. Freeport, ME: The Bond Wheelwright Company, 1957.

Chandler, Eliot J. *Ancient Sagadahoc*. Lincoln, NE: iUniverse, Inc., 2000.

Clark, Stephen. *Following in Their Footsteps: A Travel Guide and History of the 1775 Secret Expedition to Capture Quebec*. Shapleigh, ME: Clark Books, 2006.

Coffin, Robert P. Tristram. *Kennebec, Cradle of Americans*. Camden, ME: Down East Books, 2002.

Cook, David S. *Above the Gravel Bar: The Indian Canoe Routes of Maine*. Milo, ME, Milo Printing Company, 1985.

Coolidge, Olivia E. *Colonial Entrepreneur: Dr. Silvester Gardiner and the Settlement of Maine's Kennebec Valley*. Gardiner, ME: Tilbury House Publishers and the Gardiner Library Association, 1999.

Douglas-Lithgow, R. A. *Native American Place Names of Maine, New Hampshire and Vermont*. Bedford, MA: Applewood Books (originally published in Vermont in 1909).

Dow, Sterling T. *Maine Postal History and Postmarks*. Portland, ME: Severn-Wylie-Jewett Co., 1943.

Dunnack, Henry E. *Maine Forts*. Augusta, ME: Charles E. Nash & Son, 1924.

*Eckstorm, Fannie Hardy. *Indian Place Names of the Penobscot Valley and the Maine Coast*. Orono, ME: University of Maine Study Series, 1941.

Flynn, Robert V. *Map of Sagadahoc County, Maine 1858*. Harpswell, ME: King Philip Publishing, 2006.

Helmreich, Louise R. *Our Town: Reminiscences and Historical Studies of Brunswick, Maine*. Collection of the Pejepscot Historical Society, Brunswick, ME, 1967.

Hill, Mary Pelham, ed. *Vital Records of Georgetown, Maine to the Year 1892*. Maine Historical Society, Portland, ME.

Josselyn, John. *New England Rarities Discovered*. Originally printed in London, 1672. Reprinted by the Massachusetts Historical Society, Boston, 1972.

Lemont, Levi P. *1400 Historical Dates of the Town and City of Bath and Georgetown from 1604 to 1874*. Bath, ME: Published by the author, 1874.

Levett, Christopher. "A Voyage into New England, Begun in 1623 and Ended in 1624, Preformed [sic] by Christopher Levett, His Majesty's Woodward of Somersetshire, and one of the Council of New England." Collections and Proceedings of the Maine Historical Society, 2:73–109.

Little, George Thomas. *Genealogical and Family History of the State of Maine.* New York: Lewis Historical Publishing Company, 1909.

Madore, Nelson, and Barry Rodrigue, eds. *Voyages—A Maine Franco-American Reader.* Gardiner, ME: Tilbury House Publishers, 2007.

Mann, John. *Ulster-Scots on the Coast of Maine.* Bowdoin, ME: Saint Andrews Society, 2006.

McCauley, Brian. *The Many Names of Maine.* Wellesley, MA: Acadia Press, 2004.

McLane, Charles B. *Islands of the Mid-Maine Coast, Vol. IV: Pemaquid Point to the Kennebec River.* Gardiner and Rockland, ME: Island Institute, 1994.

*Noyes, Sybil, Charles T. Libby, and Walter G. Davis. *Genealogical Dictionary of Maine and New Hampshire.* Baltimore: The Genealogical Publishing Co., Inc., 1972.

*Owen, Henry Wilson, Jr. *The Edward Clarence Plummer History of Bath, Maine.* Bath, ME: The Times Company, 1936.

Owen, Moses. *Plymouth Church and Other Poems.* Portland, ME: W. S. Jones, 1873.

Patterson, William D. *The Probate Records of Lincoln County, Maine, 1760 to 1800.* Camden, ME: Picton Press, 1991.

Phippsburg Historical Society. *Phippsburg: Fair to the Wind.* Lewiston, ME: 1964.

Price, H. H., and Gerald E. Talbot. *Maine's Visible Black History.* Gardiner, ME: Tilbury House Publishers, 2006.

Proper, Ida Sedgwick. *Monhegan: The Cradle of New England.* Salem, MA: Higginson Press, 1997.

Purington, William C. *Meadowsweet.* Brunswick, ME: Privately printed by C. W. Ring.

————. *A Look into West Bath's Past.* Privately printed by the author, 1976.

Raymond, Emma Frances Harmon. *A Romance of New Meadows.* Lewiston, ME: Press of Lewiston Journal Co., 1900.

Roberts, Kenneth. *Arundel*. Camden, ME: Down East Books, 1995.

Rolde, Neil. *Unsettled Past, Unsettled Future: The Story of Maine Indians*. Gardiner, ME: Tilbury House Publishers, 2004.

Sawtelle, William Otis. *Historic Trails and Waterways of Maine*. Augusta, ME: Maine Development Commission, 1932.

Sewall, Rufus King. *Ancient Dominions of Maine*. Bowie, MD: Heritage Books, Inc., 1998.

Sloane, Eric. *Eric Sloane's Americana: American Yesterday, Our Vanishing Landscape, and American Barns & Covered Bridges*. New York: Wilfred Funk, 1956.

Spencer, Wilbur D. *Pioneers on Maine Rivers*. Baltimore: Genealogical Publishing Co. Inc., 1973.

Thayer, Rev. Henry Otis. *The Sagadahoc Colony*. New York: Benjamin Blom, Inc., 1971.

———. "Transient Town of Cork," *Collections and Proceedings of the Maine Historical Society*, Series 2, Vol. 4, 240–265.

Thorson, Robert M. *Stone By Stone*. New York: Walker and Company, 2002.

Varney, George J. *A Gazetteer of the State of Maine*. Boston: B. B. Russell, 1886.

Wahll, Andrew J., ed. *Sabino, Popham Colony Reader*. Bowie, MD: Heritage Books, Inc., 2000.

Wallace, Burnette Bailey, and Frances Soule Maher. *History of Woolwich, Maine, A Town Remembered*. Woolwich, ME: Woolwich Historical Society, 1994.

*Wheeler, George A., and Henry W. Wheeler. *History of Brunswick, Topsham and Harpswell, Maine*. Boston: Alfred Mudge & Son, 1878.

Whitney, S. H. *The Kennebec Valley*. Augusta, ME: Sprague, Burleigh & Flint, 1887.

Williamson, William D. *The History of the State of Maine*. Hallowell, ME: Glazier, Masters & Co., 1832.

Manuscripts, Documents, Booklets, and Records

Baker, Emerson W., and James Kences. "Maine, Indian Land Speculation, and the Essex County Witchcraft Outbreak of 1692." *Maine History,* Vol. 40, No. 3 (Fall 2001) 159–189.

Baxter, James Phinney. *Documentary History of the State of Maine, Vol. XXIII.* Maine Historical Society, Portland, Maine (1916) 206–207.

Fisher Mitchell Elementary School Fourth Graders. *Voices From Our Agricultural Past: The Countryside of Bath, Maine* (1999).

Gerber, William E. "Twice a Day Island," *The Best from American Canals, Number II,* American Canal and Transportation Center, York, Pennsylvania (1984).

Hawes, Edward L., Helen N. Koulouris, and Lauren Stockwell. *Between the River and the Bay: An Inventory and Evaluation of Bath's Shoreline.* Bath Waterfront Resources Committee (October 1988).

Holt, Alfred T., *Bath Families in the 19th Century.* Handwritten manuscript at the Sagadahoc History and Genealogy Room, Patten Free Library, Bath, Maine (1984, 2001).

Thayer, Henry Otis. *Sagadahoc and Kennebec: Collected Papers, Notes, Abstracts, Copies.* Maine Historical Society Collection 3046 (1928).

The Town of Brunswick, Maine in the Year 1739. Published by the town (1939)

Vose, George. *The Old Canal at New Meadows and Kennebec River.* Bath, ME: Bath Enterprise (1901).

Webber, Harry C. *Golf in Maine, Season of 1947.* Bath, ME (1947).

Field Trip Suggestions, Resources, and Associations

Abbe Museum, Bar Harbor

Bath Historical Society

Bay Bridge Landing Site, East Brunswick

Bowdoin College Library and Map Collection, Brunswick

Bowdoinham Public Library

Butler Head, North Bath

Curtis Memorial Library, Brunswick

Davistown Museum, Liberty

Day's Ferry, Woolwich

DeLorme Map Store, Freeport

Dresden Historical Society, Dresden

Freeport Historical Society

Freeport Town Hall (Vital Records back to 1789; Ancient North Yarmouth
has Freeport records prior to 1789)

Friends of Merrymeeting Bay

Gardiner Public Library

Georgetown Historical Society

Lincoln County Registry of Deeds, Wiscasset (Incorporated from York
County, 1760)

Lisbon Library

Maine Genealogical Society, Farmington

Maine Historical Society, Portland

Maine Historic Preservation Commission, Augusta

Maine Maritime Museum, Bath

Maine Old Cemeteries Association

Maine State Archives, Augusta

Maine State Library, Augusta

New England Antiquities Research Association

New Meadows Lake Association

Pejepscot Museums and Historical Society, Brunswick

Pownalborough Courthouse, Dresden

Oak and Maple Grove Cemeteries, Bath

Osher Map Library, Portland (University of Southern Maine)

Richmond Historical & Cultural Society

Sagadahoc County Registry of Deeds, Bath (Incorporated in 1854 from Lincoln County)

Sagadahoc History and Genealogy Room, Patten Free Library, Bath

Sagadahoc Preservation, Inc.

Sagadahoc Rod, Gun & Skeet Club, North Bath

Sewall Woods, Bath

Swan Island National Historic District, Richmond

Thorne Head Preserve, Bath

Topsham Public Library

Wayne Historical Society

West Bath Historical Society

Wing Cemetery, Wayne

Woolwich Historical Society

Yarmouth Historical Society

York County Courthouse, Alfred (Deeds from 1636 to present. Maine
was called New Somersetshire until 1639. The territory extended
from the Piscataqua River to the Kennebec in 1638. In 1658
Massachusetts governed the area to the edge of North Yarmouth and
the name was changed to Yorkshire, the charter including the whole
state. Lincoln and Cumberland counties were taken from York in 1760
and incorporated separately. Lincoln County separated into three districts in 1826. All properties west of the Kennebec River were
recorded in the Lincoln West district. All properties east of the
Medomack River, formerly the Muscongus River, were recorded in
the Lincoln East district. In 1854, Sagadahoc County split off from
Lincoln County.)

About the Author

Photo by Peter Gorman

Nancy Dearborn Lovetere

Nancy Dearborn Lovetere grew up in North Bath on the Kennebec River and Merrymeeting Bay. She was a lifetime member of three state Societies of Mayflower Descendants. Grandmother and marathoner, she shared a triangular existence in Connecticut, Maine, and Florida with her husband, John, until her death in 2009. She never did get a reply from her message sent adrift in a Marshmallow Fluff jar in 1954.